MW00788634

# A Clinician's Guide
# Approaches for Weight Concerns

This clinician manual presents the *Accept Yourself!* program, which is derived from empirically supported interventions (including Acceptance and Commitment Therapy and Health At Every Size) that have a demonstrated ability to enhance women's mental and physical health. This book offers a clear, research-based, and forgiving explanation for clients' failure to lose weight, helpful guidance for clinicians who are frustrated with poor client weight loss outcomes, as well as a liberating invitation to clients to give up this struggle and find another way to achieve their dreams and goals.

**Margit I. Berman** is an assistant professor of psychiatry at the Geisel School of Medicine at Dartmouth and associate professor of clinical psychology at the Minnesota School of Professional Psychology at Argosy University. She was the recipient of the 2015 Hitchcock Foundation Scholars Career Development award for her research and development of the *Accept Yourself!* intervention for women with obesity and depression. She is the past chair of the Society for Counseling Psychology's Section for the Promotion of Psychotherapy Science, and is on the editorial boards of *The Counseling Psychologist* and *Journal of Counseling Psychology*.

# A Clinician's Guide to Acceptance-Based Approaches for Weight Concerns

The *Accept Yourself!* Framework

Margit I. Berman

Routledge
Taylor & Francis Group

NEW YORK AND LONDON

First published 2018
by Routledge
711 Third Avenue, New York, NY 10017

and by Routledge
2 Park Square, Milton Park, Abingdon, Oxon, OX14 4RN

*Routledge is an imprint of the Taylor & Francis Group, an informa business*

*Library of Congress Cataloging-in-Publication Data*
A catalog record for this title has been requested

ISBN: 978-1-138-06873-5 (hbk)
ISBN: 978-1-138-06874-2 (pbk)
ISBN: 978-1-315-15765-8 (ebk)

Typeset in Goudy
by Out of House Publishing

To Jeremy and Robin McDonald, my husband and son, who bring me joy.

# Contents

# Acknowledgments

Lots of wonderful people and organizations helped make this book a reality. My mentors, Mark Hegel, Jay Hull, and Steve Bartels, were all unbelievably generous with their time, wisdom, and humor; neither this book nor I myself would have developed as well without them. The Department of Psychiatry at the Geisel School of Medicine at Dartmouth provided the early funding without which *Accept Yourself!* could never have been developed. Alan Green, Psychiatry Department chair, championed this work from the beginning and I am deeply grateful. The Hitchcock Foundation generously awarded me a 2015 Hitchcock Foundation Scholars career development award that made the research and writing behind this book possible. I owe both Jennifer Reining and Karen Jones at the Foundation my gratitude. Stephanie Morton co-authored the original self-help workbook for the *Accept Yourself!* intervention. My patients and research participants shared their experiences with candor, and made the intervention better in countless ways. Michelle Neyman Morris consulted helpfully on nutrition and health behavior change aspects of the program. My postdoctoral fellows, John Park, Evan Bick, and Monica Lindgren, all assisted with the research. Theresa Glaser, John Billig, and Linda Bacon gave important help developing treatment fidelity measures. My husband and son supported me while I wrote and worked late nights and weekends. Finally, *Accept Yourself!* was also supported by a Health Promotion and Disease Prevention Research Center supported by Cooperative Agreement Number U48DP005018 from the Centers for Disease Control and Prevention. The information and conclusions in this book are mine and do not necessarily represent the official position of the Centers for Disease Control and Prevention.

Part 1

# Why Use an Acceptance-Based Approach to Weight Management?

# Introduction

## Choosing and Using a Self-Acceptance-Based Approach: Cautions and Language

This book is written for clinicians who help clients with body image and weight concerns, and who have watched clients try and fail at various behavioral strategies to lose weight and feel better about themselves and their bodies. If you are frustrated with your inability to help clients achieve lasting improvement in their weight and body image concerns, this book is for you. You may already know that both you and your clients need a new path to wellness and self-acceptance. This book shows you that path. Inside this book you will find a clear, research-based, and forgiving explanation for clients' frequent failures to lose weight and keep it off, as well as helpful guidance for how to respond effectively to these poor outcomes, without frustration or increasing clients' shame. Finally, this book offers you and your clients a liberating invitation to give up ineffective struggles with weight loss and body image. In its place, you will be provided with a powerful and unexpected new route to help your clients achieve their dreams, wellness goals, and hope for healthy body image and self-esteem.

Part 1 of this book provides a rationale for a self-acceptance-based approach to client weight concerns and helps you understand why a radically different approach to these concerns may offer greater improvement for your clients. In Part 1, you'll find an overview of research on this and alternative approaches, as well as exercises to help you identify and remove any barriers you may have to offering self-acceptance-based treatments skillfully and ethically.

Part 2 provides a guide to conducting self-acceptance-based treatment. You'll find information and exercises to help your clients develop a new acceptance of their bodies and their relationship with food. Techniques to help clients identify and commit to their values related to food, body image, movement, and life in general are taught, including guidance to help clients tackle their most troublesome mental and practical barriers along the way.

Part 3 focuses on special problems you might encounter when implementing *Accept Yourself!* How to conduct informed consent for this treatment and effectively manage your clients' weight loss expectations are covered here, as well as termination issues at the end of treatment, and when to consider group-based versus individual treatment. This section will help you trouble-shoot common problems that arise in *Accept Yourself!* treatment, and also help you address the common situation where clients have comorbid weight-related physical health concerns for which weight loss is often recommended.

## When to Choose Accept Yourself!

Accept Yourself! is a novel treatment approach. There is preliminary evidence, reviewed in Chapter 3, to suggest that it is feasible, safe, and may be efficacious as a treatment for depression, when delivered in a group format to women with both depression and obesity. Accept Yourself! draws on both Acceptance and Commitment Therapy and Health At Every Size® treatment paradigms. These two treatment paradigms, also reviewed in detail in Chapter 3, have some evidence to suggest they may be efficacious as treatments for weight management, eating disorders, and enhancing physical wellness in a variety of populations. As such, it appears reasonable to offer the Accept Yourself! approach to clients presenting with these concerns. However, Accept Yourself! explicitly does not promise or expect client weight loss, and both clients and clinicians must understand and accept this prior to engaging in this treatment strategy. Both Chapter 4 and Chapter 13 provide clinician strategies for conducting informed consent about the Accept Yourself! approach. These chapters explore both how to help clients identify appropriate and worthwhile treatment goals, as well as how to help clients develop realistic expectations about weight loss. However, Accept Yourself! is not appropriate for clients who remain exclusively committed to weight loss as a goal following an informed consent process and completion of the strategies in Chapter 4. Such clients may benefit from a different therapeutic strategy or referral for additional help with their goals.

In addition, Accept Yourself! has not been tested as a treatment for eating disorders, such as anorexia nervosa or bulimia nervosa, and the treatment strategies contained in this book may not be sufficient to effectively treat these disorders. Because clients presenting for weight loss help or with body image concerns are likely to be at increased risk of eating disorders, clinicians should screen clients for these disorders, and may wish to refer them for multidisciplinary eating disorders treatment either in lieu of or concurrently with using the Accept Yourself! approach. The Eating Disorder Diagnostic Scale (Stice, Telch, & Rivzki, 2000) is a free brief screening tool clinicians may find helpful in identifying clients who would benefit from eating disorders treatment.

## A Word about Language

Choosing appropriate, non-judgmental, comfortable language to describe clients' bodies and their emotions and thoughts related to their bodies is complex and can be awkward. In this book, I use the word "obesity" or "obese" (or, more rarely, "overweight") when discussing research findings or classifications based on Centers for Disease Control cutoffs for body mass index (BMI) classification (see Chapter 1). These cutoffs are somewhat arbitrary and have varied substantially over time (Kuczmarski & Flegal, 2000). Apart from when I use these words in reference to the research literature which makes use of them, they are not used in this text, and I do not recommend their use with clients, although clinicians are often comfortable with these "clinical" words. The word "obesity" is problematic because it implies that obesity is in and of itself pathological, and represents a disease state. The American Medical Association did, indeed, vote in 2013 to classify obesity as a disease, hoping to increase insurance company reimbursement for obesity treatments. However, it did so against the recommendation of its own Council on Science and Public Health, which it had commissioned to study the issue and make recommendations, and the decision to classify obesity as a disease remains controversial (Stoner & Cornwall, 2014). Given that many individuals who meet the current classification for obesity in terms of BMI are metabolically (and otherwise) healthy, use of the word obesity to describe clients' body size is inappropriate. Similarly, the word "overweight" implies that, for a given individual, there is a known, optimal weight for health, which that individual exceeds. As will be discussed further in Chapter 1, evidence supporting this claim is thin, making the word "overweight" inappropriate.

In general, in this book, the words "fat" or "larger-bodied" are used to describe individuals with larger-than-average body sizes. Like "short," "tall," or "slender," "fat" can be a simple descriptive word to denote body type. However, it is also a stigmatized word that can be used, by itself, as a slur. There is a movement among size acceptance activists to "take back" this word, as lesbian, gay, bisexual, and transgender activists took back the word "queer," and I am in support of this effort. Therefore, the word "fat" is used frequently, and non-judgmentally, throughout the book. It is the position of this treatment program that being fat is not inherently problematic or pathological, and thus not a state that needs to be changed. Instead, fat is a body type, like tall, or short, that can be referred to lightly, in passing, as one might describe one's own height. Clients may or may not wish to use this word for themselves, and their wishes should be elicited and respected, although clinicians may want to discourage clients self-identifying as "overweight" or "obese." A variety of other non-judgmental or positive terms for a larger-than-average body are also possible, including "larger-bodied" (used frequently in this text as a non-judgmental synonym for "fat"), "abundant," "plus-sized," "curvy," etc. In general, words that convey judgment of body size, whether positive or negative, are avoided in this book, although positively valenced words may have clinical value for clients who have been taught that fatness is disgusting or objectionable. However, words like "abundant" or "curvy" are not used in this book or its accompanying self-help book, both because the treatment program treats weight as a neutral (neither positive nor negative) human characteristic, and because the use of euphemisms can imply judgment about the word ("fat") being avoided by their use. In addition, this book occasionally uses the term "average-weight," to describe body sizes that are close to the numerical mean for

Americans (a BMI of 27 for both men and women, which the Centers for Disease Control classifies as "overweight"). Words that denote larger-than-average body size are obviously not accurate for average-weight individuals, regardless of BMI category.

Clinicians using the *Accept Yourself!* approach should choose a non-judgmental, non-pathologizing word or set of words to use to describe client body size and shape, and should discuss their word choices with clients, who can be surprised or distressed if the clinician refers to them as "fat" without prior discussion and consent. Using positive or neutral words suggested by the client, and offering a brainstorm of possibilities, can also enhance therapeutic alliance and help encourage self-acceptance.

## References

Kuczmarski, R. J., & Flegal, K. M. (2000). Criteria for definition of overweight in transition: Background and recommendations for the United States. *The American Journal of Clinical Nutrition, 72*(5), 1074–1081.

Stice, E., Telch, C. F., & Rizvi, S. L. (2000). Development and validation of the Eating Disorder Diagnostic Scale: A brief self-report measure of anorexia, bulimia, and binge-eating disorder. *Psychological Assessment, 12*(2), 123–131.

Stoner, L., & Cornwall, J. (2014). Did the American Medical Association make the correct decision classifying obesity as a disease? *The Australasian Medical Journal, 7*(11), 462–464.

# 1 The Science of Obesity and Weight Loss
## Why Weight Control Doesn't Work

## Client Weight Loss Goals: Changing the Conversation

Clients often present to treatment hoping to lose weight. In the U.S., weight loss goals are normative in women and very common in men: 57 percent of American women and 40 percent of men report trying to lose weight within the past year (Yaemsiri, Slining, & Agarwal, 2011), and the prevalence of weight loss efforts have increased over time (Montani, Schutz, & Dulloo, 2015). Thus, therapists and helpers can expect to see clients frequently who want behavioral help with weight loss efforts. And therapists have reason to be concerned about those efforts and their role in facilitating them, because weight loss efforts affect clients' mental and physical health. Dieting failures increase clients' risk of depression (Markowitz, Friedman, & Arent, 2008) and eating disorders (Stice, 2002), as well as worsened cardiometabolic health (Montani et al., 2015). Encouraging clients to engage in weight loss efforts that are not likely to be successful thus raises important ethical questions. An unsuccessful weight loss attempt is likely to have negative effects beyond simply not achieving its aims. Thus, it is important that if clinicians offer clients weight loss help, they should have confidence that the weight loss intervention is evidence based, with data to show that it will lead to substantial long-term weight loss in line with the clients' goals. Non-evidence-based interventions, or interventions with demonstrated lack of long-term weight loss efficacy, potentially put clients' physical and mental health at risk.

What do we have to offer clients in the way of evidence-based interventions for weight loss? Both you and your clients may be surprised to discover what the scientific literature has to say about evidence-based weight loss, as well as about the causes and consequences of overweight and obesity.

## If Our Clients Feel like Failures, They're in Good Company

All weight loss interventions except bariatric surgery have poor long-term efficacy. Longitudinal, naturalistic studies of weight loss efforts undertaken by people in the "real world" find that weight loss efforts predict long-term weight *gain* and the onset of obesity even in previously normal or underweight individuals (Neumark-Sztainer, et al., 2006; 2012; Stice, Cameron, Killen, Hayward, & Taylor, 1999). Unhealthful or eating disordered behaviors, such as fasting, self-induced vomiting, or use of laxatives, predict greater weight gain, but all efforts, even more appropriate or healthful behaviors like exercise or eating more fruits and vegetables (if these behaviors are done in order to lose weight), predict weight gain (Neumark-Sztainer et al., 2006).

However, results from longitudinal, naturalistic studies cannot tell us that weight loss efforts actually cause weight gain. It's possible that biases in self-reporting dieting behavior affect the results, or that a third variable causes both dieting and weight gain, even in thin individuals. Or, it is possible that weight loss efforts do cause weight gain in naturalistic samples, but only because they are poorly implemented in uncontrolled settings. To evaluate these questions it is reasonable to look at the randomized controlled trial (RCT) literature on weight loss interventions.

An important caveat in analyzing the results of RCTs for any intervention is that RCTs likely *overstate* the benefits of any intervention, for several reasons. First, full-scale RCTs are expensive and difficult to conduct, and typically require grant funding resources to accomplish. Funders, such as the National Institutes of Health, typically require pilot trials or other concrete evidence that the intervention researchers are seeking to evaluate in an RCT is likely to be efficacious before providing funding. Thus, only interventions with demonstrated promise – interventions that have already shown they probably cause some improvement in the problem they target – are likely to ever be evaluated in an RCT.

Second, RCTs typically maximize experimental control and internal validity. This means that an intervention, when it is delivered in an RCT, is delivered as close to perfectly as possible. There are usually checks and training processes to make sure the intervention is delivered exactly as designed. Also, participants are selected so as to maximize the experimenter's ability to determine if the intervention is successful. People who are unlikely to be successful at a weight loss intervention, for example because they have an eating disorder, or depression, or another condition that might affect their ability to follow the intervention, are usually excluded from RCTs. Some RCTs even have a "run-in" period before the research begins, where participants must prove they can adhere to the intervention or some aspect of it before they can begin the trial. Participants who fail this "run-in" period are excluded from the research. For example, in the Look AHEAD trial, which evaluated a behavioral weight loss program as a treatment for cardiovascular complications of diabetes, participants had to complete a two-week run-in, which included successful self-monitoring of diet and physical activity, and they also had to pass a treadmill physical test of their physical fitness before they could be included. Anyone who couldn't successfully complete these tasks was excluded from the study (Espeland, 2007). Thus, in RCTs, interventions are delivered as close to perfectly as possible to homogenous, carefully selected, motivated participants. In other words, interventions in RCTs are delivered under ideal conditions, where we could expect maximal chances of success.

Third, if, despite the researcher's best efforts, an RCT finds no effect for the intervention, it often will be difficult to get that finding published. "Null findings," where there was no significant difference between the intervention and its control condition in an RCT, are difficult to publish in scientific journals, leading to what is known as the "file drawer" problem in intervention research, such that published research may overstate the benefits of any given intervention, because of biases in publication rates (Easterbrook, Gopalan, Berlin, & Matthews, 1991).

Because of these factors, published findings from RCTs represent an upper bound for likely outcomes from weight loss interventions, a best-case scenario in terms of predicting how your individual client will fare if she/he adopts the tested weight loss intervention. Nevertheless, despite this, RCTs for medical, dietary, exercise, and mixed weight loss interventions (all weight loss interventions except bariatric surgery) all show poor long-term efficacy overall.

Meta-analyses and comprehensive reviews of RCT of weight loss interventions, even those that analyze the same literature, come to differing conclusions about the results. Some meta-analyses and comprehensive reviews report that obesity treatments, on average, cause weight *gain* over long-term follow-up (Mann et al., 2007; Ayyad & Andersen, 2000). Others report that 3–6 percent weight loss *is* possible four years later, if participants continue all aspects of treatment (Franz et al., 2007). Nevertheless, even if this more-optimistic assessment is correct, this outcome is modest. For example, for a 200-lb patient, this represents a 6–12 lb weight loss. Health benefits of such a modest weight loss are unclear, and this is far less than clients expect or desire (Foster, Wadden, Vogt, & Brewer, 1997).

Bariatric surgery has better (but not perfect) long-term outcomes than all other weight loss interventions. Nevertheless, weight regain following bariatric surgery can be substantial: 20 percent of patients with a body mass index (BMI) of 35–49 were classified as surgical failures ten years later, and 35 percent of those with a BMI > 50 (Christou, Look, & MacLean, 2006). Bariatric surgery is also more invasive, with higher risks, than other weight loss treatments, and patients' expectations for bariatric surgery outcomes are also unrealistically optimistic in terms of amount of weight lost (Kaly et al., 2008).

It is important to note that I am not claiming that intentional weight loss never (or rarely) occurs. You may have already wondered how it could be possible that most people gain weight as a result of weight loss efforts, when you likely have clients or friends who have, or may even yourself have, successfully lost weight at some point in the past. In fact, any motivated person who follows a standard behavioral weight loss plan can likely lose weight, for a while. Weight loss outcomes in RCTs with long-term follow-up (including bariatric surgery) show v-shaped (or sometimes checkmark-shaped) outcomes, such that participants enter the trial seeking weight loss, engage in the intervention, lose weight, and then gradually regain it, sometimes regaining all

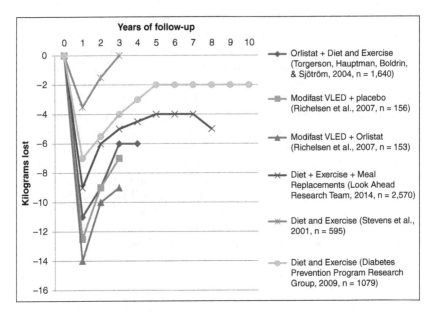

*Figure 1.1* Long-term weight loss outcomes. VLED, very-low-energy diet.

that they have lost and then some. Figure 1.1 shows an example. Displayed in the figure are the long-term weight loss outcomes (expressed as kilograms of initial weight lost; 1 kg = 2.2 lbs) for several large, high-quality, RCTs of various weight loss treatment combinations. The figure includes numbers of participants for the active treatments. Weight loss amounts shown have been rounded to nearest half-kilograms.[1] Notice that the amount of initial weight loss varies among the different interventions, but the pattern of results is the same – initial weight loss, followed by weight regain, which, in these trials, generally levels out to a stable, modest, long-term weight loss.

Long-term trials (i.e., those > 1 year in duration) often research strategies to help people maintain weight loss. In all of the trials displayed in the figure, participants continued with their initial weight loss strategies, and in some cases added additional strategies to lose weight as well. It's important to note that in the case of the one trial with the most dramatic weight loss (Richelsen et al., 2007; a trial of a very-low-energy diet (VLED) replacement followed by maintenance treatment using either a weight loss drug (Orlistat) or placebo, as well as ongoing dietary restriction), 19 percent of the sample was excluded from the analyses because they failed to lose more than 5 percent of their initial body weight in the initial 8-week trial of the VLED diet. So the larger initial weight loss in that trial represents a marked overestimate of what average patients could expect to experience. Also notice that the longer the follow-up, the more modest the weight loss, and bear in mind that all of these participants continued actively with the intensive weight loss interventions that these trials tested, in some cases adding new interventions on top of their initial weight loss strategies.

Taken together, the evidence from both the longitudinal, population-based studies and the RCT literature on weight loss suggests that, for the average patient, any weight loss action short of surgery is not evidence based. The average patient cannot expect significant long-term weight loss, and indeed bears a significant risk of long-term weight gain and the onset of obesity following a weight loss effort. Weight loss surgery, while causing larger weight losses for most patients, also carries not only substantial physical risks, but also a not-insubstantial risk of long-term weight regain. There are clearly ethical concerns involved with recommending weight loss strategies to patients, particularly if they can be expected to lead to long-term weight gain.

## Why Might Dieting Lead to Weight Gain?

Evolution has not designed human beings to lose weight (or, for that matter, to gain weight rapidly in response to overeating, either). Low body weight, weight loss (including weight loss in the range of 10–15 percent), and little body fat in women all contribute to decreased fertility, including a shortened luteal phase of the menstrual cycle, lack of ovulation, and amenorrhea (Frisch, 1987). Of course, longer-term weight loss (starvation) leads to mortality. If caloric restriction led to rapid, permanent weight loss, our evolutionary ancestors (who routinely faced caloric restriction in the form of short- and long-term famines) would not have managed to survive and reproduce. Similarly, our evolutionary ancestors would not have fared well if overeating led to massive and rapid weight gain; their famines were interrupted by periods of plenty, and major morphological changes in their bodies would have led to decreased ability to obtain food or increased death by predation (Speakman, 2008).

Thus, a predictable set of behavioral and biological responses to caloric restriction has emerged in human beings and other mammals over our evolutionary history: dietary restraint (or starvation) leads to food cravings (particularly for fat, carbohydrates, and sugar), as well as loss of self-regulation over eating, and binge eating. These responses serve to help hungry animals survive.

Indeed, dieting behavior and dietary restraint is a robust predictor of overeating and weight gain (Polivy, 1996). Hunger and food insecurity are also robustly related to weight gain and obesity, although findings are mixed with respect to whether food insecurity *causes* obesity (Franklin et al., 2012). Restrained eaters and dieters are less responsive to satiety and feelings of fullness, more responsive to the palatability of foods, and more likely to show over-eating in response to negative affect (Polivy & Herman, 1985). Some psychological factors, such as a tendency to disinhibition (Westenhoefer et al., 1994), may moderate these effects, such that people high in a personality tendency to disinhibit show more of these effects than others. However, the tendency to overeat, binge, and eat high-fat and high-sugar foods in response to dietary restriction is not solely or even mostly a psychological trait.

Patients often conceptualize binging on high-fat or high-sugar foods during a diet as an example of loss of willpower or a psychological weakness. However, it is important to observe that this is at least in part a *biological effect* of dietary restriction or food limitation. For example, laboratory rats who are exposed to intermittent dietary restriction or intermittent availability of palatable foods will increase eating (binge) when they have an opportunity, and they demonstrate a particular preference, under conditions of dietary restriction, for increased eating of high-fat, high-sugar foods, such as cookies (Hagan & Moss, 1997). (In fact, laboratory studies in rats sometimes actually use commercial cookies – Oreos are common – to demonstrate this effect.) This effect persists after the dietary restriction is removed and an otherwise-normal diet is restored (Hagan & Moss, 1997), and can lead to obesity in rats (Corwin, Aveeno, & Boggiano, 2011). It's also worth observing that this effect of dietary restriction on rat food preferences and consumption is increased by stress, such as exposure to foot shocks (Hagan et al., 2002).

For an example of this same process occurring in physically and psychologically healthy non-eating-disordered young men, consider the Minnesota Semi-Starvation Study (Keys et al., 1950). Cardiologist Ancel Keys, best known for his research into the cardiovascular benefits of the Mediterranean diet, conducted research during World War II, funded by the War Department, that was intended to establish the best methods for refeeding starving prisoners of war. Participants were conscript-age young men (age 20–33 years) who had registered as conscientious objectors to the war, and who were required, as a result, to volunteer for some form of national service, of which research participation was an option. The men were selected for their optimal physical and psychological health and hardiness, as researchers knew that the semi-starvation protocol they would be experiencing during their research protocol would be stressful and physically challenging. None of the men, of course, showed any signs of an eating disorder at the outset of the study. The semi-starvation protocol lasted 6 months, and was intended to cause participants to lose 25 percent of their body weight. (It is worth observing that patients often expect or hope to lose at least 25 percent of body weight on diets of a comparable length.) Participants ate a 1,570 calorie per day diet, an amount that patients often say is surprisingly high, comparable to what they have been prescribed for weight *maintenance* following weight-loss diets.

The effects of this diet on the men were profound. The men developed symptoms similar to what we expect to see in women with eating disorders. They became obsessed with food, subscribing to food magazines, hoarding food if they had the opportunity, and developing unusual obsessive rituals around food consumption. They experienced severe emotional distress, including increased depression, emotionality, and physical health concerns, as well as fatigue, irritability, and decreased sex drive and sociability. They reported being less able to think and concentrate. One participant amputated three of his own fingers with an axe. Physically, in addition to weight loss, decreased strength and stamina, they also experienced decreased basal metabolic rate, with lower body temperature, respiration, and heart rate.

The results of the Minnesota Semi-Starvation Study obviously raised serious ethical concerns about exposing participants to harm, and such studies are therefore no longer done. However, weight loss diets commonly recommend long-term maintenance of similar levels of semi-starvation. Scott Crow and Elke Eckert (2000), current eating disorder researchers at the University of Minnesota, where the study was done, followed up with Keys' participants 50 years later and discovered that they mainly retained the alterations in eating behavior (e.g., binging, food obsessions) caused by their brief forced period of caloric restriction in young adulthood. It is worth considering how many people are eating 1,500-calorie-a-day diets for 6 months during their twenties and early thirties, and to reflect upon the fact that the evidence suggests that they might also have similar perturbations of eating behavior for their rest of their lives.

The Minnesota Semi-Starvation Study documented both eating behavior and physical changes as a result of low-calorie diet. It is worth emphasizing that the changes experienced by human beings and animals under conditions of dietary restriction are not only behavioral, but also physical. In other words, if the behavioral changes caused by dietary restriction could somehow be avoided, physical changes would still occur that make long-term weight loss difficult to maintain. For example, dietary restraint leads to a variety of metabolic changes designed to prevent weight loss and starvation. Feedback signals from the depletion of both fat mass and fat-free mass contribute to weight regain through the modulation of energy intake and adaptive thermogenesis. This effect may actually be stronger in lean (rather than obese) individuals (Dulloo et al., 2015). Even if a patient somehow defeats the behavioral mechanisms designed to prevent weight loss, she/he might still regain weight purely via the body's biological response to starvation.

## What about Healthy Lifestyle Change?

Even Weight Watchers is aware of the growing research suggesting that dietary restriction is ineffective, crafting a recent ad campaign that suggested that "diets don't work; Weight Watchers does." Clinicians and clients wonder whether "healthy lifestyle change," that is, increased exercise and dietary modifications intended to be healthful, will help them lose weight, even though strict or prescribed dietary restriction is ineffective. However, there is little evidence that lifestyle modification leads to long-term weight loss, either.

Evaluating the effects of lifestyle modifications on health or weight outcomes is difficult. Although abundant correlational research has established such truisms as exercise (Penedo & Dahn, 2005) and healthy diet (Kant, 2004) are good for you, the magnitude of effects is often smaller than patients expect (especially for diet quality) and methodological concerns are high. Even in correlational studies, defining a healthy diet and comparing it across countries is difficult, and correlational studies do not tell you whether any associations observed are causal. Experimental studies of the effect of health behaviors are challenging to conduct, because attaining experimental control over participants' diet and exercise is difficult, particularly over the extended periods of time we would expect to observe a change. We would not necessarily expect, for example, that eating a low-fat or plant-based diet for 3 months would change future disease status, but studies that ask participants to be randomly assigned to make multi-year dietary or behavioral changes are rare. Those experimental studies that do exist obviously are highly important to enhance our understanding of the impact of healthful diet.

The Women's Health Initiative Dietary Modification Study was the largest, most extensive, experimental study of "healthy eating" ever conducted. More than 48,000 older women (aged 50–79 years) were randomly assigned to either eat their usual diet, or eat a low-fat, high fiber diet with lots of vegetables, fruits, and whole grains – the essence of what most people think of as "healthy eating." Older (rather than younger) women were chosen for the sample because they anticipated greater incidence in the diseases they wanted to observe among older women, allowing the researchers to detect differences among groups after several years of follow-up.

Women assigned to the healthy diet had intensive support to maintain their diets: an intensive initial group treatment led by nutritionists, followed by a long-term maintenance intervention group that met regularly over the course of the study, individual counseling, and personalized feedback on their dietary targets and progress. They ate the healthy diet and continued in the intervention program (and were compared with their control-group counterparts) for an average of 8 years of follow-up.

The women in the study weren't perfect at maintaining their target diets, of course, but they were pretty good: Both the usual diet and the intervention group were eating about 38 percent of their calories from fat when they entered the study. The women in the healthy-eating intervention group cut their total fat intake down to 24 percent of their calories in the first year, and were still eating 29 percent calories from fat by the sixth year of the study. The usual-diet group was at 35 percent calories from fat at 1 year, and 37 percent by the sixth year. The "healthy" dieters also increased their fruit, vegetable, and fiber intakes compared to themselves at baseline and to the comparison group, and maintained these improvements throughout the study. Although weight loss was not a focus of the study and women were not given a calorie target, by making the other changes, women in the intervention group also reduced their daily calorie intake by more than 350 calories a day from baseline to the end of the study. Women in the usual-diet group also ate fewer calories from the beginning to the end of the study, but the healthy-diet group reduced their calorie intake substantially more.

Given these changes (increased fiber, increased fruit and vegetable intake, decreased fat, decreased calories), what would you predict would be the health benefits to these women after they had adhered to these healthy lifestyle changes for 8 years?

You might be surprised to learn that researchers found no advantage in terms of cardiovascular disease, including heart disease and stroke, for the healthy-eating women (Howard et al., 2006b). There was also no advantage in terms of breast cancer (Prentice et al., 2006), colorectal cancer (Beresford et al., 2006), or any of 30 other cancers, except possibly ovarian cancer, and the researchers note that this one, modest, effect, may be due only to chance, in such a large, high-powered study (Prentice et al., 2007). And despite maintaining a restricted, lower-calorie diet for 8 years, these women lost a total of about 1 lb, on average, compared with the women who ate as they pleased (Howard, 2006a). In other words, these women successfully changed their eating lifestyles for 8 years: More fruits and vegetables, more whole grains, less fat, fewer calories. Classes, nutrition groups, hearing feedback about how they were doing. Yet they didn't do better in terms of cardiovascular health or cancer. They lost only 1 lb, for 8 years of effort. Many patients would not consider that sufficient benefit for the significant effort expended. It's also worth observing that these results mean that unrestricted eaters did not gain significant weight over time, even though they were eating more calories and food than the diet-change group.

Although the results of the Women's Health Initiative Dietary Modification Trial were persuasive, surprising and compelling, and led to fewer recommendations of low-fat diet for health change, nevertheless, it is only one study (albeit an unusually large and powerful one whose results we cannot ignore). However, other experimental studies of lifestyle changes are also striking for finding similar modest or no effects on weight loss and health.

The Look AHEAD Trial provides a useful recent example (Look AHEAD Research Group, 2013; Unick et al., 2013). This randomized, controlled, multicenter trial enrolled 5,145 overweight or obese patients with type II diabetes. Participants were randomly assigned either to an intensive lifestyle intervention, involving decreased caloric consumption and increased physical exercise, or to a control group, who received standard diabetes education. To be eligible for participation, participants had to be highly motivated, successfully passing a two-week run-in where they engaged in dietary self-monitoring, and also passing a fitness test to demonstrate that they could safely participate in exercise. Weight loss and improved diabetes control were the focus of the intervention, which was initially planned and intended to follow participants for 13.5 years. The idea behind the study was that the group receiving the lifestyle intervention would suffer fewer cardiovascular events than the control group, including heart attacks, strokes, and death related to cardiovascular issues. Instead, the trial had to be stopped after 10 years because the lifestyle modification had no effects on cardiovascular disease. Interestingly, the Look AHEAD Trial does provide the best example of which I am aware of sustained weight loss in an RCT: At the ten-year study endpoint, participants in the intervention group had maintained a weight loss of 7 percent of their initial body weight. (Intriguingly, the control group also lost about 5 percent of their initial body weight, suggesting that the highly motivated participants in this study may have been unusually successful at weight loss.) However, this modest weight loss did not translate into the health benefits researchers had hoped, and, again, it is worth considering whether these modest changes are worth the sustained effort required to maintain them, particularly if they do not lead to health benefits.

The Diabetes Care in General Practice study provides another example (Hansen, Siersma, Beck-Nielsen, & de Fine Olivarius et al., 2013; Køster-Rasmussen et al., 2016). This study was conducted in Denmark, and was a cluster RCT with an unusual (for the United States) *population-based sample* of newly diagnosed overweight and obese diabetic patients. When the study began, in the late 1980s, all patients in participating primary care practices throughout Denmark who were newly diagnosed with type II diabetes were enrolled consecutively into the study, nearly 1,400 patients in all. Then, the primary care practices were randomly assigned to either provide a program of structured care and individualized goal setting for risk factors and weight loss or treatment as usual. Weight loss didn't have to be a focus of the care in the intervention group, and not all the participants were considered overweight, but many did have weight loss as a focus. The study intervention lasted for six years. Participants were followed to assess the effects on their health for 19 years.

These researchers found that successful intentional weight loss in the intervention group was *not* associated with reduced all-cause mortality or cardiovascular morbidity or mortality (Køster-Rasmussen et al., 2016). In fact, in the intervention group, weight loss was a *risk factor* for all-cause mortality. The best health outcomes in the study were actually obtained by participants who *maintained* their weight rather than lost it. Despite these poor outcomes for intentional weight loss, there were some advantages for the intervention group: Those in the intervention group did have fewer heart attacks and less diabetes-related morbidity (Hansen et al., 2013). However, there were no differences between the two groups in all-cause mortality.

This pattern of results – modest or no health effects as a result of long-term experimental manipulation of diet and exercise – is common to nearly all of the experimental studies of diet and exercise of which I am aware, and may be an important part of informed consent for dietary changes. These studies do sometimes find some modest health benefits to dietary change, and patients should be supported to make health changes using all of the means available to them. However, their expectations should be strongly tempered, and participants who do not benefit should not be blamed or seen as having atypical outcomes. Weight loss, in particular, is modest at best, despite major efforts by researchers and motivated participants alike, with long-term weight gain likely for the average client, suggesting that prescribing weight loss to clients should not be considered an evidence-based practice and may be actively harmful.

# What Causes Obesity?

If engaging in effortful weight loss strategies does not actually result in weight loss for most people, and if, in fact, engaging in dieting is a predictor of long-term weight gain, you might be beginning to wonder what this means about the causes of obesity in the first place. There has been much media attention to the "obesity epidemic" and the childhood obesity epidemic, with most news reports focusing on presumed increases in calorie consumption or decreases in physical activity as the cause. As previously discussed, dieting and other weight loss strategies may represent one overlooked cause of the obesity epidemic: Indeed, dieting and obesity have increased in tandem, and this fits with the information already presented that implies that dieting may play a causal role over time in weight gain. But obesity as a phenomenon, and the obesity epidemic as a historical event, is likely multiply determined, with more than one cause, and different causes (or combinations of causes) for given individuals. Also, the causes of obesity for individuals are likely different than the cause of a change in obesity in the population. For example, obesity is highly heritable, so for any given fat individual, the likelihood that genetic risk contributed to her weight is high. However, the obesity epidemic was a historical event. Sometime between 1970 and 2000, the percentage of obese adults (but not overweight adults) increased by 15–20 percent, before leveling off. (You can view a graphic depicting this change at the National Institute for Diabetes and Digestive and Kidney Disease's webpage on Overweight and Obesity Statistics: www.niddk.nih.gov/health-information/health-statistics/Pages/overweight-obesity-statistics.aspx.) Obviously, our gene pool did not change between 1970 and 2000, so, even though genetic risk is likely the most important causal factor to explain any given individual's weight, it is useless to explain the increase in obesity in the population that occurred at the end of the twentieth century. In the following sections, we'll consider both causal factors that contribute to individuals' weight, as well as factors that may contribute to historical changes in weight.

## *Does Decreased Physical Activity Cause Obesity?*[2]

Many people believe that decreased physical activity caused the obesity epidemic, although it's worth noting that this idea fits with weight-based stereotypes that fat people are lazy. However, physical activity has, indeed, fallen over time in the general population, whereas "screen time" has increased. However, screen time began to increase rapidly with the invention of television – well before obesity increased. Figure 1.2 displays average screen time over the decades since the advent of television, with the timing of the "obesity epidemic" highlighted. If increased screen time caused the obesity epidemic, we would expect to see the rapid rise in obesity rates occurring beginning in the 1940s, not in the 1970s. In fact, to date, no direct causal relationship between inactivity and obesity has been demonstrated. Correlational studies do sometimes show a relationship, but

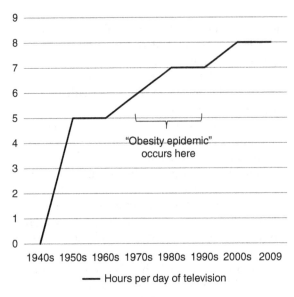

Figure 1.2   Screen time and obesity.
Sources: Television Bureau of Advertising, Inc. (2010) and Ogden & Carroll (2010).

they have mixed results and methodological flaws. Physical activity has a variety of benefits, both mental and physical, for people of all weights, but it does not appear either to be responsible in its absence for increasing prevalence of obesity nor an effective weight loss method.

### Does Overeating Cause Obesity?

Research has investigated possible associations between obesity and caloric intake, as well as the intake of macronutrients, such as fat and carbohydrates. There is little evidence that increased carbohydrate intake is associated with obesity. Some studies suggest that dietary fat intake is associated with obesity, but the association is highly variable across studies, with evidence mixed overall. And, in general, large-scale studies of eating behavior in the U.S.A. and Europe suggest that calorie and fat intake fell slightly or remained steady during the period that the obesity epidemic occurred (Ladabaum et al., 2014; Weinsier et al., 1998). For example, in a large-scale study that made use of a wide variety of databases of survey data representative of the U.S. population, such as the National Health and Nutrition Examination Survey (NHANES II and III), the U.S. Department of Agriculture Nationwide Food Consumption Survey, the Behavioral Risk Factor Survey System, and the Calorie Control Council Report, researchers found that in the adult U.S. population, the prevalence of overweight rose 31 percent from 1976 to 1991. However, during the same period, average fat intake dropped

11 percent, and average total daily calorie intake also decreased by 4 percent. Simultaneously, there was a dramatic rise in the percentage of the population consuming low-calorie products, whereas the prevalence of sedentary lifestyle did not change (Heini & Weinsier, 1997). European studies during the same period also found that obesity increased while caloric intake fell (Prentice & Jebb, 1995; Rolland-Cachera, Deheeger, & Bellisle, 1996). Studies comparing "healthy" to "unhealthy" eating patterns likewise find inconsistent results, with some studies finding a food intake pattern consisting mainly of meat, fatty, sweet, and energy-dense foods to be associated with BMI and obesity, and other studies finding that the same pattern was negatively associated with BMI and obesity. Many studies also find no association between food intake pattern and BMI or obesity. Food intake patterns are also less positively associated with BMI and obesity in women than in men (Togo et al., 2001).

Now, most food consumption research relies on self-reported data, and it is at least possible that people have become more inaccurate in reporting their dietary intake over time in a fashion that systematically underestimates the calories or fat grams consumed to an increasing degree. (However, it is worth noting that the studies described thus far are all well done methodologically, using survey methods designed and demonstrated to produce reliable and valid results.) One way to look at food consumption changes over time without self-report biases is to look at food disappearance data. Food disappearance data provide an estimate of how many food commodities a nation produced and consumed, corrected for waste and other uses (e.g., animal feed). These corrections can introduce their own biases, but combined with self-report data, food disappearance data give a sense of what foods a nation consumed.

To identify a candidate food that might have caused an increase in obesity, you will be looking for a change in Americans' diets that happened between (or just before) 1970 and 2000. (One obvious candidate is diet foods, which, as previously noted, increased dramatically in consumption during this time. Diet soda, for example, was introduced as a product for diabetics in the 1950s, and was not widely consumed until the 1960s, with the introduction of Tab, Diet Rite, and Diet Pepsi.) Before going on, take a moment and jot down what you think has changed in Americans' diets since 1970 that might explain the increase in obesity since that time.

Barnard (2010) summarizes U.S. food disappearance data from 1909 to 2007. If you want to explain the "obesity epidemic" using diet, you should be looking for foods that saw big increases or decreases between 1970 and 2007. Here's what changed during that time: Between 1970 and 2007 meat consumption increased. Specifically, red meat fell, poultry consumption more than doubled, and fish and shellfish consumption increased slightly.

In terms of dairy products: Egg consumption fell, as did consumption of fluid milk, which fell more than 30 percent. Much of that drop was accounted for by whole milk, which fell by 75 percent, whereas low-fat and skim milk consumption more than doubled. Cream consumption had fallen substantially after World War II, but increased somewhat between 1970 and 2007, but not back to levels seen prior to World War II. Butter consumption also fell dramatically after the war, but did not change between 1970 and 2007. Cheese consumption tripled. Frozen dairy consumption (ice cream) did not change significantly. Disappearance data for milk products such as cottage cheese, evaporated and condensed milks, and powdered milks, never a big part of the food supply, suggested that these also decreased slightly.

Added fats and oils did increase quite substantially, almost entirely driven by an increase in consumption of salad and cooking oils, which tripled during this time. Fruit consumption increased nearly 25 percent; both fruit juice and whole-fruit consumption increased. Vegetable consumption increased by about a third, mostly fresh and frozen vegetables.

Flour and cereal consumption also increased by about a third, mostly driven by the increase in restaurant meals during this time, as restaurants serve a disproportionate amount of inexpensive grain-based foods, such as pizza, pasta, and breads. Sweeteners increased, but less than 10 percent overall; sugar fell substantially, whereas corn-based sweeteners (corn syrup) increased nearly four times. Bottled waters increased dramatically, and carbonated soft drinks also increased, driven almost entirely by increased consumption of diet soda. Juices, beer, and wine also increased, whereas milk fell.

So, to summarize, there were reasonably big increases in the following foods between 1970 and 2007: poultry, low-fat and skim milk, cheese, salad and cooking oils, whole fruit and fruit juices, vegetables (mainly fresh and frozen), grains, corn syrup, and non-milk beverages, especially diet soda, water, and beer and wine. There were big decreases in the consumption of milk, especially whole milk, red meat, eggs, and sugar.

In general, in looking at these changes, one gets the impression that Americans were attempting to follow dietary recommendations, consuming more liquid oils, vegetables, fruits, and fewer high-fat meats and dairy products. Some changes in food production are observed, such as the increase in grains that probably signals more restaurant food consumption and the increase in corn syrup sweeteners and diet sodas. Which of these changes plausibly relate to the change in obesity, and why? Perhaps the increase in diet soda, the use of which may also be a marker for dietary restriction, which itself may lead to weight gain. The increase in poultry might be responsible, if antibiotic residues in poultry are causing changes in the human gut microbiome (e.g., see Riley, Raphael, & Faerstein, 2013). Research on fat and carbohydrate consumption might lead us to point at the increase in cooking oils or grains, but as we've previously noted, this research either has negative (carbohydrates) or mixed (fat) results. High-fructose corn syrup has been implicated as a cause of the obesity epidemic (Bray, Neilsen, & Popkin, 2004), although this claim has been controversial (Klurfield et al., 2013). In general, however, it is difficult to make a compelling case that any of these changes is a clear candidate for a causal role in the obesity epidemic, since the changes overall during this time are relatively small, and overall calorie consumption appears to have remained level. However, if neither lack of physical exercise nor overeating caused the obesity epidemic, what did?

### Uncontrollable Factors That Cause Obesity: Genetics

One factor that definitely did not cause the obesity epidemic (since it cannot have changed between 1970 and 2000), but that plays a powerful role for many or most individuals with obesity, is genetics. Obesity is highly heritable. As Vögele (2005) notes, heritability levels for identical twins, fraternal twins, or twins reared apart tend to cluster around 70 percent of the variation in BMI. In contrast, adoption studies have generated the lowest heritability estimates (30 percent or less), with heritability levels from family studies falling in between. Genetic factors affect resting energy expenditure, the thermic effect of food, and body fat response to overfeeding in complex ways, and genetic inputs may exert their influence on body weight through multiple and interacting biological and biopsychosocial mechanisms. As Vögele (2005) reports, there is some evidence for specific gene mutations (specifically mutations of the melanocortin-4-receptor) in a small number (3–5 percent) of obese individuals with BMIs over 40. For most fat people, however, obesity is likely caused by interactions among several genes and epigenetic interactions with the environment.

### Prenatal and Other Factors

Vögele (2005) also notes that there is some evidence for "metabolic programming" or "fetal priming" in obesity. Caloric deprivation in utero, low birth weight, high birth weight, and having a mother with insulin-dependent diabetes are all risk factors for later obesity.

One of the most intriguing explanations for the obesity epidemic involves the work of researcher David Allison. Allison observed that during the same years that human beings were struggling with the obesity epidemic, low-calorie pet food began to be marketed. He became curious about this phenomenon, and wondered if the obesity epidemic extended to animals. In his research with laboratory animals (e.g., lab rats, mice, and monkeys), domesticated animals (e.g., dogs and cats), and feral animals with some exposure to humans (e.g., city rats), he and his team documented that average weight (and obesity) has increased since the 1980s not only in humans, but also in animals (Klimentidis et al., 2011). Although the explanation for this change in animals is unclear, Allison's team has suggested that a variety of causes, including endocrine-disrupting chemicals, infectious agents, and epigenetic factors could all provide possible explanations. Imagining obesity being transmitted from a virus may seem far-fetched, but at least one possible infectious agent contributing to obesity has been identified. Monkeys infected in the lab with human adenovirus 36 gain both weight and increased fat (Dhurandhar et al., 2002), and antibodies to this virus are correlated with obesity in human beings (Atkinson et al., 2005).

Regardless of the specific cause ultimately identified for the obesity epidemic in animals, however, it seems clear that laboratory rats did not appreciably change either their diet or their exercise regimen between 1970 and 2000. In general, what is known currently about the causes of obesity suggests that apart from avoiding dietary restriction and the associated dysregulation of eating that can occur as a result (e.g., binging), most causes of obesity are beyond our clients' control, and not resolvable by increasing the restrictive or self-punitive lifestyle changes that are associated with dietary restriction. This is not to say that patients shouldn't be encouraged to move their bodies and become physically active and vital, nor that they should be discouraged from making health-promoting dietary changes. But these activities should be explored with patients outside the paradigm of weight loss, so that clients both understand that weight loss is not to be expected from making these changes, and also that they are freed from feeling responsible or shamed for their weight. Avoiding stigmatizing weight or shape is of essential importance, because weight stigma may also play an important-but-overlooked causal role in obesity and in worsening clients' health, both directly and indirectly through its impact on health care and the therapeutic relationship, as will be discussed in Chapter 2.

## If Clients Remain Fat, What Are the Risks to Their Health?

At this point, you may be persuaded that obesity is not your clients' fault or the result of their personal weaknesses and that weight loss efforts are likely to be ineffective or even actively counterproductive. However, you (and your clients) may still be concerned that if they do not somehow lose weight, there will be serious risks to their health.

Obesity, as readers surely already know, is associated with a variety of health problems, including hypertension, type II diabetes, obstructive sleep apnea, certain cancers, and cardiovascular diseases (Lavie et al., 2014). What does this mean for mortality?

### Does Obesity Increase Your Risk of Death?

Classification systems for overweight and obesity have changed over time. The National Heart, Lung, and Blood Institute, a division of the National Institutes of Health, changed the definition of overweight and obesity to be more stringent in 1998. Prior to the change, a man was classified as overweight if he had a BMI > 28, and a woman if she had a BMI > 27. After the change, both men and women were classified as overweight at a BMI of ≥ 25. (Readers may be amused to realize this surprising source for the "obesity epidemic." Many Americans went to bed normal weight one night in 1998 and woke up overweight!) Researchers have been interested in whether this change helped us understand actual mortality risk from obesity, and you may be interested, too. So take a guess: Which BMI category has the highest mortality risk?

Which has the lowest? Take a moment and put these categories in order, from the highest risk to the lowest. Maybe use a pencil in the margin to put a number 1 by the riskiest category (high risk of death), a 2 by the second-highest risk, and so on.

- Underweight (BMI < 18.5)
- Normal weight (BMI 18.5–24.9)
- Overweight (BMI 25–29.9)
- Obese (BMI 30–34.9)
- Moderately/extremely obese (BMI > 35)

Now, before I tell you the answers, it's important to discuss the methodological issues that might cloud your understanding of these results. If researchers wanted to, they could "cheat" in several ways with mortality and weight data that would make it appear as if obesity was not as harmful as it actually is. For example, when reviewing these kinds of epidemiological studies, it's important to know whether the researchers controlled for disease status. Many diseases, as part of their pathology, cause weight loss, so if you do not correct for disease status, lower weight might appear more harmful than it is in a healthy person free of disease. Also, researchers should correct for smoking status, because smokers both weigh less and are at elevated risk of death. In the case of the research I review below, researchers have controlled for disease status and smoking status.

### The Underweight Category Loses

Across studies, the greatest risk of death, by a long way, is consistently in the underweight category. Studies tend to find that underweight individuals are at about twice the risk of death than normal-weight individuals (Orpana et al., 2010; Strawbridge, Wallhagen & Shema, 2000). Are you surprised? In the U.S., we refer to a BMI < 18.5 as "underweight," which, because of weight stigma, sounds neutral or perhaps even positive in tone. But the World Health Organization refers to the same BMI as "malnourished," which helps makes sense of why this BMI is so strongly predictive of mortality. Note that the stringent International Classification of Diseases weight criteria for anorexia nervosa lists a BMI < 17.5 as required for an anorexia diagnosis, a full BMI point below the malnourished/underweight cutoff.

### Moderate-To-Extreme Obesity and Risk of Death

The risk of death *is* somewhat elevated in people with BMI ≥ 35 (classified as "moderate to extreme," or Class 2 or 3, obesity) versus normal-weight people, but the elevation is not as high as it is for those who are underweight. The hazard ratio for mortality among people with a BMI ≥ 35 is about 1.3 (Flegal et al., 2013). (If you are not familiar with hazard ratios, they are a measure of risk that compares one group to an arbitrarily chosen reference category. In this case, the reference category is normal-weight individuals. A hazard ratio of 2 means "twice as likely to die as those of normal weight," a hazard ratio of 3 means "three times as likely," and so on.). It's also interesting to note that across studies, the risk of being overweight or obese for mortality is higher if BMI was self-reported, rather than measured by the researchers, suggesting either that methodological quality is lower in studies that find greater risks of obesity, or perhaps that obesity self-stigma is interacting with both mortality and people's reports of their own weight. In any event, the risks of greater BMI for mortality are lower when BMI is measured more accurately, by researchers, rather than self-reported by participants (Flegal et al., 2013).

### "Normal Weight" and Risk of Death

The third-likeliest category to die across studies is the normal-weight category, which should leave you scratching your head. Normal weight (currently a BMI of 18.5–24.9), if it is correctly classified, should be the lowest-risk category, but it isn't. This suggests that the move to make the BMI category more stringent in 1998 was a mistake, and perhaps the underweight category should be expanded to include the lower part of the current "normal-weight" category.

### Mild Obesity and Risk of Death

The fourth category is "mild" obesity or obesity class 1, a BMI of 30–34.9. Across studies, this category's risk of death is similar to the normal-weight category.

### "Overweight" and Risk of Death

The lowest risk category across studies is the "overweight" category, a BMI from 25 to 29.9. People in this category have a modestly lower risk of death than those in the normal-weight category. Taken together, these findings suggest that the BMI categories are overall not accurate proxies for health and mortality as they are currently constituted. More accurate categories (that actually reflected risk) would probably have an at-risk or malnourished category that included people with a BMI < 20 or so, a normal-weight category, including BMIs from 20–35, and an overweight category that included those with a BMI > 35. Such categories would not address stigma, the inaccuracy of using BMI as a measure of adiposity, the complexities of cardiometabolic fitness as they interact with weight, or the impossibility of weight loss for the average fat client. However, they would at least reflect mortality risk accurately, which the current categories do not.

*Implicit Mental Models of Risk and Obesity*

Many people imagine that a "malnourished" or "anorexic" person must appear emaciated, but most celebrities and models fall into the underweight category, and the fact that we are constantly surrounded by images of "fit" or "healthy" celebrities, selling running shoes or fitness clothes, for example, creates a risk of our holding implicit biases about weight and health that are inaccurate. Most people who would – based on their BMIs alone – fall into the underweight or anorexia nervosa categories have body types that appear attractive and "healthy" to us based on media exposure alone. It is worth making the mental adjustment to remind yourself that, for example, actress Angelina Jolie, whose BMI likely falls in the "underweight" category, therefore has a risk of death (based on that fact alone) that is substantially higher than the largest-bodied person you know (who perhaps would fall into the moderately to extremely obese category). Obviously, the comparison is ridiculous, because you and I both likely know nothing about either Jolie's health or the health of the largest-bodied person you know, and epidemiological research isn't useful for quantifying individual risks. However, it is useful as a mental heuristic and corrective: If you are more concerned about the health of your fattest clients than you are about the health of the celebrities you see on television or at the movies, and more ready to recommend weight loss to your fat clients than you would be to recommend that celebrities gain weight for their health, your health concerns may be based more on weight stigma than on scientific evidence. The scientific evidence is at variance with pop cultural messages about weight and shape, which, as we have seen, overstate both the risks of being fat, and the ease and benefits of weight loss.

### Health Effects of Being Fat

Readers might be surprised to learn that besides the well-known health risks of obesity, there are some benefits associated with fatness. Extensive research has been conducted on the "obesity paradox," which is the widely replicated finding that, especially for cardiovascular disease, obesity is a protective factor against disease-related mortality and morbidity. In other words, although higher weight is associated with increased risk of cardiovascular disease, overweight/obese patients with cardiovascular disease have better prognoses (Lavie et al., 2014). Why this obesity paradox occurs is not known. It may be that greater adiposity serves as a physical reserve the body can draw upon as it copes with disease.

## Does Weight Loss Enhance Health?

The health effects of even successful weight loss are controversial. Some studies find that intentional weight loss is associated with increased, not decreased, mortality (Allison et al., 1999; Sørensen, 2003), and other studies find that intentional weight loss does not improve survival, as we have already described. It's not clear that the risk profile of someone who has success-fully and intentionally lost weight resembles that of someone who always maintained a lower weight.

Regardless of whether or not obesity is a health risk or a health benefit, or a neutral factor with respect to health, I would argue that it is often and perhaps generally inappropriate to counsel patients to engage in weight loss. Safe, effective weight loss strategies that cause a significant amount of long-term weight loss are not currently available, and it is not clear whether inten-tional weight loss, even if successful, improves or harms health, especially among those who already have diseases where better prognoses among those of greater weight have been observed (Horwich et al., 2001). Even if obesity is robustly associated with health risk and mortality (as we have seen that it often is not), the situation resembles that faced by men.

Consider this: Maleness, like fatness, is a human trait that is not readily or easily changeable. It's also a trait strongly associated with disease and mor-tality. Men die seven years earlier, on average ,in developed nations (Regan & Partridge, 2013). They have greater cardiovascular disease risk, and greater risk of certain cancers, alcoholism, death by suicide, death from influenza, and other infectious diseases. Nevertheless, despite these obvious and clinically important risks to your health of being male, if you are male, your doctor has never said you should consider a sex change to improve your health, nor (if you are female) congratulated you on this fact as something positive you are doing for your health. Why not?

Both you and your doctor recognize that changing your gender would not necessarily affect your disease risk positively. (A transgender woman may not resemble cisgender women in terms of her future disease risk.) Insisting men become women so that their disease risk resembled women's is absurd, and would be discriminatory and unethical, as well as invasive and expensive. However, unlike with weight loss, if someone were to come to me as a med-ical professional and say, "I want to change my sex, what is the empirically supported, safe and effective means of doing so?" I can actually answer that question. If someone asks me, "how do I become thin instead of fat?" how-ever, that question does not have a low-risk, effective, scientifically supported answer. Even if it did: We consider it obvious that men don't need to turn into women to be considered to have done enough for their health. Similarly, fat people don't need to turn into thin ones to have done enough for their health, either.

### Notes

1  Note that the Look Ahead Research Team (2014) data were reported as per-centage body weight lost, but these estimates are converted to kilograms lost based on a participant mean initial weight in the Look Ahead sample of 100.86 kg.

2  I am indebted to Vögele's (2005) excellent chapter on the causes of obesity for much of the discussion in this section.

# References

Allison, D. B., Zannolli, R., Faith, M. S., Heo, M., Pietrobelli, A., Vanltallie, T. B., ... & Heymsfield, S. B. (1999). Weight loss increases and fat loss decreases all-cause mortality rate: results from two independent cohort studies. *International Journal of Obesity, 23*(6), 603–611.

Atkinson, R.L., Dhurandhar, N.V., Allison, D.B., Bowen, R.L., Israel, B.A., Albu, J.B., & Augustus, A.S. (2005). Human adenovirus-36 is associated with increased body weight and paradoxical reduction of serum lipids. *International Journal of Obesity, 29*(3), 281–286.

Ayyad, C., & Andersen, T. (2000). Long-term efficacy of dietary treatment of obesity: A systematic review of studies published between 1931 and 1999. *Obesity Reviews, 1*(2), 113–119.

Barnard, N. D. (2010). Trends in food availability, 1909–2007. *The American Journal of Clinical Nutrition, 91*(5), 1530S-1536S.

Beresford, S. A., Johnson, K. C., Ritenbaugh, C., Lasser, N. L., Snetselaar, L. G., Black, H. R., ... & Brunner, R. L. (2006). Low-fat dietary pattern and risk of colorectal cancer: The Women's Health Initiative Randomized Controlled Dietary Modification Trial. *Journal of the American Medical Association, 295*(6), 643–654.

Bray, G.A., Nielsen, S.J., & Popkin, B.M. (2004). Consumption of high-fructose corn syrup in beverages may play a role in the epidemic of obesity. *The American Journal of Clinical Nutrition, 79*(4), 537–543.

Christou, N. V., Look, D., & MacLean, L. D. (2006). Weight gain after short-and long-limb gastric bypass in patients followed for longer than 10 years. *Annals of Surgery, 244*(5), 734–740.

Corwin, R. L., Avena, N. M., & Boggiano, M. M. (2011). Feeding and reward: Perspectives from three rat models of binge eating. *Physiology and Behavior, 104*(1), 87–97.

Crow, S., & Eckert, E. D. (2000, April). *Follow-up of the Minnesota Semistarvation Study participants*. Paper presented at the Ninth International Conference on Eating Disorders, New York.

Dhurandhar, N. V., Whigham, L. D., Abbott, D. H., Schultz-Darken, N. J., Israel, B. A., Bradley, S. M., ... & Atkinson, R. L. (2002). Human adenovirus Ad-36 promotes weight gain in male rhesus and marmoset monkeys. *The Journal of Nutrition, 132*(10), 3155–3160.

Diabetes Prevention Program Research Group. (2009). 10-year follow-up of diabetes incidence and weight loss in the Diabetes Prevention Program Outcomes Study. *The Lancet, 374*(9702), 1677–1686.

Dulloo, A. G., Jacquet, J., Montani, J. P., & Schutz, Y. (2015). How dieting makes the lean fatter: From a perspective of body composition autoregulation through adipostats and proteinstats awaiting discovery. *Obesity Reviews, 16*(S1), 25–35.

Easterbrook, P. J., Gopalan, R., Berlin, J. A., & Matthews, D. R. (1991). Publication bias in clinical research. *The Lancet, 337*(8746), 867–872.

Espeland, M. (2007). Reduction in weight and cardiovascular disease risk factors in individuals with type 2 diabetes: One-year results of the Look AHEAD trial. *Diabetes Care, 30*(6), 1374–1383.

Flegal, K. M., Kit, B. K., Orpana, H., & Graubard, B. I. (2013). Association of all-cause mortality with overweight and obesity using standard body mass index categories: A systematic review and meta-analysis. *Journal of the American Medical Association, 309*(1), 71–82.

Foster, G. D., Wadden, T. A., Vogt, R. A., & Brewer, G. (1997). What is a reasonable weight loss? Patients' expectations and evaluations of obesity treatment outcomes. *Journal of Consulting and Clinical Psychology*, 65(1), 79–85.

Franklin, B., Jones, A., Love, D., Puckett, S., Macklin, J., & White-Means, S. (2012). Exploring mediators of food insecurity and obesity: A review of recent literature. *Journal of Community Health*, 37(1), 253–264.

Franz, M. J., VanWormer, J. J., Crain, A. L., Boucher, J. L., Histon, T., Caplan, W., ... & Pronk, N. P. (2007). Weight-loss outcomes: A systematic review and meta-analysis of weight-loss clinical trials with a minimum 1-year follow-up. *Journal of the American Dietetic Association*, 107, 1755–1767.

Frisch, R. E. (1987). Body fat, menarche, fitness and fertility. *Human Reproduction*, 2(6), 521–533.

Hagan, M. M., & Moss, D. E. (1997). Persistence of binge-eating patterns after a history of restriction with intermittent bouts of refeeding on palatable food in rats: Implications for bulimia nervosa. *International Journal of Eating Disorders*, 22(4), 411–420.

Hagan, M. M., Wauford, P. K., Chandler, P. C., Jarrett, L. A., Rybak, R. J., & Blackburn, K. (2002). A new animal model of binge eating: Key synergistic role of past caloric restriction and stress. *Physiology and Behavior*, 77(1), 45–54.

Hansen, L. J., Siersma, V., Beck-Nielsen, H., & de Fine Olivarius, N. (2013). Structured personal care of type 2 diabetes: A 19 year follow-up of the study Diabetes Care in General Practice (DCGP). *Diabetologia*, 56(6), 1243–1253.

Heini, A. F., & Weinsier, R. L. (1997). Divergent trends in obesity and fat intake patterns: The American paradox. *The American Journal of Medicine*, 102(3), 259–264.

Horwich, T. B., Fonarow, G. C., Hamilton, M. A., MacLellan, W. R., Woo, M. A., & Tillisch, J. H. (2001). The relationship between obesity and mortality in patients with heart failure. *Journal of the American College of Cardiology*, 38(3), 789–795.

Howard, B. V., Manson, J. E., Stefanick, M. L., Beresford, S. A., Frank, G., Jones, B., ... & Vitolins, M. (2006a). Low-fat dietary pattern and weight change over 7 years: the Women's Health Initiative Dietary Modification Trial. *Journal of the American Medical Association*, 295(1), 39–49.

Howard, B. V., Van Horn, L., Hsia, J., Manson, J. E., Stefanick, M. L., Wassertheil-Smoller, S., ... & Lewis, C. E. (2006b). Low-fat dietary pattern and risk of cardiovascular disease: The Women's Health Initiative Randomized Controlled Dietary Modification Trial. *Journal of the American Medical Association*, 295(6), 655–666.

Kaly, P., Orellana, S., Torrella, T., Takagishi, C., Saff-Koche, L., & Murr, M. M. (2008). Unrealistic weight loss expectations in candidates for bariatric surgery. *Surgery for Obesity and Related Diseases*, 4(1), 6–10.

Kant, A. K. (2004). Dietary patterns and health outcomes. *Journal of the American Dietetic Association*, 104(4), 615–635.

Keys, A., Brozek, J., Henschel, A., Mickelsen, O., & Taylor, H. L. (1950). *The biology of human starvation*. Minneapolis, MN: University of Minnesota Press.

Klimentidis, Y. C., Beasley, T. M., Lin, H. Y., Murati, G., Glass, G. E., Guyton, M., ... & Allison, D. B. (2011). Canaries in the coal mine: A cross-species analysis of the plurality of obesity epidemics. *Proceedings of the Royal Society of London B: Biological Sciences*, 278(1712), 1626–1632.

Klurfield, D. M., Foreyt, J., Angelopoulos, T. J., & Rippe, J. M. (2013). Lack of evidence for high fructose corn syrup as the cause of the obesity epidemic. *International Journal of Obesity, 37*(6), 771–773.

Køster-Rasmussen, R., Simonsen, M. K., Siersma, V., Henriksen, J. E., Heitmann, B. L., & de Fine Olivarius, N. (2016). Intentional weight loss and longevity in overweight patients with type 2 diabetes: A population-based cohort study. *PLOS ONE, 11*(1), e0146889.

Ladabaum, U., Mannalithara, A., Myer, P. A., & Singh, G. (2014). Obesity, abdominal obesity, physical activity, and caloric intake in US adults: 1988 to 2010. *The American Journal of Medicine, 127*(8), 717–727.

Lavie, C. J., McAuley, P. A., Church, T. S., Milani, R. V., & Blair, S. N. (2014). Obesity and cardiovascular diseases: implications regarding fitness, fatness, and severity in the obesity paradox. *Journal of the American College of Cardiology, 63*(14), 1345–1354.

Look AHEAD Research Group. (2013). Cardiovascular effects of intensive lifestyle intervention in type 2 diabetes. *The New England Journal of Medicine, 369*(2), 145–152.

Look AHEAD Research Group. (2014). Eight-year weight losses with an intensive lifestyle intervention: The Look AHEAD study. *Obesity, 22*(1), 5–13.

Mann, T., Tomiyama, A.J., Westling, E., Lew, A.M., Samuels, B., & Chatman, J. (2007). Medicare's search for effective obesity treatments: Diets are not the answer. *American Psychologist, 62*, 220–233.

Markowitz, S., Friedman, M. A., & Arent, S. M. (2008). Understanding the relation between obesity and depression: Causal mechanisms and implications for treatment. *Clinical Psychology: Science and Practice, 15*(1), 1–20.

Montani, J. P., Schutz, Y., & Dulloo, A. G. (2015). Dieting and weight cycling as risk factors for cardiometabolic diseases: Who is really at risk? *Obesity Reviews, 16*(S1), 7–18.

Neumark-Sztainer D, Wall, M., Guo, J., Story, M., Haines, J., & Eisenberg, M. (2006) Obesity, disordered eating, and eating disorders in a longitudinal study of adolescents: How do dieters fare 5 years later? *Journal of the American Dietetic Association, 106*, 559–568.

Neumark-Sztainer, D., Wall, M., Story, M., & Standish, A. R. (2012). Dieting and unhealthy weight control behaviors during adolescence: Associations with 10-year changes in body mass index. *Journal of Adolescent Health, 50*(1), 80–86.

Ogden, C. L. & Carroll, M. D. (2010). Prevalence of overweight, obesity, and extreme obesity among adults: United States, trends 1960–1962 through 2007–2008, NCHS Health E-Stats. Hyattsville, MD: National Center for Health Statistics. Retrieved from www.cdc.gov/NCHS/data/hestat/obesity_adult_07_08/obesity_adult_07_08.pdf

Orpana, H. M., Berthelot, J. M., Kaplan, M. S., Feeny, D. H., McFarland, B., & Ross, N. A. (2010). BMI and mortality: results from a national longitudinal study of Canadian adults. *Obesity, 18*(1), 214–218.

Penedo, F. J., & Dahn, J. R. (2005). Exercise and well-being: A review of mental and physical health benefits associated with physical activity. *Current Opinion in Psychiatry, 18*(2), 189–193.

Polivy, J. (1996). Psychological consequences of food restriction. *Journal of the American Dietetic Association, 96*(6), 589–592.

Polivy, J., & Herman, C. P. (1985). Dieting and binging: A causal analysis. *American Psychologist, 40*(2), 193.

Prentice, A.M. & Jebb, S.A. (1995). Obesity in Britain: Gluttony or sloth? *British Medical Journal, 311*, 437–439.

Prentice, R. L., Caan, B., Chlebowski, R. T., Patterson, R., Kuller, L. H., Ockene, J. K., ... & Paskett, E. (2006). Low-fat dietary pattern and risk of invasive breast cancer: The Women's Health Initiative Randomized Controlled Dietary Modification Trial. *Journal of the American Medical Association, 295*(6), 629–642.

Prentice, R. L., Thomson, C. A., Caan, B., Hubbell, F. A., Anderson, G. L., Beresford, S. A., ... & Singh, B. (2007). Low-fat dietary pattern and cancer incidence in the Women's Health Initiative Dietary Modification Randomized Controlled Trial. *Journal of the National Cancer Institute, 99*(20), 1534–1543.

Regan, J. C., & Partridge, L. (2013). Gender and longevity: why do men die earlier than women? Comparative and experimental evidence. *Best Practice & Research Clinical Endocrinology & Metabolism, 27*(4), 467–479.

Richelsen, B., Tonstad, S., Rössner, S., Toubro, S., Niskanen, L., Madsbad, S., ... & Rissanen, A. (2007). Effect of Orlistat on weight regain and cardiovascular risk factors following a very-low-energy diet in abdominally obese patients. *Diabetes Care, 30*(1), 27–32.

Riley, L. W., Raphael, E., & Faerstein, E. (2013). Obesity in the United States: Dysbiosis from exposure to low-dose antibiotics? In R. P Hunter, C. F. Amábile-Cuevas, J. Lin, J. D. Nosanchuk, & R. Aminov (Eds.), *Frontiers research topics: Low-dose antibiotics: current status and outlook for the future* (pp. 61–68). Lausanne: Frontiers.

Rolland-Cachera, M.F., Deheeger, M., & Bellisle, F. (1996). Nutritional changes between 1978 and 1995 in 10 year old French children. *International Journal of Obesity, 20*(Suppl. 4), 53.

Sørensen, T.I.A. (2003). Weight loss causes increased mortality: Pros. *Obesity Reviews, 4*(1), 3–7.

Speakman, J. R. (2008). Thrifty genes for obesity, an attractive but flawed idea, and an alternative perspective: The "drifty gene" hypothesis. *International Journal of Obesity, 32*(11), 1611–1617.

Stevens, V. J., Obarzanek, E., Cook, N. R., Lee, I. M., Appel, L. J., West, D. S., ... & Millstone, M. (2001). Long-term weight loss and changes in blood pressure: Results of the Trials of Hypertension Prevention, phase II. *Annals of Internal Medicine, 134*(1), 1–11.

Stice, E. (2002). Risk and maintenance factors for eating pathology: A meta-analytic review. *Psychological Bulletin, 128*(5), 825–848.

Stice, E., Cameron, R.P., Killen, J.D., Hayward, C., & Taylor, C.B. (1999). Naturalistic weight-reduction efforts prospectively predict growth in relative weight and onset of obesity among female adolescents. *Journal of Consulting and Clinical Psychology, 67*, 967–974.

Strawbridge, W. J., Wallhagen, M. I., & Shema, S. J. (2000). New NHLBI clinical guidelines for obesity and overweight: will they promote health? *American Journal of Public Health, 90*(3), 340–343.

Television Bureau of Advertising, Inc. (2010). TV basics: A report on the growth and scope of television. Retrieved from www.tvb.org/media/file/TV_Basics.pdf

Togo, P., Osler, M., Sørensen, T. I., & Heitmann, B. L. (2001). Food intake patterns and body mass index in observational studies. *International Journal of Obesity, 25*(12), 1741.

Torgerson, J. S., Hauptman, J., Boldrin, M. N., & Sjöström, L. (2004). Xenical in the prevention of diabetes in obese subjects (XENDOS) study. *Diabetes Care, 27*(1), 155–161.

Unick, J. L., Beavers, D., Bond, D. S., Clark, J. M., Jakicic, J. M., Kitabchi, A. E., ... & Look AHEAD Research Group. (2013). The long-term effectiveness of a life-style intervention in severely obese individuals. *The American Journal of Medicine, 126*(3), 236–242.

Vögele, C. (2005). Etiology of obesity. In S. Munsch & C. Beglinger (Eds.), *Obesity and binge eating disorder* (pp. 62–73). Basel: Karger.

Weinsier, R. L., Hunter, G. R., Heini, A. F., Goran, M. I., & Sell, S. M. (1998). The etiology of obesity: Relative contribution of metabolic factors, diet, and physical activity. *The American Journal of Medicine, 105*(2), 145–150.

Westenhoefer, J., Broeckmann, P., Münch, A. K., & Pudel, V. (1994). Cognitive control of eating behavior and the disinhibition effect. *Appetite, 23*(1), 27–41.

Yaemsiri, S., Slining, M. M., & Agarwal, S. K. (2011). Perceived weight status, overweight diagnosis, and weight control among US adults: The NHANES 2003–2008 Study. *International Journal of Obesity, 35*(8), 1063–1070.

# 2 Clinician Stigma in Weight Management Treatment

## First, Do No Harm

### What Fat Clients Experience When They Seek Care

Fat people face intense stigma and discrimination in most aspects of life, including medical and psychological care and obesity treatment (Puhl & Heuer, 2009). Fat patients certainly perceive discrimination from healthcare providers. Body mass index (BMI) in and of itself is associated with poorer patient satisfaction in medical care overall (Fong, Bertakis, & Franks, 2006; Wee et al., 2002). Obese and overweight women seeking weight loss treatment report that healthcare providers are the second most common source of size stigma (after family members), and most report a history of receiving inappropriate comments about their weight from a doctor (Puhl & Brownell, 2006). Similarly, patients seeking bariatric surgery feel their doctors do not understand how difficult it is to be overweight (Anderson & Wadden, 2004). Women seeking behavioral weight loss treatment report that weight is blamed for most of their medical problems, that no one investigates the cause of their obesity, but simply puts them on diets, and that medical providers see them as second-class citizens (Thompson & Thomas, 2000).

A medical student I mentored at Dartmouth became interested in what patients in our pilot research of the *Accept Yourself!* program said about their interactions with doctors related to their weight, and carried out a qualitative analysis of interviews we had conducted with these patients about their experiences with our program (Morton, Hegel, & Berman, 2014). Weight stigma and interactions with healthcare providers were not the focus of these interviews. Instead, we were looking to evaluate and improve the program described in this book. However, in comparing their experience in our program to other efforts they had made to improve their physical and mental health, they offered up unsolicited examples of weight stigma, enough that my student, Stephanie Morton, was able to create a research project from these comments alone.

Participants described experiences of feeling shamed by physicians related to their weight, to such a degree that they were nearly unable to communicate with their physicians. For example, one participant described it this way (the letter P refers to comments made by patient participants, whereas the letter T refers to the comments from the therapist-researcher conducting the interview):

P: How to handle when you meet with your doctor about your weight and stuff … how do you handle that situation with them? And they have very distinct ideas of where you need to be and what should be happening, and then you feel like everything that you may have is being blamed on yourself – that [your obesity]. Any bariatric or whatever type physician, they just want you to have surgery. I never know how to handle that one. I go in and I sort of end up curling into a ball and nodding my head yes.

T: It's just such a shaming experience.

P: Yeah. And it's like, well, do you think I don't understand every day when I look in the mirror?

T: Do you think that's invisible to me?

P: Right. You think that if it was so easy to do, I wouldn't just do it? I don't know. Do physicians get any kind of training for sensitivity or … understanding all of that, and what it does to…?

Other participants described the "false hope" offered by weight loss interventions, and how the process of going through weight loss interventions or seeking medical care interacted with weight stigma to produce shame and anxiety. One participant, when asked to compare *Accept Yourself!* with other interventions she had tried, had this to say:

P: Other than that, it's either scolding by your physician, or, you know, I tried some medication, but the rest was on my own.

T: And so how did it [*Accept Yourself!*] compare either to the meds for the obesity or being scolded or the things you tried on your own to lose weight?

P: Well, scolding is horrible.

T: This was less horrible.

P: I don't think it's helpful at all because you just beat yourself up and hate yourself even more and wonder why you aren't strong enough to be able to do this, and, so, I think it's sort of counter-effective. [Medications are] like false hope, because you take the medicine and then as soon as you stop taking it, you just put the weight back on and then that feels twice as bad. So I guess it's maybe because this treatment wasn't focused on weight loss, and how successful or unsuccessful you were. It wasn't like the fear of coming in every week and having to step on a scale and being nauseous on your way there, wondering, starving yourself the day before, so that you can try to be okay when you step on the scale, and feeling like you have to justify or you're a failure.

Participants also noted how stigma impaired care providers' ability to see them clearly and to assess what they were already doing to improve their health. One highly physically fit participant, who happened to be a Pilates teacher, described an experience where a doctor gave her a book about Pilates unprompted, and suggested that reading it might help the patient lose weight:

P:  I think just generally being okay with that aspect, and being able to now go back to the doctor and say, look, your crazy little book that you recommended is not the solution ... But, I have to say, in her defense, most people don't believe that I exercise all the time, and I think they think that's just a quick fix, you know? Oh, yeah, do some Pilates and you'll be fine. I'm like, I've been doing Pilates for 10 years. It's not that I haven't been doing it.

## Explicit Weight Stigma among Clinicians and Medical Professionals

When I train therapists and healthcare providers about weight stigma, they frequently point out to me that patients' perceptions of care do not necessarily reflect reality, and that just because a patient perceives a healthcare provider comment about her weight as inappropriate, it doesn't mean that comment actually was intended to be stigmatizing. Is there evidence that medical professionals actually hold biases based on patients' size? Unfortunately, the answer is yes. Medical professionals hold consistently negative attitudes about fat patients (Puhl & Heuer, 2009; Phelan et al., 2015), including physicians, allied healthcare providers such as nurses, physical trainers, and dieticians, and students in health professions. Several studies also suggest that psychologists, therapists, and social workers, as well as mental health students, hold biased, explicit anti-fat attitudes and sometimes engage in size-based discrimination against their clients as well (Agell & Rothblum, 1991; Davis-Coelho et al., 2000; Pascal & Kurpius, 2012).

Yalom (1968) provides a stark, classic example of the way his own hatred of larger bodies (and its intersection with his misogyny) affected his psychotherapy process with a fat female client:

The day Betty entered my office, the instant I saw her steering her ponderous two-hundred-fifty-pound, five-foot-two-inch frame toward my trim, high-tech office chair, I knew that a great trial of countertransference was in store for me. I have always been repelled by fat women. I find them disgusting: their absurd sidewise waddle, their absence of body contour – breasts, laps, buttocks, shoulders, jawlines, cheekbones, everything, everything I like to see in a woman, obscured in an avalanche of flesh.

(pp. 87–88)

Yalom appears unaware of how his stigma, misogyny, and fat hatred may have harmed his client, even as he identifies his countertransference. He describes their work together, and her ultimate weight loss during treatment, as an unqualified success. His blindness to the seriously problematic aspects of his weight stigma may be common, or even normative, among healthcare providers. Even obesity experts attending obesity specialty care conferences display these biases (Schwartz et al., 2003; Teachman & Brownell, 2001), and there is evidence that biases among obesity experts may be actually increasing rather than decreasing over time (Tomiyama et al., 2015).

### Explicit Stereotypes

In considering biases and stereotyping toward patients' weight, it is important to consider both implicit and explicit stereotypes about fat people. Explicit stereotypes consist of the things medical professionals say they think and believe about fat patients. Explicit stereotypes are consciously held attitudes that can be articulated and defended by the person who holds them. Implicit stereotypes, however, may not be properly described as "stereotypes" at all. Implicit stereotypes are unconscious associations that people may hold between ideas – for example, a medical provider who denies any conscious negative attitudes toward fat patients may still hold the unconscious association between being fat and being lazy, simply through being exposed repeatedly to this idea from his or her community or media sources. Medical professionals hold both explicit and implicit anti-fat biases.

You might imagine, or hope, that medical professionals would consciously endorse few explicit anti-fat attitudes. However, you would be wrong. Medical professionals commonly report that obese patients are non-compliant with treatment (Foster et al., 2003), unmotivated to make life changes (Brown, 2006), frustrating to treat, and to blame for their obesity (Campbell & Crawford, 2000). Medical professionals appear to believe that fat patients are not just bad patients, but also bad people. They endorse explicit beliefs that they are ugly, lazy, sloppy, and unattractive (Andrade, et al., 2011; Foster et al., 2003). In a study of humor used in training and critical care medical settings, medical students reported that both they and their attending and training physicians considered fat patients presenting for emergency care to be "fair game" for humorous, derogatory remarks, based on the fact that they felt fat patients were to blame for their difficulties and that they felt caring for them was more difficult than for other patients (Wear et al., 2006). Finally, medical professionals report that fat patients make them feel ineffective at their jobs: They feel poorly trained and ill-equipped to help fat patients, feel that their efforts are less effective with these patients, and dislike working with them (Puhl & Heuer, 2009). Even when responding to such explicit, obviously biased items such as "I really don't like fat people much," a substantial minority of both medical professionals and medical students endorse agreement (Berman & Hegel, 2017; Phelan et al., 2014).

### Implicit Weight Stigma among Professionals

Medical professionals also have implicit (unconscious) anti-fat biases. Even if you do not hold any explicit anti-fat stereotypes and enjoy working with fat clients, you may hold these biases without being aware of them. Implicit biases are much more difficult to identify and study than explicit biases. Explicit biases are verbal behavior; people are conscious of them and can report on them if you ask. But how do you measure a bias someone isn't even aware that they have? Does it even count as a bias if the person who holds it isn't aware of it and consciously disagrees with it?

Social psychologists measure implicit biases in a number of different ways, often by measuring how much more quickly people can associate stereotypical compared with counter-stereotypical ideas. For example, if you can more quickly and accurately associate the word "fat" (or an image of a fat person) with the word "lazy" than you can with the word "hard-working," that might suggest that unconsciously you find the stereotypical association easier to make. One of the most commonly used measures of implicit bias is the Implicit Associations Test (IAT). Instead of explaining in detail how the IAT works, I'd encourage you to try it for yourself. You can take the weight IAT at the Project Implicit website, located at: https://implicit.harvard.edu/implicit/selectatest.html. The Project Implicit website also has several dozen other IATs that assess other kinds of bias, and also opportunities to participate in research or use the IAT yourself, in research or for other purposes. Take a moment now, take the weight-based IAT, and briefly record your score and the interpretation the website provides you on the lines below.

*My Weight-Based IAT Results*

Today's date _____

_____

_____

_____

_____

_____

_____

In later chapters, we'll discuss how and whether you can alter your implicit biases, but for now, you should know that most people score as having some degree of implicit anti-fat bias, whereas a minority show neutral implicit attitudes or anti-thin biases. If you scored with the majority, you shouldn't feel surprised or guilty; implicit anti-fat biases do not reflect your consciously held beliefs, and may arise, at least in part, from mere exposure to these biases, which are readily available in our culture.

However, even though such a score is not unusual, it does potentially have consequences for your clients that need to be ameliorated so they don't cause your clients harm. Measures of implicit and explicit biases predict different types of biased behavior. Explicit stereotypes about stigmatized groups generally predict verbal behavior and conscious decision-making, which makes sense, given that measures of explicit stereotypes essentially assess verbal attitudes. Implicit measures, however, generally predict non-verbal behavior, and decision-making under cognitive burden (Wilson, Lindsey & Schooler, 2000). We might expect a clinician who endorses explicit anti-fat biases to behave in a more overtly discriminatory way to fat clients, encouraging weight loss regardless of the client's presenting concern, or making treatment recommendations or conceptualizations primarily on that client's weight. However, we would expect different behavior from a clinician who did not hold explicit anti-fat biases, but did hold strong *implicit* anti-fat biases. Such a clinician could be expected to show subtle non-verbal differences with fat clients, perhaps making less eye contact or spending less time developing rapport, and such a clinician might make biased treatment decisions as well, especially at the end of the day or workweek, when tired, or when facing a heavy client load.

## Discrimination against Fat Clients

Both implicit and explicit biases are most important to the degree they affect behavior. We might be less concerned with clinician or healthcare provider anti-fat stigma if we knew that even highly biased providers treated all patients fairly. Unfortunately, however, this is not the case. Physicians offer less information about health to fat patients, and spend more time on technical tasks during patient visits (Bertakis & Azari, 2005). They build less rapport with fat patients, spend less time with them, and look at them less during the patient interaction (Gudzune et al., 2013; Hebl & Xu, 2001; Persky & Eccleston, 2011).

Some studies find that physicians order more and different diagnostic tests for fat patients (Hebl & Xu, 2001), but other studies find no differences except in weight-related diagnostic recommendations, such as ordering a blood glucose test (Wigton & McGaghie, 2001; Persky & Eccleston, 2011). However, physicians do make different recommendations to fat than to thin patients with the same symptoms, offering more medical solutions and symptom management (e.g., prescribing medicine) to thin patients, but more lifestyle change recommendations (e.g., exercise) to fat patients (Persky & Eccleston, 2011).

Patients also receive a message from the objects and tools in healthcare settings, including chairs, blood pressure cuffs, gowns, exam tables, etc., that are not functional for size, and which send the message to patients that they do not belong and should get out (Malterud & Ulrickson, 2011). Incorrectly sized equipment does more harm than simply communicating bias, however. As early as the 1980s, researchers were aware that too-small blood pressure cuffs overestimated blood pressure in obese patients, and that the differences were large enough that the well-known correlation between obesity and hypertension that had been long established even at that time could be nothing but an artifact of measurement error (Maxwell et al., 1982).

While implicit and explicit biases may be difficult to eradicate, one simple measure you can take immediately to improve care for your fat clients is to evaluate your office setting for functionality and ability to welcome people of all sizes and abilities. Is your space fully accessible, including entrances, bathrooms, reception desk at height for all users, etc.? Do you have comfortable seating, without arms, in your office and waiting areas? If you make any medical assessments, is your equipment appropriate (e.g., scales that accommodate > 400 lbs with accuracy, blood pressure cuffs in various sizes, gowns that provide full coverage to all bodies, exam tables that are accessible to all, etc.)? Do the magazines and artwork in your office and waiting area reflect human diversity, or do they send weight loss and size-shaming messages? If people are depicted in artwork in your office, are people of all colors, sizes, shapes, and abilities displayed on the walls in positive ways?

## How Weight Stigma Harms Client Health

Ameliorating the impact of your own biases on your patients is not just the right thing to do, or a nicety. Provider weight bias may negatively affect healthcare outcomes (including psychotherapy outcomes) in a variety of ways, as Phelan et al. (2015) observed. Confronted with a fat patient, health providers may simply make poor diagnostic or treatment decisions based on their biases, leading directly to poor health outcomes for the patient. But a variety of indirect effects are also possible. Poor provider attitudes or stigmatizing treatment of the patient (even when clinical recommendations are appropriate) may lead to poor provider–patient communication, poor adherence by the patient to the provider's recommendations, or simply avoidance of care. Even if provider interactions are appropriate, threatening environmental or situational cues can have these same effects, all leading to poor health outcomes. In addition, the stress of coping with stigma (whether real or anticipated) by either a provider or the social and physical environment itself has direct negative effects on health, including weight gain.

There is evidence that weight stigma does affect health outcomes both indirectly and directly. In terms of indirect effects, fat patients do avoid and underutilize health care, and they do specifically attribute their underutilization to embarrassment, shame, and stigmatizing interactions related to their weight (Phelan et al., 2015; Puhl & Heuer, 2009). Fat patients avoid breast, cervical, and colorectal cancer screenings (Amy et al., 2006; Ferrante et al., 2006: Wee et al., 2000). They also avoid preventative and primary care visits

(Drury, Aramburu, & Louis, 2002). Obviously both morbidity and mortality are likely to be worsened for fat patients if they don't receive adequate preventative care. Most chronic and serious conditions are less treatable if caught late rather than early in the disease process; avoiding cancer screenings obviously leads to mortality. It is impossible to speculate how much delayed care may contribute to the association between obesity and various diseases, but it seems possible that this association may be significant.

However, the effects of weight stigma on health are not only mediated through patient avoidance. In fact, the stress of stigma and discrimination appears to have *direct* negative effects on obesity-associated diseases, especially when stigma is internalized and becomes self-stigma (Muennig, 2008). For example, weight *dissatisfaction* is a stronger predictor of physical health outcomes than BMI, and both within and across cultures, groups with lower fat stigma experience less obesity-associated disease mortality and morbidity (Muennig et al., 2008). Weight bias internalization also relates to metabolic syndrome across the weight spectrum (Pearl et al., 2017), whereas weight stigma and discrimination mediates the relationship between BMI and self-reported physical health and quality of life (Hunger & Major, 2015; Latner et al., 2014). Finally, there is mounting evidence that the stress of weight stigma also causes *weight gain*, making obesity stigma itself an unrecognized causal factor in obesity and the obesity epidemic (Tomiyama, 2014).

## Weight Gain and Mental Health: A Vicious Cycle?

The experience of obesity stigma affects not only physical health, but also mental health, perhaps especially in women. Obesity and depression commonly co-occur and are reciprocally related in women. Obesity is a risk factor for the development of depression in women (Roberts, Deleger, Strawbridge, & Kaplan, 2003). In addition, for women, but not men, depression predicts later weight gain and obesity (Richardson et al., 2003). And when depression and obesity co-occur, they affect treatment for both conditions: Weight loss interventions are less effective among depressed individuals, and a history of unsuccessful dieting is associated with depression (Clark et al., 1996). Depressed individuals in weight loss programs lose less weight (Roberts et al., 2003), are more likely to drop out (Clark et al., 1996), and regain more weight (McGuire et al., 1999). Overweight and obesity also predict poorer depression treatment response, and there is some evidence that stress and inflammatory processes may be factors mediating this relationship (Woo et al., 2016).

Researchers have begun to suggest that obesity and depression may constitute a "metabolic-mood syndrome," a distinct disease subtype, with specific biopsychosocial processes that reciprocally influence metabolic function and mood, as well as treatment response (Mansur, Brietzke & McIntyre, 2015). Psychosocial stress, and specifically the psychosocial stress caused by weight stigma, has been implicated as one such process, and researchers have been interested in whether weight stigma affects hypothalamic–pituitary axis and immunological dysfunction in ways that might promote both metabolic and mood dysfunction (Tomiyama, 2014).

Tomiyama's (2014) Cyclic Obesity Weight-Based Stigma (COBWEBS) model is an example. COBWEBS theorizes that weight stigma causes stress (and perhaps also depressive symptoms), which then cause eating and cortisol changes that promote weight gain, fueling additional weight stigma and restarting the cycle. This model provides an explanation for the poor treatment response observed for both obesity and depression when these conditions co-occur. Depression or obesity treatments that ignore (or worsen) weight stigma may set the stage for long-term weight gain and depression relapse.

There is indirect evidence that weight loss interventions and efforts can worsen weight stigma: Weight loss intervention advertisements worsen weight stigma in experiments (Geier, Schwartz, & Brownell, 2003), and repeated dieting is also associated with depression, perhaps because of stigmatizing attributions related to dieting failure (Markowitz, Friedman, & Arent, 2008). Weight loss interventions are predicated on the assumption that weight is controllable, a belief commonly targeted as inaccurate in interventions to reduce weight stigma (Danielsdottir, O'Brien, & Ciao, 2010). Depression interventions, whether medical or psychotherapeutic, likely do not worsen weight stigma, but also do not directly target it. The COBWEBS model offers a possible explanation for why current treatments deliver discouraging outcomes: If weight stigma promotes depression, which in turn promotes increased eating behavior and increased cortisol response, leading to long-term weight gain, interventions that fail to address (or even worsen) weight stigma are likely to promote long-term weight gain and depression relapse even if they initially offer some therapeutic benefit.

Weight stigma also affects eating-disordered behaviors and diagnoses across the client weight spectrum. Weight stigma predicts eating disordered behaviors among women of all weights, and this relationship is mediated by both internalization of weight biases, as well as negative emotions (O'Brien et al., 2016). Stigma also worsens the course of eating disorders (including eating disorders characterized by underweight, such as anorexia) and has emotional and eating behavior consequences (Puhl & Suh, 2015). Some clinicians wonder, if clients are encouraged to accept their weight and no longer feel ashamed of it, will this lead to poor health because they are no longer motivated to make health changes? The evidence suggests that this supposition could not be further from the truth.

## Why Providing Weight Control Treatments is an Ethical Concern

If you have read thus far, you have now absorbed some essential and stereotype-busting information relevant to working with weight-concerned clients of all shapes and sizes. You have learned that being "overweight" does not increase risk of death and that being moderately to extremely obese increases mortality risk less than being underweight. You have discovered that the likelihood of clients permanently achieving their weight loss goals following a weight loss effort is slim, and that weight gain may even be the most typical outcome of a weight loss effort. You have learned that the health benefits of intentional weight loss are not as clear cut as we might have hoped, and that for clients with health problems (regardless of weight), structured interventions and goal setting to improve health may have benefits but do not need to be linked to weight loss. You have also learned that for otherwise healthy clients (regardless of weight), eating unrestrictedly for nutrition and pleasure is not harmful. Finally, you have discovered that weight stigma and discrimination have harmful effects on health that may worsen obesity-associated diseases and cause further weight gain, and that health professionals, including mental health professionals, are a major source of harmful weight stigma, especially for fat patients.

What are the ethical implications of this knowledge? There have been relatively few articles considering the ethical implications of weight loss. One early critique noted the ethical risks associated with blaming individuals for body weight (as is done implicitly in weight loss programs), as well as the problems associated with promoting a culture of thinness, supporting weight loss product merchants, and promoting treatments of dubious efficacy (Hawks & Gast, 2000). I have also written a previous analysis of the ethical implications for psychologists, in particular, of promoting weight loss (Berman, 2017), which I will briefly summarize here. (Readers can find the complete analysis online at the Society for the Advancement of Psychotherapy website: http://societyforpsychotherapy.org/weight-loss-psychotherapy.)

Ethical principles of beneficence, nonmaleficence, integrity, justice, as well as associated enforceable ethical standards for psychologists, may all be threatened by psychotherapy for weight loss. For example, with respect to the American Psychological Association (APA) Code of Ethics for Psychologists, Ethical Principle A, Beneficence and Nonmaleficence: The Code (2010) states that "psychologists strive to benefit those with whom they work and take care to do no harm." Psychologists take the issue of avoiding client harm sufficiently seriously that avoiding harm is also an enforceable ethical standard, as well as a general aspirational principle. Specifically, standard 3.04, Avoiding Harm, states that, "psychologists take reasonable steps to avoid harming their clients/patients, students, supervisees, research participants, organizational clients, and others with whom they work, and to minimize harm where it is foreseeable and unavoidable."

As we have discussed, the typical outcome of weight loss efforts is controversial. If behavioral weight loss causes long-term weight gain for typical clients, recommending it appears to be a relatively clear-cut case of causing potential client harm, and clients with early dieting experiences and multiple dieting failures may be at the highest risk of harmful outcomes (Ikeda et al., 2004).

However, clinicians may be reassured by research that concludes instead that a modest long-term weight loss is possible. These clinicians should consider the fact that typical clients seeking weight loss expect to lose about a third of their initial body weight (Foster, Wadden, Vogt, & Brewer, 1997; Masheb & Grilo, 2002), not the 3–6 percent that represents a best-case scenario for long-term weight loss for most clients. Weight losses typical clients say would be "disappointing" following treatment are still far in excess of typical outcomes of behavioral weight loss, and, in fact, researchers have noted that an amount of weight loss treatment-seekers rate as "disappointing" represents a typical *successful* outcome of bariatric surgery, the most invasive and potent weight loss intervention available (Kaly et al., 2008). This situation means that even though the clinician may see the client as improved, the client may feel she has failed. Dieting failures, whether objective or perceived, increase clients' risk of depression (Markowitz et al., 2008), negative affect, and eating pathology (Stice, 2002). It's also important to note that modest weight loss is only possible if the weight loss efforts are maintained. However, unrealistic expectations for weight loss predict treatment drop-out (Grave et al., 2005), and the intense, substantial sustained effort required over many years may be more than clients will be willing to continue to maintain such a "disappointing" weight loss. Weight cycling, which might be expected following "disappointing" but successful weight loss, predicts worsened cardiometabolic health (Montani, Schultz, & Dulloo, 2015). The risk of harm to clients from engaging in weight loss strategies in psychotherapy is thus considerable, even if clients successfully lose a best-case-scenario-predicted amount of weight and keep that weight off.

With respect to Ethical Principle C: Integrity, the Code (APA, 2010) states that "psychologists seek to promote accuracy, honesty and truthfulness in the science, teaching and practice of psychology," a principle that psychologists and therapists may be manifesting when they engage in the informed consent process with psychotherapy clients. For therapists who are considering helping clients with weight loss, assessing and correcting expectations for treatment seems an essential part of informed consent, including information about the risks of weight gain as a result of treatment, the risks of weight cycling as a result of treatment (with associated mental and physical health ricks), the modest likely outcomes of even successful treatment, and the requirement that clients continue with all aspects of the treatment indefinitely. It is difficult to imagine that many clients who received fully informed consent for weight loss services would be willing to engage indefinitely in the sustained and intense behavioral changes required for long-term weight loss, especially given that the likely losses offer uncertain health benefits and are probably visually undetectable.

Ethical Principle D: Justice, states that "Psychologists ... take precautions to ensure that their potential biases ... do not lead to or condone unjust practices." The Code does not list size-based discrimination as a form of discrimination that psychologists strive to eliminate. However, the risk that therapist's size-based prejudice will affect their services of all kinds to larger-bodied clients, as well as affect their recommendations for weight loss, in ways that are unjust is substantial, as we have already described. Women generally report that they were placed on their first diets by family or healthcare providers, generally in adolescence, and most report that they did not want to be on a diet and describe their diets in overwhelmingly negative terms (Ikeda et al., 2004). Justice requires that psychologists and therapists assess and ameliorate the effects of their own implicit and explicit anti-fat biases, and also would suggest that they be alert to the possibility that clients are being coerced into weight loss as a presenting concern.

In general, it appears that the ethical risks of offering behavioral weight loss services to clients are substantial. Most weight loss interventions cannot be considered evidence-based treatments for weight loss or obesity-related health problems. In fact, clinicians who seek to engage in the highest level of ethical and just practice should work to encourage size acceptance and advocate against size discrimination, not only with individual clients, but also in their advocacy work and cultural activities as a whole.

# References

Agell, G., & Rothblum, E. D. (1991). Effects of clients' obesity and gender on the therapy judgments of psychologists. *Professional Psychology: Research and Practice*, 22(3), 223–229.

American Psychological Association. (2010, as amended 2016). Ethical principles of psychologists and code of conduct. Retrieved from www.apa.org/ethics/code/index. aspx

Amy, N. K., Aalborg, A., Lyons, P., & Keranen, L. (2006). Barriers to routine gynecological cancer screening for White and African-American obese women. *International Journal of Obesity*, 30(1), 147–155.

Anderson, D. A., & Wadden, T. A. (2004). Bariatric surgery patients' views of their physicians' weight-related attitudes and practices. *Obesity*, 12(10), 1587–95.

Andrade, A. D., Ruiz, J. G., Mintzer, M. J., Cifuentes, P., Anam, R., Diem, J., ... & Roos, B. A. (2011). Medical students' attitudes toward obese patient avatars of different skin color. *Studies in Health Technology and Informatics*, 173, 23–29.

Berman, M.I. (2017, April 16). The ethics of helping clients with weight loss in psychotherapy [Blog post]. Retrieved from http://societyforpsychotherapy.org/weight-loss-psychotherapy/

Berman, M. I., & Hegel, M. T. (2017). Weight Bias Education for Medical School Faculty: Workshop and Assessment. *Journal of Nutrition Education and Behavior*, 49(7), 605–606.

Bertakis, K. D., & Azari, R. (2005). The impact of obesity on primary care visits. *Obesity Research*, 13(9), 1615–1623.

Brown, I. (2006). Nurses' attitudes towards adult patients who are obese: Literature review. *Journal of Advanced Nursing*, 53(2), 221–232.

Campbell, K., & Crawford, D. (2000). Management of obesity: Attitudes and practices of Australian dietitians. *International Journal of Obesity*, 24(6), 701–710.

Clark, M. M., Niaura, R., King, T. K., & Pera, V. (1996). Depression, smoking, activity level, and health status: Pretreatment predictors of attrition in obesity treatment. *Addictive Behaviors*, 21(4), 509–513.

Danielsdottir, S., O'Brien, K. S., & Ciao, A. (2010). Anti-fat prejudice reduction: A review of published studies. *Obesity Facts, 3*(1), 47–58.

Davis-Coelho, K., Waltz, J., & Davis-Coelho, B. (2000). Awareness and prevention of bias against fat clients in psychotherapy. *Professional Psychology: Research and Practice, 31*(6), 682–684.

Drury, A., Aramburu, C., & Louis, M. (2002). Exploring the association between body weight, stigma of obesity, and health care avoidance. *Journal of the American Academy of Nurse Practitioners, 14*(12), 554–561.

Ferrante, J. M., Ohman-Strickland, P., Hudson, S. V., Hahn, K. A., Scott, J. G., & Crabtree, B. F. (2006). Colorectal cancer screening among obese versus non-obese patients in primary care practices. *Cancer Detection and Prevention, 30*(5), 459–465.

Fong, R. L., Bertakis, K. D., & Franks, P. (2006). Association between obesity and patient satisfaction. *Obesity, 14*(8), 1402–1411.

Foster, G. D., Wadden, T. A., Makris, A. P., Davidson, D., Sanderson, R. S., Allison, D. B., & Kessler, A. (2003). Primary care physicians' attitudes about obesity and its treatment. *Obesity Research, 11*(10), 1168–1177.

Foster, G. D., Wadden, T. A., Vogt, R. A., & Brewer, G. (1997). What is a reasonable weight loss? Patients' expectations and evaluations of obesity treatment outcomes. *Journal of Consulting and Clinical Psychology, 65*(1), 79–85.

Geier, A. B., Schwartz, M. B., & Brownell, K. D. (2003). "Before and after" diet advertisements escalate weight stigma. *Eating and Weight Disorders – Studies on Anorexia, Bulimia and Obesity, 8*(4), 282–288.

Grave, R., Calugi, S., Molinari, E., Petroni, M. L., Bondi, M., Compare, A., & Marchesini, G. (2005). Weight loss expectations in obese patients and treatment attrition: an observational multicenter study. *Obesity, 13*(11), 1961–9.

Gudzune, K. A., Beach, M. C., Roter, D. L., & Cooper, L. A. (2013). Physicians build less rapport with obese patients. *Obesity, 21*(10), 2146–2152.

Hawks, S. R., & Gast, J. A. (2000). The ethics of promoting weight loss. *Healthy Weight Journal, 14*(2), 25–26.

Hebl, M. R., & Xu, J. (2001). Weighing the care: Physicians' reactions to the size of a patient. *International Journal of Obesity, 25*(8), 1246.

Hunger, J. M., & Major, B. (2015). Weight stigma mediates the association between BMI and self-reported health. *Health Psychology, 34*(2), 172.

Ikeda, J. P., Lyons, P., Schwartzman, F., & Mitchell, R. A. (2004). Self-reported dieting experiences of women with body mass indexes of 30 or more. *Journal of the American Dietetic Association, 104*(6), 972–974.

Kaly, P., Orellana, S., Torrella, T., Takagishi, C., Saff-Koche, L., & Murr, M. M. (2008). Unrealistic weight loss expectations in candidates for bariatric surgery. *Surgery for Obesity and Related Diseases, 4*(1), 6–10.

Latner, J. D., Barile, J. P., Durso, L. E., & O'Brien, K. S. (2014). Weight and health-related quality of life: The moderating role of weight discrimination and internalized weight bias. *Eating Behaviors, 15*(4), 586–590.

Malterud, K., & Ulriksen, K. (2011). Obesity, stigma, and responsibility in health care: A synthesis of qualitative studies. *International Journal of Qualitative Studies on Health and Well-being, 6*(4), 10.3402/qhw.v6i4.8404.

Mansur, R. B., Brietzke, E., & McIntyre, R. S. (2015). Is there a "metabolic-mood syndrome"? A review of the relationship between obesity and mood disorders. *Neuroscience & Biobehavioral Reviews, 52*, 89–104.

Markowitz, S., Friedman, M. A., & Arent, S. M. (2008). Understanding the relation between obesity and depression: Causal mechanisms and implications for treatment. *Clinical Psychology: Science and Practice, 15*(1), 1–20.

Masheb, R.M., & Grilo, C.M. (2002). Weight loss expectations in patients with binge-eating disorder. *Obesity Research, 10*(5), 309–314.

Maxwell, M., Schroth, P., Waks, A., Karam, M., & Dornfeld, L. (1982). Error in blood-pressure measurement due to incorrect cuff size in obese patients. *The Lancet, 320*, 33–36.

McGuire, M. T., Wing, R. R., Klem, M. L., Lang, W., & Hill, J. O. (1999). What predicts weight regain in a group of successful weight losers? *Journal of Consulting and Clinical Psychology, 67*(2), 177.

Montani, J. P., Schutz, Y., & Dulloo, A. G. (2015). Dieting and weight cycling as risk factors for cardiometabolic diseases: Who is really at risk? *Obesity Reviews, 16*(S1), 7–18.

Morton, S.N., Hegel, M.T. & Berman, M.I. (2014, October). Evaluating the effectiveness of combined Health At Every Size and Acceptance and Commitment Therapy to treat women with obesity and depression. Poster presented at the Geisel School Research Poster Night, Hanover, NH.

Muennig, P. (2008). The body politic: The relationship between stigma and obesity-associated disease. *BMC Public Health, 8*(1), 128.

Muennig, P., Jia, H., Lee, R., & Lubetkin, E. (2008). I think therefore I am: Perceived ideal weight as a determinant of health. *American Journal of Public Health, 98*(3), 501.

O'Brien, K. S., Latner, J. D., Puhl, R. M., Vartanian, L. R., Giles, C., Griva, K., & Carter, A. (2016). The relationship between weight stigma and eating behavior is explained by weight bias internalization and psychological distress. *Appetite, 102*, 70–76.

Pascal, B., & Kurpius, S. E. R. (2012). Perceptions of clients: Influences of client weight and job status. *Professional Psychology: Research and Practice, 43*(4), 349–355.

Pearl, R. L., Wadden, T. A., Hopkins, C. M., Shaw, J. A., Hayes, M. R., Bakizada, Z. M., … & Alamuddin, N. (2017). Association between weight bias internalization and metabolic syndrome among treatment-seeking individuals with obesity. *Obesity, 25*(2), 317–322.

Persky, S., & Eccleston, C. P. (2011). Medical student bias and care recommendations for an obese versus non-obese virtual patient. *International Journal of Obesity, 35*(5), 728–735.

Phelan, S. M., Burgess, D. J., Yeazel, M. W., Hellerstedt, W. L., Griffin, J. M., & Ryn, M. (2015). Impact of weight bias and stigma on quality of care and outcomes for patients with obesity. *Obesity Reviews, 16*(4), 319–326.

Phelan S.M., Dovidio, J.F., Puhl, R.M., Burgess, D.J., Nelson, D.B., Yeazel, M.W., et al. (2014). Implicit and explicit weight bias in a national sample of 4,732 medical students: The medical student CHANGES study. *Obesity, 22*, 1201–1208.

Puhl, R. M., & Brownell, K. D. (2006). Confronting and coping with weight stigma: An investigation of overweight and obese adults. *Obesity, 14*(10), 1802–1815.

Puhl, R. M., & Heuer, C. A. (2009). The stigma of obesity: A review and update. *Obesity, 17*(5), 941–964.

Puhl, R., & Suh, Y. (2015). Stigma and eating and weight disorders. *Current Psychiatry Reports, 17*(3), 1–10.

Richardson, L. P., Davis, R., Poulton, R., McCauley, E., Moffitt, T. E., Caspi, A., & Connell, F. (2003). A longitudinal evaluation of adolescent depression and adult obesity. *Archives of Pediatrics and Adolescent Medicine, 157*(8), 739–745.

Roberts, R. E., Deleger, S., Strawbridge, W. J., & Kaplan, G. A. (2003). Prospective association between obesity and depression: evidence from the Alameda County Study. *International Journal of Obesity, 27*(4), 514–521.

Schwartz, M. B., Chambliss, H. O. N., Brownell, K. D., Blair, S. N., & Billington, C. (2003). Weight bias among health professionals specializing in obesity. *Obesity Research, 11*(9), 1033–1039.

Stice, E. (2002). Risk and maintenance factors for eating pathology: A meta-analytic review. *Psychological Bulletin, 128*(5), 825–848.

Teachman, B. A., & Brownell, K. D. (2001). Implicit anti-fat bias among health professionals: Is anyone immune? *International Journal of Obesity, 25,* 1525–1531.

Thompson, R. L., & Thomas, D. E. (2000). A cross-sectional survey of the opinions on weight loss treatments of adult obese patients attending a dietetic clinic. *International Journal of Obesity and Related Metabolic Disorders, 24*(2), 164–170.

Tomiyama, A. J. (2014). Weight stigma is stressful. A review of evidence for the Cyclic Obesity/Weight-Based Stigma model. *Appetite, 82,* 8–15.

Tomiyama, A. J., Finch, L. E., Belsky, A. C. I., Buss, J., Finley, C., Schwartz, M. B., & Daubenmier, J. (2015). Weight bias in 2001 versus 2013: Contradictory attitudes among obesity researchers and health professionals. *Obesity, 23*(1), 46–53.

Wear, D., Aultman, J. M., Varley, J. D., & Zarconi, J. (2006). Making fun of patients: Medical students' perceptions and use of derogatory and cynical humor in clinical settings. *Academic Medicine, 81*(5), 454–462.

Wee, C. C., McCarthy, E. P., Davis, R. B., & Phillips, R. S. (2000). Screening for cervical and breast cancer: Is obesity an unrecognized barrier to preventive care? *Annals of Internal Medicine, 132*(9), 697–704.

Wee, C. C., Phillips, R. S., Francis Cook, E., Haas, J. S., Louise Puopolo, A., Brennan, T. A., & Burstin, H. R. (2002). Influence of body weight on patients' satisfaction with ambulatory care. *Journal of General Internal Medicine, 17*(2), 155–159.

Wigton, R. S., & McGaghie, W. C. (2001). The effect of obesity on medical students' approach to patients with abdominal pain. *Journal of General Internal Medicine, 16*(4), 262–265.

Wilson, T. D., Lindsey, S., & Schooler, T. Y. (2000). A model of dual attitudes. *Psychological Review, 107*(1), 101–126.

Woo, Y. S., Seo, H. J., McIntyre, R. S., & Bahk, W. M. (2016). Obesity and its potential effects on antidepressant treatment outcomes in patients with depressive disorders: A literature review. *International Journal of Molecular Sciences, 17*(1), 80.

Yalom, I. D. (1968). The fat lady. In I.D. Yalom (Ed.), *Love's executioner and other tales of psychotherapy* (pp. 87–117). New York: Basic Books.

# 3 A New Alternative

## Acceptance-Based Approaches to Client Weight Concerns

If behavioral weight loss interventions are not evidence-based care for clients with weight concerns, what do we have to offer instead? Two acceptance-based approaches, and one approach that integrates them, offer promise for enhancing the physical and mental health of weight-concerned clients willing to try a non-weight-loss approach. Acceptance-based interventions can be used to decrease weight stigma and increase values-driven, healthful lifestyles among clients with weight and body image concerns. These approaches include: (1) Acceptance and Commitment Therapy (ACT); (2) Health At Every Size® (HAES); and (3) a new, integrative approach for women with weight and mental health concerns described in this book, *Accept Yourself!* In this chapter, these approaches will be described, including the theoretical and empirical support for their use with weight-concerned clients.

### An Overview of Acceptance and Commitment Therapy for Weight and Body Image Concerns

ACT (Hayes, Strohsahl & Wilson, 2011) is a third-wave cognitive behavioral therapy (CBT), which means it focuses on clients' thoughts and behaviors, arises out of scientific research on human behavior, emotion, and cognition, and weaves mindfulness and Buddhist principles into a behaviorist understanding of human suffering. A detailed consideration of the historical and theoretical underpinnings of ACT is beyond the scope of this chapter, but a few notes of background will be helpful in understanding the approach and how it applies to clients with weight concerns. ACT focuses on accepting and mindfully experiencing negative private events, including thoughts, emotions, or sensations that a person finds painful. For example, ACT focuses on accepting and mindfully experiencing thoughts of failure, body hatred or disgust, "feeling fat," sadness, tearfulness, and physical pain, without seeking to control or eliminate these experiences. ACT also encourages clients to choose, commit to, and act on important life values, such as values related to family, love, or work, while experiencing negative private events.

ACT takes a unique perspective on psychopathology. In most forms of psychological or psychiatric treatment, we tend to assume that emotional or physical pain are abnormal and need to be corrected to return the client to optimal mental health. In contrast, ACT assumes that psychological pain is a normal and inescapable part of the human condition. Psychopathology arises then, not because of the experience of pain, but out of psychological inflexibility. This inflexibility arises out of the unique human capacity to learn and use language.

ACT therapists observe that people know much of what we know not by direct, lived experience, but by learned verbal and social rules that guide our behavior. This has distinct advantages: You can learn, verbally and socially, important information that it would be dangerous, or even fatal, to learn by direct lived experience, such as the fact that certain snakes or spiders are poisonous, or that touching a downed power line after a rainstorm might cause an electrocution. You can also learn verbally and socially to persist in situations where the reinforcement for participation is not immediate, but far in the future, such as working hard in a class to earn a grade or a degree. However, ACT therapists point out that this ability to learn and follow verbal and social rules has a distinct downside. In particular, we may continue to follow these rules even when our experience is telling us that the rules are unhelpful or counterproductive.

The experience of many clients with weight control is an excellent example. Clients often have learned a series of verbal and social rules about food, movement, appearance, and their overall relationship with their bodies that are ineffective. For example, clients have often been taught how many calories they "should" consume or need. This arbitrary, socially learned number, when consumed, often leads to immediate negative experiential feedback: feelings of hunger, or even symptoms of starvation, or binge behavior. And yet the rule, "You should only eat 1,200 calories per day," overrides these experiences. The client may continue to follow (or try to follow) the rule, despite what her experience is telling her.

Similar rules have often been learned for emotions, leading to similar insensitivity to one's own experience, and negative outcomes. For example, many people have been taught that certain emotions or emotional expressions are unacceptable. "Don't cry or I'll give you something to cry about," "Don't be scared," and "God hates a coward" are all possible examples. If clients feel or express an "unacceptable" emotion (or feel it more frequently or more intensely than the rule states is acceptable), then they may make efforts to get rid of these emotions by any number of strategies: distraction, numbing (e.g., with alcohol or drugs), avoidance, or control of the environment so it will not elicit emotions. Emotions still emerge despite these efforts, leading to anger, frustration, and shame that the person cannot control the emotion as she/he "should" be able to, and the control strategies themselves often have harmful effects (e.g., avoidance leading to disengagement from enjoyable activities, substance use leading to addiction). Nevertheless, the person may go on following the rule "sadness or fear is unacceptable," without ever noticing that following this rule has led to a situation where the sadness and fear remain, are increased, and are joined by even more unpleasant emotions and experiences.

Clients often have similar unhelpful, socially and media-learned rules about body image and living in their bodies that are adhered to inflexibly, regardless of feedback from their contexts or environments. Rules about how bodies should look, for example, are generally derived from wholly unattainable, idealized media images: Even celebrities and models whose full-time paid job is to conform to beauty ideals are not depicted in media images without first being extensively made up, costumed, posed, airbrushed, and Photoshopped to look like an ideal of beauty and body image that even they cannot attain. As supermodel Cindy Crawford said, "I wish I looked like Cindy Crawford" (Jhally, 2010). Following the rule "I should look like media imagery of Cindy Crawford" may lead to lack of attainment in career, personal life, or other valued domains, as well as increasing frustration, shame, self-hatred, and anger, as one fails to attain this unattainable ideal, no matter how much time or energy is invested in it. Again, clients may follow the rule so rigidly that they do not even notice the actual outcomes of rule adherence, instead focusing on the importance of following the rule at any cost.

ACT therapists observe that following social and verbal rules like these in spite of negative feedback from their direct, lived experience may lead to a variety of problems. Instead of being guided by personal goals, values, and life experience, clients suffering from psychological inflexibility are guided by these learned verbal rules. When pain emerges, as it does for all people at some point, clients who hold rules about emotions being harmful struggle with the pain they are experiencing and what it means about them, rather than simply experiencing their pain, and this struggle may prolong and intensify their misery. ACT describes several processes that drive this inflexibility.

Figure 3.1 displays the ACT Hexaflex with examples common among clients who struggle with weight and body image. The Hexaflex is a graphic depiction of psychopathology in ACT. It is called the Hexaflex because it is hexagonal in shape, with six primary processes noted, and because the emphasis is on psychological flexibility or inflexibility. Six processes that drive psychological inflexibility are illustrated on the Hexaflex.

Sticking to rules that don't work we have already described. These rules can take almost any form or be relevant to many domains of life. The unifying feature of these rules is that following them leads to unpleasant consequences or leads the client away from a goal or valued life activity. For example, the client following the rule "eating pizza means I've failed" may find herself unable or unwilling to go out for pizza with friends she enjoys, or to participate in a pizza fundraiser for a child's activity she values, or may find that she does choose to participate in these activities, eats pizza, feels like a failure, and fails to experience the enjoyment or accomplishment and lack of bad outcomes the activity of eating pizza in the context might otherwise afford. Following the rule leads to poor outcomes, and not following the rule would lead the client closer to experiences she wants and enjoys.

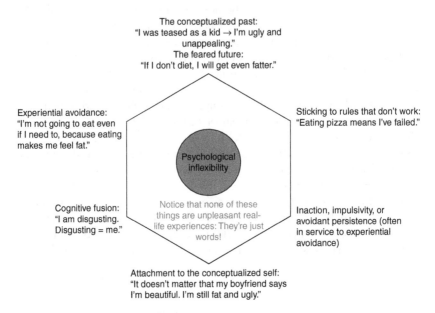

The conceptualized past:
"I was teased as a kid → I'm ugly and
unappealing."
The feared future:
"If I don't diet, I will get even fatter."

Experiential avoidance:
"I'm not going to eat even
if I need to, because eating
makes me feel fat."

Sticking to rules that don't work:
"Eating pizza means I've failed."

Psychological
inflexibility

Cognitive fusion:
"I am disgusting.
Disgusting = me."

Notice that none of these
things are unpleasant real-
life experiences: They're just
words!

Inaction, impulsivity, or
avoidant persistence (often
in service to experiential
avoidance)

Attachment to the conceptualized self:
"It doesn't matter that my boyfriend says
I'm beautiful. I'm still fat and ugly."

*Figure 3.1* The Hexaflex.

The conceptualized past and the feared future represent thoughts the client has about what has or will happen. For example, a client who struggles with weight may say, "I was teased for being fat all the way back in grade school. I've *always* been fat, ugly, and undesirable." Intriguingly, clients may continue to struggle with the conceptualized past in this fashion regardless of past or current body size. For example, when I have worked with childhood photographs of fat clients who were teased for being "fat" as children, they have often been able to observe that they were not, in fact, fat when they were teased or treated cruelly by peers or family members about their weight, and they often also observe the difference between what their mind tells them about their memories of that time ("I was a fat and ugly kid") and what the photographs show ("Actually I was normal weight, an adorable little girl. Why would anyone say I was fat? Why did I think I was fat?"). Clients who are currently in thin or average-sized bodies, however, will sometimes insist that they are "*really*" fat; I've *always* been fat" because of a conceptualized past of being fat, and will express fear that if they relinquish control over their weight or stop engaging in weight loss strategies they will return to the size specified in their conceptualized past as "theirs." Similarly, the feared future, often of becoming fat or more fat (with a highly negative, stigmatized conceptualization of what fatness means), dominates clients' behavior and self-understanding.

Experiential avoidance refers to situations where a client avoids something that may bring up unpleasant private experiences (e.g., unpleasant

## Why Should a Therapist Consider Using ACT for Weight-Concerned Clients?

ACT is efficacious for a variety of client concerns, including depression (Forman et al., 2012; Markanday et al., 2012). There is preliminary evidence that suggests that ACT is also helpful for eating and weight-related concerns. Several small, non-experimental studies suggest ACT may be safe and efficacious for eating disorders (Berman, Boutelle, & Crow, 2009; Heffner et al., 2002; Juarascio et al., 2013; Martín-Murcia, Díaz & Gonzalez, 2011). In addition, two small, randomized controlled trials have shown ACT to be efficacious for general eating pathology and body dissatisfaction (Juarascio, Forman, & Herbert, 2010; Pearson, Follette, & Hayes, 2012); one of these found that ACT was more effective than cognitive therapy (Juarascio et al., 2010). A case series has also demonstrated feasibility and possible efficacy of ACT in treating binge eating disorder (Hill et al., 2015). Some research has also found that ACT interventions decreased obesity stigma, and improved quality of life for obese weight-loss-seeking participants and bariatric surgery patients compared to behavioral weight loss strategies alone (Forman et al., 2009; Lillis et al., 2009; Weineland et al., 2012). However, ACT is a psychotherapy, and it has been used primarily to improve mental health concerns. ACT does not specifically target or teach physical wellness strategies. In addition, even though ACT is an acceptance-based treatment, it has been used as an adjunct to behavioral weight loss. There are other self-acceptance-based approaches that focus more tightly on physical wellness, and that have a more consistent message of self-acceptance related to weight.

## An Overview of HAES for Weight and Body Image Concerns

HAES represents a self-acceptance-based, non-stigmatizing, non-weight-loss approach to physical wellness. HAES is not a psychotherapy. Instead, it is a wellness paradigm that encourages people of all sizes to address health directly (i.e., without waiting for weight loss) by adopting healthy behaviors. HAES encourages people to adopt health habits for the sake of health and well-being (rather than for weight control), and HAES doesn't promise or prioritize weight loss. In fact, from a HAES perspective, weight gain would be a perfectly acceptable outcome of treatment, provided the patient's mental and physical wellness also improved. HAES is weight neutral, and does not place a positive or negative judgment on any particular weight or weight-change outcome. Instead, HAES teaches clients to accept and respect their bodies as they are, and also to respect and appreciate the natural diversity of body sizes and shapes among the population in general. HAES helps clients eat flexibly, in a manner that values (rather than shames) pleasure and honors internal cues of hunger, satiety, and appetite. HAES encourages clients to enjoy moving their bodies and becoming more physically vital, rather than rigidly focusing on exercise as a means of penance or control. Although we have already made the point, it is central to understanding the HAES paradigm, and thus bears repeating: *HAES is not a weight loss program. It neither expects nor encourages weight loss.*

HAES is not a particular treatment or program. Instead, it is a wellness paradigm that can be adapted to a variety of treatment contexts and activities. What makes a treatment HAES is adherence to the HAES Guiding Principles (Association for Size Diversity and Health, 2017), which were created and are maintained by the Association for Size Diversity and Health, an organization of professionals who promote the HAES Principles and use them in their work. These principles include:

1. Weight Inclusivity: Accept and respect the inherent diversity of body shapes and sizes and reject the idealizing or pathologizing of specific weights.
2. Health Enhancement: Support health policies that improve and equalize access to information and services, and personal practices that improve human well-being, including attention to individual physical, economic, social, spiritual, emotional, and other needs.
3. Respectful Care: Acknowledge our biases, and work to end weight discrimination, weight stigma, and weight bias. Provide information and services from an understanding that socio-economic status, race, gender, sexual orientation, age, and other identities impact weight stigma, and support environments that address these inequities.
4. Eating for Well-being: Promote flexible, individualized eating based on hunger, satiety, nutritional needs, and pleasure, rather than any externally regulated eating plan focused on weight control.
5. Life-Enhancing Movement: Support physical activities that allow people of all sizes, abilities, and interests to engage in enjoyable movement, to the degree that they choose.

The HAES Principles are periodically revised; more information about them is available from the Association for Size Diversity and Health (www.sizediversityandhealth.org). HAES represents a productive alternative to non-evidence-based behavioral weight loss approaches because HAES has been demonstrated to cause improvements in physiological health outcomes (e.g., blood pressure and lipids), health behaviors (e.g., physical activity), and psychosocial outcomes (e.g., depression and quality of life) among overweight and obese participants that are longer-lasting than weight loss programs. In addition, participants are more adherent to HAES than weight loss interventions (Bacon & Aphramor, 2011). However, HAES is a wellness paradigm, not a psychotherapy or treatment program, and, although it has demonstrated some psychosocial benefits, it does not directly address psychological concerns or struggles.

# An Integrative Self-Acceptance-Based Treatment for Obese Women with Depression and Psychological Concerns: *Accept Yourself!*

ACT and HAES appeared to me and my research team to be ripe for integration to help women (and perhaps also men) with weight concerns and related psychological problems. Both treatments independently have shown promise for body-image-related distress, mood, and improved physical health and wellness, and both treatments have shown promise where other interventions have failed. Combined, these interventions represent a paradigm shift in treatment for obesity and related psychological distress *away* from treatments that emphasize weight and emotional control and *toward* acceptance-based approaches. Combined, they each address the limitations of the other: adding ACT's coherent theoretical framework for self-acceptance, and its well-fleshed-out interventions that comprise a cohesive treatment program, to HAES' clear ethical insistence on providing evidence-based care that addresses weight stigma and enhances physical well-being for people of all shapes and sizes. Because we believed that the two treatments would be well integrated, my research team and I have spent the past decade developing and beginning to test the integrated self-acceptance approach described in this book and known as *Accept Yourself!*

## The Accept Yourself! Research Treatment Program

The *Accept Yourself!* program grew out of research I had conducted on ACT as a treatment for eating disorders, including anorexia nervosa, as well as teaching and advocacy I had been doing related to size acceptance, beginning in 2006. My team and I began developing a treatment manual for *Accept Yourself!* in 2011, and we received preliminary funding for pilot research from a Gary Tucker Junior Investigator Research Award I received from the Geisel School of Medicine at Dartmouth in 2013. With that pilot funding, we conducted a preliminary investigation to determine if *Accept Yourself!* was safe, feasible, and to see if there were signs it might be helpful for obese women who also had major depressive disorder (MDD). Our primary interest was in depression symptoms, but we also monitored some physical health outcomes and other psychosocial outcomes as well.

A qualitative study describing pilot participants' reactions to the program, as well as a clinical description of the intervention, was initially published (Berman, Morton, & Hegel, 2016a). We learned that women who had participated in the program felt it was helpful, and we made changes to the program based on their feedback, including developing a self-help manual, which we have expanded upon in the companion volume to this text.

We also published the outcomes of that pilot trial (Berman, Morton, & Hegel, 2016b). The study used an uncontrolled, pre-treatment to post-treatment design, with a 3-month follow-up, to evaluate the feasibility and outcome of *Accept Yourself!* As evaluated in the pilot trial, *Accept Yourself!* was an 11-week manualized, group-based HAES/ACT intervention. Twenty-one obese women with MDD received the intervention; 18 completed at least seven sessions, which we chose a priori as representing a minimal dose of the intervention. We assessed depressive symptoms, depression diagnosis, physical health outcomes (including physical activity and blood pressure), and obesity-related quality of life at baseline, post-treatment, and at the three-month follow-up. Although we did not expect it to change, we also monitored participants' weight. We found that depression, blood pressure, and obesity-related quality of life all significantly improved from pre-treatment to post-treatment, and those improvements were sustained over the brief 3-month follow-up. We also found that participants did not gain significant weight during the intervention or at follow-up. Thus, the pilot data suggested that *Accept Yourself! could* be a promising treatment for obese, depressed women, although these data were not experimental, so we have no way of knowing whether the intervention actually caused the improvements we observed.

With the support of these promising pilot data, in 2015, the Hitchcock Foundation awarded me a two-year, $250,000 career development award to conduct a small, pilot, randomized controlled trial comparing *Accept Yourself!* to Weight Watchers, a group-based behavioral weight loss program, as a treatment to enhance the mental and physical health with obese women with MDD. Data collection for this trial is now complete, and we are analyzing the data as of this writing. We followed the participants in this trial for a full year after the intervention, so we hope to gain information about the longer-term effects of both Weight Watchers and *Accept Yourself!*

Neither we nor anyone else has conducted research on whether *Accept Yourself!* is helpful for women who are not obese, for men, or for people who do not have MDD, although we suspect it could be helpful for women of all sizes and for other psychological problems related to poor body image. We are uncertain whether it would work equally well for men, as much of the content relates to women's experiences of cultural discrimination, self-objectification, and internalization of thin and beauty ideals for women. However, men also experience body image concerns and exposure to unattainable body image ideals, and we suspect and hope that *Accept Yourself!* can be adapted for men. If you adapt this program for use with male clients, I hope you will get in touch with me and let me know how it goes; you will find contact information and options in Chapter 13.

For now, it is appropriate to consider the research support for *Accept Yourself!* for obese women with depression to be promising but very preliminary, and to admit that there is no empirical information to support its use with other populations. Nevertheless, clinically it may represent a powerful and novel approach for you to consider with your clients, and it may represent an improvement over behavioral weight loss approaches, which, as we have reviewed, cannot be considered evidence based and have some evidence that they may cause harm for some clients under some circumstances.

# References

Association for Size Diversity and Health (2017). *HAES® Principles*. Retrieved from www.sizediversityandhealth.org/content.asp?id=76

Bacon, L., & Aphramor, L. (2011). Weight science: Evaluating the evidence for a paradigm shift. *Nutrition Journal, 10*(9), 2–13.

Berman, M. I., Boutelle, K. N., & Crow, S. J. (2009). A case series investigating acceptance and commitment therapy as a treatment for previously treated, unremitted patients with anorexia nervosa. *European Eating Disorders Review, 17*(6), 426–434.

Berman, M.I., Morton, S.N., & Hegel, M.T. (2016a). Health At Every Size and Acceptance and Commitment Therapy for obese, depressed women: Treatment development and clinical application. *Clinical Social Work Journal, 44*(3), 265–278.

Berman, M.I., Morton, S.N., & Hegel, M.T. (2016b). Uncontrolled pilot study of an Acceptance and Commitment Therapy and Health At Every Size intervention for obese, depressed women: Accept Yourself! *Psychotherapy, 53*(4), 462–467.

Forman, E. M., Butryn, M. L., Hoffman, K. L., & Herbert, J. D. (2009). An open trial of an acceptance-based behavioral intervention for weight loss. *Cognitive and Behavioral Practice, 16*(2), 223–235.

Forman, E. M., Shaw, J. A., Goetter, E. M., Herbert, J. D., Park, J. A., & Yuen, E. K. (2012). Long-term follow-up of a randomized controlled trial comparing acceptance and commitment therapy and standard cognitive behavior therapy for anxiety and depression. *Behavior Therapy, 43*(4), 801–811.

Harris, M. A., Brett, C. E., Johnson, W., & Deary, I. J. (2016). Personality stability from age 14 to age 77 years. *Psychology and Aging, 31*(8), 862–874.

Hayes, S. C., Strosahl, K. D., & Wilson, K. G. (2011). *Acceptance and Commitment Therapy: The process and practice of mindful change (2nd Ed)*. New York: Guilford.

Heffner, M., Sperry, J., Eifert, G. H., & Detweiler, M. (2002). Acceptance and commitment therapy in the treatment of an adolescent female with anorexia nervosa: A case example. *Cognitive and Behavioral Practice, 9*(3), 232–236.

Hill, M. L., Masuda, A., Melcher, H., Morgan, J. R., & Twohig, M. P. (2015). Acceptance and commitment therapy for women diagnosed with binge eating disorder: A case-series study. *Cognitive and Behavioral Practice, 22*(3), 367–378.

Jhally, S. (Director). (2010). *Killing us softly 4* [Motion picture]. U.S.A.: Media Education Foundation.

Juarascio, A. S., Forman, E. M., & Herbert, J. D. (2010). Acceptance and commitment therapy versus cognitive therapy for the treatment of comorbid eating pathology. *Behavior Modification, 34*(2), 175–190.

Juarascio, A., Shaw, J., Forman, E., Timko, C. A., Herbert, J., Butryn, M., … & Lowe, M. (2013). Acceptance and commitment therapy as a novel treatment for eating disorders: an initial test of efficacy and mediation. *Behavior Modification, 37*(4), 459–489.

Lillis, J., Hayes, S. C., Bunting, K., & Masuda, A. (2009). Teaching acceptance and mindfulness to improve the lives of the obese: a preliminary test of a theoretical model. *Annals of Behavioral Medicine, 37*(1), 58–69.

Markanday, S., Data-Franco, J., Dyson, L., Murrant, S., Arbuckle, C., McGillvray, J., & Berk, M. (2012). Acceptance and Commitment Therapy for treatment-resistant depression. *Australian and New Zealand Journal of Psychiatry, 46*(12), 1198–1199.

Martín-Murcia, F., Díaz, A. J. C., & Gonzalez, L. P. (2011). A case study of anorexia nervosa and obsessive personality disorder using third-generation behavioral therapies. *Clinical Case Studies, 10*(3), 198–209.

Pearson, A. N., Follette, V. M., & Hayes, S. C. (2012). A pilot study of acceptance and commitment therapy as a workshop intervention for body dissatisfaction and disordered eating attitudes. *Cognitive and Behavioral Practice, 19*(1), 181–197.

Weineland, S., Arvidsson, D., Kakoulidis, T. P., & Dahl, J. (2012). Acceptance and commitment therapy for bariatric surgery patients, a pilot RCT. *Obesity Research & Clinical Practice, 6*(1), e21–e30.

# Part 2

# *Accept Yourself!* Skills and Techniques

Now that you have considered the evidence supporting the *Accept Yourself!* approach, as well as the rationale for rejecting behavioral weight loss approaches and for destigmatizing client body size, both within yourself as a professional and as an intervention for your client, you may be ready to consider how, in practice, to implement the approach. Part 2 of this book provides a detailed framework of techniques and interventions that together comprise the *Accept Yourself!* program. *Accept Yourself!* has been evaluated in research as a group intervention, and the group format may be ideal for delivering it, but it is also possible to implement it as an individual psychotherapy, and this manual assumes you are delivering the intervention in a one-on-one format. Chapter 13 provides guidance if you are interested in conducting *Accept Yourself!* groups. Chapter 4 explores how you might begin *Accept Yourself!* treatment, but assumes that you and your client(s) have completed the informed consent process and mutually decided to take this approach, rather than a weight loss or other psychotherapy approach. See Chapter 13 for guidance about the informed consent process for *Accept Yourself!* and how to help clients decide if this therapy is right for them.

# 4   Exploring Weight Control as a Problem

## Evaluating What Has Already Been Tried

*Accept Yourself!* begins with a functional assessment of clients' previous experiences with efforts to control their bodies and improve their self-image. Even after clients understand the research on weight and shape reviewed in Chapter 1 and with clients during the informed consent process (see Chapter 13), many often still believe that their personal failure to lose weight and achieve control over *their* bodies is the result of poor motivation or personal failings. Partly, this is the result of cultural programming related to weight and shape, which suggests, contrary to the available evidence, that weight is under one's personal control. However, this belief may also be based on clients' personal observations and experiences of weight loss in the real world. Even though, as we have already discussed, for the average client, weight loss efforts are ineffective and may even lead to weight gain over the long term, effortful weight loss in the short term is clearly possible, and many clients have achieved it repeatedly. When asking clients to add up the number of pounds they have lost on diets over the course of their lives, cumulative losses of hundreds or even thousands of pounds are not unusual. In addition, even though long-term weight loss is clearly ineffective for the average client, on an individual basis, weight loss treatment outcomes are highly heterogeneous, with standard deviations in weight loss as large or larger than means (MacLean et al., 2015). Thus, clients often know people who have successfully lost weight, whether in the short- or long-term. Clients may take others' experiences as a barometer for what is possible for themselves, and temporarily or permanently successful weight losers may also work to convince clients that they need only try harder or try their effective approach to lose weight for good this time. This combination of factors: cultural messages about weight and shape control as an attainable goal, personal experiences of repeated temporary weight loss, observation of others' successful weight loss, and pressure from others to emulate their successful permanent or temporary weight losses, all combine to make it difficult to abandon weight loss efforts, even when they are obviously ineffective.

In addition, these same factors may make it difficult for clinicians to commit to a self-acceptance-based non-weight-loss focused treatment. When clients want weight loss, came to treatment asking for weight loss, and when weight dissatisfaction appears to be harming clients' health and well-being, it is tempting for both clinicians and clients to re-engage in familiar weight loss strategies. Offering a self-acceptance-based approach can feel like "giving up" to clients or clinicians, and it may be unclear whether self-acceptance is a preferable recommendation for a particular weight-concerned client. Therefore, beginning treatment with a detailed functional assessment of the role of weight loss, body change, and other efforts to improve self-image in a client's life history may help clarify the value of a self-acceptance based approach for both client and clinician.

In ACT, this type of functional assessment is part of the creative hopelessness process. The goal of creative hopelessness is to avoid repeating previous therapeutic and treatment mistakes with clients, while also experiencing directly how well or poorly previous efforts to control the problem have worked. This exercise can be presented to clients as a means of confirming that *Accept Yourself!* is the best strategy for them now, and also as a way of avoiding reinventing the wheel: If clinicians understand what strategies have already been tried and how they worked, they can avoid wasting clients' time with strategies that are already known to be unworkable.

In *Accept Yourself!* creative hopelessness begins by asking the client to name or label her problem in a word or phrase so that both client and clinician have a convenient shorthand way of talking about it. I ask clients what they call the problem that brought them to treatment. Choosing a perfect or ideal name is not important, and, as a clinician, I usually go along with whatever name clients propose. Some clients choose straightforward names with clear relevance to weight and shape, like "my weight," or "my body image," or "hating my body." Others choose more global names, like "my self-esteem" or "my relationship with myself." Some names may be quite abstract and of unclear relevance to the clinician, like "feeling stuck." All of these are reasonable names for the problem as clients see it.

Next, clients are asked to make a list that will help flesh out *why* the problem is a problem. Specifically, clients are asked to list the costs of the problem in their lives, in broad terms. Clients are encouraged to be exhaustive, and to consider costs of the problem in various life domains, such as in relationships, at work, with self-esteem, in leisure time, financial costs, costs of time and energy, anything that the client feels has been taken from her by the presence of the problem. These lists of costs can be quite lengthy, and painful for clients when considered all at once. It is important to validate any pain, grief, or tearfulness that emerges as clients contemplate the harm that their problems have caused them. Clinicians can also validate that these costs explain why clients sought treatment, and the importance of achieving real change in the problem. "No wonder you are here," the clinician can say. "This problem is costly. No wonder you need it to change."

After naming the problem and identifying and grieving its costs, the next step of creative hopelessness involves making an exhaustive list of all the strategies that clients have already tried to solve the problem. The important aspect of this list is that it be comprehensive, and include every strategy the client has tried, whether it worked or not, whether it was a "good" or "healthful" or "bad/unhealthy" strategy or not, whether the client liked or disliked the strategy. Many different kinds of strategies may have been tried, including psychotherapies, cognitive strategies (like trying to "get over myself" or "pull myself up by my bootstraps"), medical strategies, including antidepressant or weight loss medications, surgeries, non-surgical medical interventions, diets, exercise programs, etc. Strategies may have been formal, such as involvement in a group like Weight Watchers or Overeaters Anonymous, or they may have been informal, such as trying to "eat healthy," give oneself pep talks, or bike daily. Variations on the same strategy may have been tried more than once, such as seeing five different therapists or trying six different antidepressant medications. When making this list, strategies should be listed separately. For example, if the client lists "diets," the clinician should ask for the names of specific diets she has tried, gently encouraging the client to think of and list specifics, rather than being overwhelmed by the number of different failed attempts and thus not being willing to explore the details. Instead of "diet pills," clients should generate the names of each different pill they tried. Each diet tried should be listed separately, each therapist, each different medication, and so on. Some clients experience shame in making this list, or they may expect to be shamed for the length of the list and their perceived failure to do well at such a long list of strategies. A curious, open stance from the clinician is helpful in navigating through this potential source of shame.

These lists can be even more lengthy and extensive than the list of costs already generated. Twenty to 30 items is common. When a comprehensive list has been generated, the next step is to evaluate each strategy on the list, one at a time. The question clinicians should use in evaluating strategies is: "How far has [strategy] taken you to solving [client's problem name]?" This question is very important, and should not be deviated from by the clinician. That is, the focus in evaluating strategies needs to be on how well the strategy has worked to *solve* the problem. The clinician should *not* help the client evaluate *why* the strategy did or did not work, and reasons-giving by clients should be observed as a possible way of avoiding shame and embarrassment that the strategy was a failure. Clinicians do not need to confront reasons-giving by clients, but instead should simply fail to engage in this activity with the client, returning the client again to the question: "Yes, I understand, but how far did [strategy] take you to *solving* your problem?"

In addition, clinicians should note instances where a client describes benefits to the strategy that did not include problem solution. For example, asked to evaluate Overeaters Anonymous, a client may say that it "helped me achieve insight into my food addiction and why I overeat." Clinicians should be careful not to note this as a successful strategy. Instead, if the same client has labeled her problem as "my weight," clinicians should gently acknowledge the client's evaluation, but return to the question: "So Overeaters Anonymous helped you achieve some insight into how the problem worked. But how far did it take you to solving your problem with your weight?"

At that point, the client may say, "I lost 20 pounds over the first six months I did OA [Overeaters Anonymous], and felt better about myself. But then I gained it back, and, in fact, even gained five more pounds, even though I was still avoiding sugar and carbs. I was so embarrassed I stopped going to meetings."

The clinician might then respond, "OK, so it sounds like it helped you achieve insight, and temporarily the problem got better, but then it returned, so that overall, after OA, the problem was worse than before?" If the client agrees that this was the case, the client and clinician can note that OA made the problem worse, rather than better.

The process of identifying and evaluating strategies using this key question should be completed in writing so that clients have a record of it and can see it on paper, in black and white. A worksheet may be useful, or this can be done on a note pad. (See the client self-help workbook that accompanies this volume for pre-prepared worksheets to help clients with this process.)

Clients can complete all or part of this process as homework, or they can complete it in session with the clinician. Whether done as homework or in session, however, clinicians should review and discuss how clients have evaluated strategies.

Clinicians should be careful to avoid common pitfalls of this strategy-listing and evaluating process. Both clients and clinicians have likely engaged in similar processes where the goal was problem-solving, and clients were listing strategies chiefly to find new, more effective angles or insufficiently tested strategies. (This previous experience may prime clients for shame during the process, as they are expecting clinicians to point out various strategies that they did not try hard enough to implement or that they should go back to, as well as expecting clinicians to brainstorm new strategies that will work better this time.) Clinicians, too, may be tempted to point out perceived flaws in the client's efforts or to help problem-solve why strategies didn't work or how they could be implemented better. All of these clinician behaviors are actively counterproductive to the creative hopelessness process. Clinicians should not engage with clients in reasons-giving about, or problem-solving of, their ineffective solutions. Instead, the clinician's goal here is simply to list strategies and evaluate their workability for the client.

*Accept Yourself!* clinicians assume that clients have made good-faith efforts to solve their problems, and that if the problem is not solved after 30 or more logical, good-faith attempts to solve it, the problem is not the client's motivation or poor solution implementation. Instead, the goal in this process is to validate the client's hard work, and to observe that if the problem were able to be solved through effort and logic alone, the client would have already solved it long before. Clients deserve an "A for effort" in their attempts to solve their weight and body image problems. The failure to solve the problem is not because clients have not tried hard enough, as the very existence of such a long list of strategies should make obvious. Clinicians should state as much explicitly to clients; should acknowledge their hard work, their sincere, reasonable efforts to change; and should note that the clinician sees clearly that the problem cannot be solved through hard work and effort alone. A group format for this process can be especially powerful for clients, as many clients are more readily able to observe that another client's failure to lose weight after 30 or more strategies attempted is clearly not the result of this other client's poor motivation or effort, even when she finds it difficult to see this point for her own efforts.

In considering the evaluation of strategies clients have placed on their lists, there are several common evaluations:

1. Clients may note that the strategy simply didn't work,
2. Or, it made the problem worse,
3. Or, it made the client feel better temporarily, but didn't do anything to solve the problem,
4. Or, it worked temporarily, but the problem returned (and sometimes returned worse than it was before starting the strategy),
5. Or, it worked for some parts of the problem, but not others (e.g., the client reports that her exercise program solved her problem with hypertension, but did not cause any weight loss),
6. Or, the solution worked, but the client had to give it up because it was too costly in terms of time, money, energy, or otherwise to continue with it,
7. Or, rarely, clients may report that they have a sincere expectation that a strategy will totally solve their problem, but that they have not yet had the opportunity to give the solution a fair shot.

Clinicians should exercise particular caution in considering strategies evaluated in these last two categories. Strategies that were given up because of cost are particularly difficult for clients, because they lead to self-blame. Clients feel that they ought to have been able to solve the problem using costly strategies, and that they ought to have been able to pay the price of time, money, energy, or whatever other barrier made continuing with that strategy difficult. Clinicians should point out that a workable strategy is one that clients can implement, and that if a strategy was too costly to implement that suggests a flaw in the strategy, not the implementation.

Strategies that haven't been fully evaluated require particular caution on the part of the clinician. In fact, often strategies that appear to be in this category belong in category six; that is, the strategy has been tried, but was abandoned because it was too costly to implement (and the client still feels grief and guilt that this seemingly workable strategy was not, in fact, workable). I have never seen a client seeking weight loss that truly had a strategy that belonged in category seven. However, I have seen such strategies emerge occasionally with other presenting concerns.

For example, once I worked with a client whose problem was chronic pain. This particular client had tried literally everything I could ever have thought of, as well as many strategies I would never have considered, to alleviate her pain. Her list of strategies had more than 50 items on it, all of which were unworkable and fell into one of the above six categories except one: Acupuncture. What that patient told me about acupuncture was this: She noted that she had tried acupuncture, and that, for her, it had been a miracle cure. Her pain had been completely (albeit temporarily) eliminated after the acupuncture treatments, and each subsequent treatment her acupuncturist had recommended had lasted longer and seemed more efficacious than the last. However, her insurance had a strict cap on acupuncture sessions, and she had not been able to afford to follow the acupuncturist's recommendations for treatment. I asked her, with all of her history of initially promising treatments that ultimately failed or even made the problem worse, if she sincerely believed that acupuncture might totally solve her problem. She noted that she had mostly lost hope for treatments and felt cynical about them, but that the help from this technique had been so clear, dramatic, and improving over time that she really did think it might totally solve her problem. At that point, I paused my efforts to do ACT psychotherapy with her. Instead, my role in her life shifted to advocating for her needs with her insurance company. Those efforts were successful – we were able to convince the insurer to pay for the number of acupuncture sessions her acupuncturist had recommended, and I advised her to follow through on these recommendations until either her problem was solved or acupuncture moved into one of the other categories, at which point she should return to see me and resume ACT therapy. She never returned, and hopefully the acupuncture was helpful to her.

To make a similar choice – that is, to pause *Accept Yourself!* treatment while the client attempts another weight loss or body control strategy – both the client and clinician should be convinced that the strategy under consideration is accessible, not too costly, and that it really will be different from all other strategies on her list and will completely and permanently *solve* her problem. Clinicians should carefully consider why a promising strategy like this has not been already tried, and whether there is scientific evidence supporting the client's intuition that the strategy could solve her problem. Clinicians should further be certain that whatever barriers stopped successful past implementation are *completely eliminated* now. As mentioned earlier, I have never met a client presenting for weight loss who met these criteria, so clinicians should consider this possibility a rare one. Also, clinicians should not themselves help clients implement the promising non-self-acceptance-based strategy. Instead, they should refer clients to the strategy, with the caveat that clients will check in and return if the strategy does not live up to its promise.

### Another Way to Evaluate Body Change Strategies: Timelines

Heffner and Eifert (2006) have developed another innovative way to help clients with anorexia nervosa explore how well their efforts to change their bodies and achieve good body image have worked over time. They have the client create a body image timeline to graphically illustrate changes over time in their relationships with their bodies. I often use body image timelines in conjunction with strategy lists as another way to develop a shared understanding of the client's struggle and her history with it. When using timelines, I ask clients to take a sheet of paper with an arrow drawn widthwise down the center of the page, representing time's forward motion. I will ask them to place on the timeline any significant events in their history with their bodies. These might be experiences of weight stigma, change strategies and their outcomes, general life experiences both positive and negative. Whatever the client thinks is important can be placed on the timeline. Some clients enjoy putting photographs or artwork on their timelines; for others, this may be a quick in-session exercise.

There are several items to observe about timelines. One is whether clients place weight numbers on their timelines. Most do not, but some do. Usually, these weights represent not victories or positive achievements, but ongoing milestones in the client's struggle with herself. If clients did place weight numbers on their timelines, it is worth observing trends over time. In general, weights increase over time. Another area of observation has to do with evidence of valued life activities on the timeline, apart from body image. Clients will often place on their timelines significant achievements or happy life events, such as marriages, or career or personal goals achieved. Noticing that these items are present and do not represent weight-based achievements can also be useful in highlighting that perhaps the struggle with weight is not the most important aspect of life to the client. If clients place pictures on their timeline, these can also be interesting to observe. Clients, looking at old pictures of their bodies, often spontaneously notice that there is a difference between what their minds told them about how they looked then, and how their bodies appear to them now. Many observe that they were "normal" weight at times when others were stigmatizing them based on weight, that they *felt* "fat" and ugly, but that they were *not*, in fact, fat or ugly. Clinicians should comment on or ask about these various possibilities as they emerge, but there is no particular agenda or end goal to the timeline exercise, beyond simply observing the client's history with her struggle, however that appears.

## The Problem so Far

Having completed the strategy evaluation and timeline exercises, clinicians should take some time to help the client sum up and make sense of what has been learned and experienced during the creative hopelessness process. Clinicians should ask clients, "How old were you when your problem with weight, shape, food, or body image first came into your life?" and should compare this to the client's present age, to get a sense of how long this problem has been present in her life, and how many years have passed since the problem began. Clinicians should inquire, "Since the problem began, has it gotten better, gotten worse, or stayed about the same?" For most clients, the problem has gotten worse over time, despite their long list of strategies to change it. Although both weight and self-image have likely fluctuated substantially over time, if considered simply as two points in time, the beginning of the problem and now, most clients both weigh more and feel less satisfied with their bodies now compared with when the problem first came into their lives. Noting this clearly can often be an extremely powerful (and painful) experience for clients.

At this point, clients are often expecting or hoping that I will offer them the exciting, fabulous, secret body control strategy that will work where all others have failed. Thus, at this point, it is essential to be clear that you as a clinician do not have the answer. It is important to validate that the client has, indeed, done all of the logical things you can think of, and perhaps many things you would never have thought to try, to solve her weight, shape, and body image problems, and that you as a professional believe that she has tried hard enough to solve the problem and that you cannot think of anything else logical to try. It is important to be clear and humble, and tell the client explicitly, "I do not have the answer." Clinicians should resist the urge to sugarcoat this essential truth, if in fact this is what the creative hopelessness functional analysis has revealed for the client, and clinicians should allow themselves, as well as their clients, to face up to the reality (if this is what has been uncovered through this process) that weight loss efforts have not been successful and may have been counterproductive for this individual client. Clients and clinicians should allow themselves to feel, with full force, the feelings that arise from the fact that there is no evidence that weight loss efforts will work more effectively in the future. Clinicians are often concerned that clients may feel hopeless or even suicidal as a result of realizing that their body image control strategies have not worked. But one goal of *Accept Yourself!* treatment is for clients to get in closer touch with what their own personal life experiences are telling them about what works for them. Clinicians *do* want clients to feel hopeless about hopeless strategies. Feeling hopeful about a hopeless strategy will lead only to continued engagement in that strategy, which necessarily means not engaging in any strategies that might *not* be hopeless. Clinicians should, of course, assess for suicidality and engage in crisis intervention for clients for whom this is a concern. But clinicians should avoid sugarcoating the results of the creative hopelessness process, or promising clients that the clinician has better or more novel strategies which they will learn in treatment. Allow clients to sit with this new discovery that weight and body change has not worked, by being clear that you yourself do not know entirely what this means and do not have the answer for it.

What the clinician *can* offer the client at this point is a useful metaphor to help make sense of her situation. Many standard ACT metaphors used during creative hopelessness can be employed effectively here, such as the story of the child in the hole or the story of the tug of war with a monster (Hayes, Strohsahl, & Wilson, 2011). My personal favorite metaphor to share with clients at this point, however, is the metaphor and image of the casino.

Imagine the Las Vegas strip. Have you ever been there? Do you have a favorite casino? Picture the casino floor, the blackjack and craps tables, the slot machines. The situation of the client who has spent many years trying to control her weight (and, by extension, her body image) reminds me of this casino. When you go into a casino, go up to a slot machine and insert a coin: What do you hope will happen? Of course, you hope that you will win! And if you take a roll of coins to the slot machine and play for a while, it is likely that you *will* win – a little bit, here and there, just enough, typically, that you may feel tempted to keep playing, even after your initial budget is gone. In fact, casinos employ mathematicians to develop algorithms that will pay out exactly enough money exactly as often as necessary to keep you playing longer. Not only that, in a casino, some people *do* win life-changing amounts of money: If you look around the casino, you will see posters, and – if you're lucky – flashing lights and clinking coins announcing that some people win, and win big. A tiny number of people go to a casino, win an enormous fortune, and, one hopes, never return. But what happens if *you* keep playing, roll after roll of quarters, for days, weeks, and months on end?

You lose money. And the longer and harder and more faithfully you play, the more you lose, even though, as gambling addicts can tell you, from time to time you may be ahead – you may be winning. And why is this? Why is it that most people can confidently tell me that they are likely to lose in the casino, even though some people win? Why is it that gambling addicts always lose money, even their entire fortunes, despite dedicated effort, over many years, in a place expressly designed to address their hopes to win big?

The reason is simple and you have already thought of it: *Because the game is rigged.* The house will always win in the end, and the more money the gambling addict puts in, the more she/he will lose in the end. It is worth sharing this imagery and set of questions with clients, and asking them, "Could it be that the same is true for your game? Your depression, dieting, weight loss, self-hatred game?"

Clinicians can ask clients to look back over their timelines and their list of strategies and to check whether this is true: Did their problems ultimately get worse every time they tried to make them better? (Clients sometimes have to be reminded to avoid being like the gambler, who brags about his small wins without admitting to the much bigger losses! Clients should be prompted to look at the net change for themselves over time in answering this question.) The clinician can point out: "If the problem got worse every time you tried to make it better, then *is it possible that the solutions may be part of the problem?*" This question is not one I answer for clients, and it is frequently one I will leave them to ponder at the end of a session, as homework. It is a powerful image and set of questions, and clients typically need some time to digest it.

## The Magic Wand: Weight Loss as a Means to an End

After clients have had some time to consider and discuss with the clinician the meaning of the creative hopelessness process, the clinician can introduce another new (and for some clients, amusing) idea: The client does not actually want weight loss! In fact, nobody wants weight loss! Not only that, speaking of winning large sums of money: Nobody wants to win a million dollars in the lottery, either! And the clinician can prove it. Here is how.

Imagine you have won a million dollars in the lottery. Your luck has arrived! The lottery office is ready to pay out your winnings. However, there is just one catch: You will receive one million dollars, in fresh, crisp, ten-dollar bills. However, you are required, as terms of the win, to keep all of these ten-dollar bills, in perpetuity, encased in a column of glass somewhere in your home. They cannot be removed from the case for any purpose. They cannot be spent. However, you are still the proud new owner of one million dollars. Are you satisfied? Aren't you excited?

No? Why not? You don't actually want to win a million dollars, or 100 million dollars, in the lottery. You don't want money. You don't want a stack of crisp ten (or 100) dollar bills. You want the *things money can buy*. Isn't this true?

Is this also true for weight loss? To answer that question, try a second mental experiment. You can pretend I am a gameshow host like Monty Hall, and I will offer you a choice. Behind door number one is weight loss: The permanent attainment of your goal weight, whatever that is. However, the catch is that although your weight will change – if you step on a scale, you will see that your gravitational mass in relationship to Earth has changed to be whatever you are wishing it will be – nothing else about your life changes. Your body image, how you see yourself, how others see you, will not change. Your health will not change. Your mobility and level of fitness and physical abilities will not change. Your self-confidence and sex appeal will not change. Your relationships with food, with other people, at work, at school, in other domains of life will not change. Nothing will change except your gravitational mass in relationship to Earth. That is door number one.

Behind door number two, your weight will remain exactly the same. However, you will receive instead all of the benefits that you imagine weight loss will bring you: Your health and physical abilities will improve in all of the ways you are imagining. You will feel more confident, sexier. Your body image will be confident and healthy; you will feel attractive. Your life will improve in whatever ways you imagine are linked to weight loss. You will be able to travel, engage in physical adventures, have sex and relationships, get promotions, and whatever other benefits you imagine would accrue if you could reach your desired weight. You will not experience weight-based discrimination; others will see you as you imagine and hope they will. The only catch is that your weight will not change. Which door will you choose? Is the situation similar to the lottery win of unspendable money? Is it possible that you do not actually want weight loss, but instead want the benefits that you imagine weight loss will bring?

Asking clients these questions can rapidly clarify what the goals of therapy are and ought to be. At this point, I ask clients to flesh out their weight-and-shape-related hopes and dreams in more detail. I ask them to imagine that I have a magic wand that will instantly and permanently make them their goal weight. They will remain at this magical goal weight no matter what they do, whether or not they exercise or eat "right," for the rest of their lives. Once they've imagined this scenario, I ask them to write a narrative describing how their life would be different after I waved my magic wand and performed this trick. This is their magic wand fantasy, and it will serve as your blueprint for the rest of treatment. Size-acceptance blogger Kate Harding writes about the fantasies people have about getting thin, in an essay called "The Fantasy of Being Thin," which you can find here: https://kateharding.net/2007/11/27/the-fantasy-of-being-thin. She taps into the fact that, in a culture that highly values the thin ideal, many women (and men) have detailed fantasies about what life will be like once they have succeeded in making themselves thin and physically attractive. Clients' fantasies about what life will be like when they successfully lose weight typically include a number of domains of valued living: Sex, physical activity, social life, relationships, self-confidence, health, work, and leisure are all areas that clients imagine and hope will improve with weight loss. Clients' goals and values are revealed in these fantasies, and that is what is meant by stating that the magic wand fantasy provides a roadmap for the remainder of the *Accept Yourself!* program. The simple truth is that *these goals and values can be pursued directly, without waiting for weight loss.*

It is worth pointing out to clients that they have believed up until this point that they could not attain the goals, values, and desirable aspects of life contained in their magic wand fantasies until they successfully lost weight. Unfortunately, neither you nor they know how to pursue that path to attaining their fantasies: The road to weight loss appears blocked, and efforts to follow it have appeared to lead clients further away from weight loss, not closer. In the meantime, clients should observe whether it is true that they *also* have not gotten any closer to the elements of their fantasy. If this is the case, it may be time to abandon the (closed) road to weight loss, and to pursue attaining their fantasies by a different (and more direct) road entirely. That is the *Accept Yourself!* program in a nutshell: to help clients pursue their dreams and goals and values directly, without waiting for weight loss as a prerequisite.

The remainder of this book (as well as its companion self-help volume) is designed to help you as a clinician pursue clients' magic wand fantasies directly, coping with barriers that emerge along the way and can take clients off course. However, one important barrier is your own weight stigma, which may manifest itself at this point in the form of a suspicion that clients cannot achieve some aspects of their magic wand fantasies without first losing weight. This same suspicion, or argument, may show up for clients when you present this rationale for and understanding of the goals of treatment to them: How can I treat my diabetes/be seen as sexy to a partner/ever love my body/go surfing/ride on airplanes/go rock climbing/etc. in the body I have now? As a clinician, your commitment to helping clients achieve their goals regardless of weight is essential, as clients may need your resources and assistance to navigate around systemic and institutionalized weight stigma (and self-stigma) in pursuit of their goals.

Both clients and clinicians will encounter institutionalized weight bias and abuse in their efforts to achieve clients' dreams. It is the job of the clinician to model navigating through this discrimination for the client, advocating for herself and finding or creating resources that are free of stigma and support her dreams. How to do that will be introduced in the following chapters, but clinicians must make a commitment to engage in this work and to be dogged in the face of size discrimination for the resources contained in this book to be maximally effective.

If you as a clinician struggle with your own body image and desire to lose weight, completing the magic wand fantasy (and other exercises in this and the companion volume) may be an essential way to bolster your own commitment to self-acceptance-based approaches, to help you understand experientially how to help your clients, and to help you model goal and dream attainment and values pursuit in the face of weight, stigma, and other barriers. I encourage you to pause and complete the magic wand exercise now if it is relevant for you, and to make an initial plan for how you will pursue the items you list on your fantasy in your present body.

## References

Hayes, S. C., Strosahl, K. D., & Wilson, K. G. (2011). *Acceptance and Commitment Therapy: The process and practice of mindful change (2nd Ed)*. New York: Guilford.

Heffner, M. & Eifert, G.H. (2006). *The anorexia workbook: How to accept yourself, heal your suffering, and reclaim your life.* Oakland, CA: New Harbinger.

MacLean, P. S., Wing, R. R., Davidson, T., Epstein, L., Goodpaster, B., Hall, K. D., … & Rothman, A. J. (2015). NIH working group report: Innovative research to improve maintenance of weight loss. *Obesity, 23*(1), 7–15.

# 5 Identifying and Producing Programming

## Identifying Weight and Food Programming

The experience of being human is one of learning. As you move through your life, you learn an enormous amount; in fact, everything you know about being human and how to live has been learned. Some of what you have learned and now know you learned by experience. How to walk, for example: Probably, no one told you how to walk. If they had tried, you would not have understood, if you learned to walk as most people do, around one year of age. Instead, if you learned to walk as an infant, you learned by a variety of experiments you initiated, attempted, failed at, modified, and re-attempted. You taught yourself to move around on your hands and feet, perhaps by crawling, or creeping, in some way you yourself invented. You pulled yourself up on the furniture and discovered you could use your hands to steady your feet to move. Perhaps a grown-up who loved you held your hands and let you experiment with moving your feet forward. You took your brave first steps, fell, and got up and tried again, right then, or later on, eventually. In an important way, you invented walking and learned to walk all by yourself. There is no book entitled *How to Walk* because its most important audience doesn't know how to talk, let alone read. But even after infancy, there are other tasks since you may have also learned, at least in part, by experience: How to comfort a baby. How to drive a car. How to lead a group of other people. How to swim. Some things are so variable and idiosyncratic (e.g., babies) or so difficult to put into words (e.g., how to swim) that the only way to learn the important details of how to do them is by experience.

But many things you have learned, you did not learn by experience. Many things you know – perhaps even most things – you were taught, with words. You've learned some things that would be dangerous or even fatal to learn by direct experience: Which snakes are poisonous, how to avoid being electrocuted by a downed power line, what to do when you hear tornado sirens, how to interact with police during a traffic stop. You've perhaps learned some behaviors that are simply too difficult and elaborate to learn by direct experience or trial and error: The value of good grades in school, manners, slang, cultural customs for various situations, financial planning, computer programming, how to make *injera* or *coq au vin*, how to read, and the entire miraculous system by which sounds correspond to letter shapes and letter shapes and sounds both correspond to an infinite number of concepts and ideas in the world.

Besides all this: You've also learned a wide variety of arbitrary (and even contradictory) rules and ideas for living depending on the culture you have grown up in, what media you have been exposed to, what your family was like, and a variety of other arbitrary accidents of your existence that dictated what learning opportunities and materials you were exposed to throughout your life. All of this verbal and symbolic learning, all of the things you learned not by experience but by arbitrary social accident, is your programming.

Some of this programming, some of the time, may be useful and workable information that furthers your values and goals. For example, perhaps you are thumbing through a magazine in a doctor's office waiting room when you see a picture of a cake that inspires you to make something similar to delight a new friend. (The idea that a friendship would be advanced by bringing a home-made sweet treat to a visit is itself a piece of programming you likely have not even considered. You might also never have considered the gender or cultural aspects of this rule about bringing a sweet treat to a friend: That it was probably a women's magazine you were thumbing through, that if it inspired you to make cake you were likely socialized female in a culture where "bake a treat to build goodwill" is a rule taught more to women rather than men.) But regardless: This tiny brush with programming has an effect that serves your values. You make the cake using the photo or the recipe as your guide, you bring it to your friend, your friend is delighted, and you are pleased to have built upon and strengthened your new friendship in this way.

Other pieces of programming may actually lead you away from your values if you follow them. For example, the fat client who loves to swim, enjoys swimming, was a talented swimmer as a kid, and wants to swim now, may have learned or been taught the arbitrary social rule "Fat women do not have the right to wear swimwear in public." She may feel fear or shame as a result of this rule when she considers putting on her bathing suit and going to the beach or pool. She may obey the rule and stay away from the valued activity of swimming. Interestingly, many clients who have been taught a rule like this, and who follow this rule, if you ask whether they *believe* this rule or think it is a worthwhile rule to teach to others, such as their children or other women, they will reject the rule clearly and outright. No, your client may tell you, I think all women have the right to go to the beach! I'd want my fat daughter, or niece, or friend, to feel completely welcome at the pool. They often don't actually believe this rule or consider it an appropriate rule for living, even though they may follow it faithfully and to their own detriment.

It is a worthwhile aim of therapy to explore and identify clients' programming related to weight, shape, body image, emotions, mental and physical health, and eating. The goal in identifying programming is not to dispute the programmed ideas, rules, and thoughts, or to determine their accuracy.

The goal is simply to notice the arbitrary nature of this mental material, and to consider whether it serves the client's goals and values. In addition, by observing the arbitrary nature of programming and the lack of fit between what the client believes, wants, and intends to pursue versus where the programming leads her, clients can begin to experience *defusion*. That is, through this process, clients can begin to come unstuck from these arbitrary rules, noticing that they are rules, and begin to exercise a free choice, if they wish, to behave based on their values instead of what this arbitrary rule suggests.

There are a variety of ways to explore and begin to identify client programming. Clients and therapists can begin by looking at influential childhood experiences and memories for what rules about the world, the self, the body, and how to live are contained therein. For example, a client might re-read her favorite chapter or picture books from childhood, asking herself or writing down what messages she sees taught in the pages. Similar exercises can also be done by recalling important childhood memories at home and at school and noting what these experiences taught the client about herself, her body, the world. Looking again at favorite childhood or adolescent TV shows, music, magazines, or other media represents another opportunity to identify programming, as does considering what sayings were common or passed around in her family or among her friends. Considering what was said during moments relevant to body image, food, or intense emotion in her family or among her friends provides another possible source of programming. Identifying programming can be easier if clients contrast the programming they received with programming dissimilar to what they received. For example, if a client is reading her favorite childhood picture book to identify programming, she may also wish to read a childhood picture book from the same era aimed at or popular with boys, or a childhood picture book from a different country or culture. Noticing the differences in implicit messages she received versus those sent to children of another gender or culture can sometimes help highlight both the arbitrary nature of such messages and also their varying content. It is also worth noticing the current programming surrounding clients. Favorite TV shows; their Facebook, Twitter, Instagram, or Tumblr feeds; favorite books; and spousal, family, and friend messages can all be investigated to identify programming. The accompanying self-help volume has written exercises to help clients identify both childhood and contemporary programming of various kinds. Clinicians should also work through the experience of investigating and identifying their own programming, paying particular attention to the messages they have received about weight, shape, body image, and food. Can you identify the messages you have been exposed to around these issues? Do you obey these arbitrary rules? Are they workable (do they lead you closer to or further away from your personal values and goals)? Do you believe them, that is, would you recommend them or sell them to others, including children?

Exploring your own and your clients' programming offers the opportunity to explore the difference between programming and beliefs. As noted already, often clients can recognize that they hold and even obey pieces of programming that they definitely *do not* believe, and, in fact, can even identify and label as harmful or counterproductive thoughts that they actively reject (even while obeying them!). At other times, clients may express that they *do* believe programming, particularly negative programming, about the self. Often you can identify programming as it emerges in session because clients will respond to questions about a piece of programming's workability by saying that even though the programming was counterproductive or unhelpful, it is still "the truth." Arguing about whether a piece of programming is "true" or "false" is generally unworkable, although the urge to get into such an argument with your client may be a sign that the piece of programming in question is particularly sticky and the client is fused with it. ACT therapists do not concern themselves with the "truth" or falsity of client thoughts, but instead explore their workability for helping the client move toward her values. Refocusing on the workability of a thought the client insists is "true," on what the thought leads her to do, feel, and want, and whether or not this is consonant with her wishes and values can be more productive than arguing with a client or trying to get her to abandon the thought. In fact, all learning in the human brain is additive. It is not possible to unlearn what one has been taught, and it is not necessary to unlearn programming in order to live an effective life. Asking clients where a thought was picked up or learned can also help clarify its arbitrary nature. Asking whether the client made up herself or creatively chose a piece of programming she believes is "the truth" can also be useful in observing that even "true" pieces of programming were arbitrarily learned somewhere, and are not the result of clients' creative generativity and values.

## Media Portrayals and Body Image: Altering How Clients See Themselves

Media images of the thin ideal for both men and women are a major source of programming for all of us. Exposure to the thin ideal in media is related to body image disturbance in women (Grabe, Ward, & Hyde, 2008) and also affects men in a variety of ways (Johnson, McCreary, & Mills, 2007). The importance placed by media on female physical beauty for success by both men and women in the most valued domains of life has been documented by psychologists and researchers for more than 60 years (Ellis, 1951), and products designed to change or enhance the female figure have been sold in the U.S. for more than 100 years. (Interestingly, such products have been sold to promote weight gain, as well as weight loss. Victorian-era advertisements for Fat-Ten-U and Corpula Foods sold women insecurities based on a too-thin body type. The specifics of what type of body is fashionable have varied across time, whereas the message that women's bodies are inadequate and require expensive improvements have remained constant.)

Books, websites, and documentaries that explore how media affect women's body image can all be useful resources for clients exploring their programming. The website About Face (www.about-face.org), for example, has as its mission to "equip women and girls with tools to understand and resist harmful media messages that affect their self-esteem and body image." Visitors to the site can view a "gallery of offenders" (advertisements with harmful, objectifying messages) and a "gallery of winners" with more positive and empowering messages. The website helps users develop critical thinking and observation skills related to body image media programming, and also helps users act on their values by offering tools for advocacy. Workshops and activism opportunities related to healthy body image are all available on the site. The Media Education Foundation, a documentary production house and distributor, has a variety of documentary films available (https://shop.mediaed.org/representations-of-women-c63.aspx), with companion readings and resources, that explore media influences on gender and body image. For example, the *Killing Us Softly* series of documentaries by Jean Kilbourne is a detailed exploration across four films and several decades of how media portrayals of women's bodies affect us. Jean Kilbourne's author website also has a diverse list of resources relevant to media and body image (www.jeankilbourne.com/resources).

Experiential exercises can also help clients begin to explore the arbitrary nature of their programming related to their own body images and appearances. The companion self-help book describes one example in detail: A media diet, where clients take a one-week break from all forms of media consumption apart from work requirements. Turning off social media, television, movies, music, reading, and other sources of media input for one week is quite challenging, and provides an opportunity to practice accepting discomfort, mindfully observing silence and one's own thoughts. In addition, this exercise can provide unique insight into the nature of the programming one is currently experiencing. I recommend clinicians try the media diet themselves before prescribing it for clients, to have an awareness of the difficulties in implementing it, some tools for navigating those barriers, and to develop an experiential sense of the power of fasting from media consumption, for even a brief period, in terms of what it reveals about the role of programming in our lives.

A media diet is obviously best assigned as homework, but in-session experiential exercises can be powerful as well, to illuminate how arbitrary body image programming can get in the way of connecting and even seeing other women. For example, many women engage in body size and shape comparisons and judgments of other women's bodies, both socially, out loud with peers, and individually, in the privacy of their minds. Looking at another woman and wondering "Am I that fat?" or thinking "I'm not as fat as she is," and feeling a mix of fear, guilt, and relief are common experiences for many clients (and clinicians). Clinicians can observe and point out that these thoughts occur in our minds, even though we actually have no data by which to make the comparison accurately. The mind judges another woman's body as attractive, unattractive, fat, thin, larger or smaller, or the same as one's own, but these thoughts are all simply thoughts, not facts. Other women do not wear signs broadcasting their heights and weights, and there is no objective "truth" about how attractive or unattractive one is to be uncovered. The mind's chatter about this is just that, chatter. It is also worth observing that this chatter is based on media programming: Ideas about the appropriate size, shape, and appearance women should have are based on pervasive media imagery of idealized female figures who may not even be human: Photo-illustration software is often used not only to retouch photographs past the point of recognizability, but also to invent whole new composite images of women who never existed. Media also provide rules about what women's bodies should look like, sometimes in specific numeric form, such as the long-standing idea that a woman's figure should measure "36–24–36," or the idea that a size zero is the most desirable clothing size. Comparisons women make with other women are altered by these thoughts and entirely fact-free. The My Body Gallery website (www.mybodygallery.com) offers one means of exploring these comparisons and observing shifting thoughts in an individual session. The website allows you to search pictures uploaded by women and labeled with height, weight, body shape, age, and clothing size. You can search for women who match you on any or all of these parameters and notice what thoughts arise. You can search for women who are at a weight you want to attain, or a weight you fear attaining. The images uploaded to the website are diverse: Some feature headless shots of women wearing swimwear or underwear so the belly is highlighted; others show fully clothed women and faces. The women themselves choose what photos to upload. Some weight and height combinations, especially at high weights, are not represented or well represented, so the clinician may wish to preview the site for a client's height and weight to make sure a selection of images are available for her.

What typically occurs when women use the My Body Gallery website in session? You might imagine without trying it that this exercise would increase fusion with body shaming, judgmental thoughts, and perhaps that is possible (an outcome to be mindfully observed). More commonly, however, what is striking about the images at both one's own weight and at higher or feared weights is that the diversity of women's appearances within a given weight/shape/size are often substantially larger than the differences in the photographs between categories. There are "attractive," "flattering," "pretty" photos at the highest weights, and "unattractive," "unflattering" photos at the lowest weights. Observing this allows women to experience defusion from the idea of a weight *per se* as a meaningful judgment about the self. Women also often judge their own weight as "acceptable" on another woman's body as depicted on the site, while still thinking that this weight is "unacceptable" for themselves. Clients are often able to observe the difference between the lack of judgment they feel looking at a woman who shares their height and weight, in contrast to the intense judgment the mind provides for their own (similar) bodies. Looking at women who are at feared weights can reveal that these women are not markedly different in appearance than the women at one's present weight, and also to again notice the variability in the judgments the mind provides for different photos of women who are all the same weight. In addition, observing that the women on the site are "just people" and that their bodies would not be notable to us as we walk down the street offers another opportunity to notice the contrast between mental chatter about ideal female beauty versus the actual experience of encountering others' humanity in real life.

In a group setting, My Body Gallery is generally not appropriate, as the pictures viewed cannot be tailored to women's own thoughts about their own individual weights, and judgmental comments can arise that are unhelpful to the group process. The mirror exercise is an excellent alternative for a group format. It allows clients to observe the differences between their own chatter about appearance versus others' chatter, and to notice the arbitrary nature of both types of chatter. To do the mirror exercise, women in the group are first given a small hand mirror and asked to use it to observe their own faces as accurately as possible. They are asked to write down the observations, and to go for accuracy, as well as noting down any thoughts that arise, such as "I have a nice smile" or "My eyebrows are too thin." After describing their own faces, women turn the page in their notebooks to a blank page, so their answers cannot be seen, and pass the notebook to a partner. The partner's job is to describe the woman's face as accurately as possible, for example as if she were describing her partner's face for a forensic artist. That is, the partner will try to describe the face in such detail that an artist who had never seen her could reconstruct an image from the description. Then the partner returns the notebook to the woman, and she is invited to read both descriptions and see what she notices (and discuss this in the group). Women are able to observe that there are often striking differences between the two descriptions (and sometimes that the observer's description is less nega-tively judgmental). The group leader invites the women to consider which description is more accurate, and women often struggle with answering this question. This gives the group leader the opportunity to observe that neither description is accurate, and that, in fact, it is not possible for anyone to have an "accurate" view of anyone's appearance. Even very skilled photo-realistic artists, asked to draw the same person, produce different images. The ideas and mental chatter we carry about how we look is just that, not a gospel truth about ourselves.

In fact, although we might like to turn off our programming, or make it accurate, it isn't possible to be free of our programming. Although you could, at least in theory, stop using all media from this day forward, there is no button to turn off the programming that was picked up, arbitrarily and essentially at random, and that is already in your head chattering away. Instead of turning programming off, you might consider turning it down. Not "turning it down" in the sense of *decreasing its volume*, because again, there is no way to control these thoughts when they show up in your mind. Instead, "turning it down" here means *refusing it*. You can turn down arbitrary programming as a means of guiding your life choices. You can refuse to live your life by the gospel of the thin ideal.

## Owning the Airwaves by Producing a No-Self-Judgment Channel

One means of turning down programming in a creative, empowering fashion is via the *Airwaves* metaphor. It's interesting to consider how many channels of actual media programming are literally floating in the room with you as you read this. You may not be aware of any of them except the words you are reading now in the book (or it may be you have a radio or YouTube channel on, or a television on in the background, so that you are at least dimly aware of two channels of programming coming into your mind at once). But whether you are aware of being programmed in this moment or not, it is probably still the case that radio and television and telecommunications broadcasts are all literally "in the air" in the room where you sit. You can't hear them – you're not tuned in – but they are there. And if you switch on your television, or your radio, or pick up your cell phone and call or text a friend, you can tune in, instantly, to one or another stream of programming that was there all along, outside of your awareness. You can also change channels, if you see something objectionable or uninteresting – you can turn your attention elsewhere, although the airwaves carrying the content you have switched away from are still right there in the room, regardless of what you are attending to. And, ultimately, you have no control over what is broadcast over the airwaves, even in the privacy of your own home. Except in one way: In most towns and cities, there is a public access television channel or radio station. These stations often offer classes in video or radio production, and it's actually possible to take one of those classes, and produce your own programming, which will then be broadcast out to everyone over the airwaves just like all the other programming, and which will be available to be tuned into, and will even, inevitably, program someone else. You can become a public-access producer of your own programming, and, in that way, add creative messages of your own, which reflect your own values and wishes, to the cultural stream of programming from which we all drink.

I'm not literally suggesting that clients or clinicians should all produce public-access TV shows, although, of course, that might be one way to produce one's own creative programming. But the airwaves metaphor allows clinicians and clients to discuss the reality that the client is not only an unwitting consumer of programming, but also has the right to intentionally produce it, shaping cultural ideas for herself and others, based on her dreams, values, or even efforts at self-acceptance. Producing one's own programming in either a metaphorical or literal way represents an opportunity to deal with weight, shape, and gender discrimination and practice self-acceptance at the same time. In addition, it may allow clients and clinicians the opportunity to be helpful to others, providing alternative, values-driven programming to tune into alongside cultural messages about the thin ideal.

In treatment, the clinician can discuss with clients the idea of creating a "no-self-judgment channel" of programming for themselves. It is important to note that the idea is not to eliminate negative or judgmental thoughts about the self, which will float in the air regardless of what clients tune into or program for themselves, but to allow clients to notice that they can create their own chosen, affirming programming to go *alongside* the more familiar programming they did not choose. HAES therapist Deb Burgard has created a "body disparagement-free zone" doorhanger (available here: www.bodypositive.com/doorhangers.htm) that clients can order for free if they wish to designate a physical space within their homes to practice engagement in non-self-judgmental behavior and produce countercultural programming (while still experiencing whatever thoughts and programming they experience). These doorhangers can also be hung on the clinician's door or given as a gift to clients to symbolize the beginning of their self-acceptance journey. The doorhangers are most appropriate for average-sized or smaller women, as they feature an admonition against saying the phrase "I'm so fat," which obviously is not appropriate for larger-bodied women who are practicing reclaiming the word "fat" as a non-judgmental term. However, clients and clinicians can create similar tools for women of diverse body sizes using symbols and language that feel appropriate to them.

Clients and clinicians can seek out books, websites, social media channels, blogs, online communities, films, and videos that feature themes of body acceptance and use these to inspire programming for the "no-self-judgment" channel. The list of resources and additional readings in the accompanying self-help manual includes options useful for this purpose.

## References

Ellis, A (1951). *The folklore of sex.* Oxford: Charles Boni.

Grabe, S., Ward, L. M., & Hyde, J. S. (2008). The role of the media in body image concerns among women: A meta-analysis of experimental and correlational studies. *Psychological Bulletin, 134*(3), 460–476.

Johnson, P. J., McCreary, D. R., & Mills, J. S. (2007). Effects of exposure to objectified male and female media images on men's psychological well-being. *Psychology of Men and Masculinity, 8*(2), 95–102.

# 6   Mindfulness and Self-Acceptance

## Tuning in to Programming: Mindfulness as a Self-Acceptance Tool

Although creating one's own programming and actively disrupting unhelpful cultural messages about weight, shape, and food are useful means of creatively responding to negative body image or emotion-related messages, it can still be difficult for clients to recognize that they also have the power to "turn down" (i.e., refuse to be guided by) these messages, which continue to play loudly inside their minds. Clients are used to engaging actively with these messages, either by arguing against them, trying to control them, or being guided by their commands away from their values and wishes. Given that these thoughts cannot be controlled or removed – there is no way to unlearn what has been learned – what is an effective way to experience and co-exist with these thoughts without being controlled by them?

Mindfulness provides one answer. Mindfulness is frequently misunderstood. In this program, mindfulness is not a relaxation technique, nor is it a means to develop a "quiet" mind or to stop the mind from becoming distracted. It is not a skill in the sense of being an activity you can do well or poorly. Mindfulness is simply the act of being aware of one's own experience. To engage in mindfulness, you simply attend to one or another aspect of your experience, noticing and experiencing it fully, without trying to distract yourself or change the experience in any way. Mindfulness can be difficult to introduce to clients, because it can sometimes seem to be either an abstract, foreign concept, or a new-agey fad, which clients may have already tried, embraced, or rejected. However, we all have moments of mindfulness in our lives all the time: If you have ever been completely consumed by the sensations of a kiss, or fully focused on the taste of a delicious chocolate truffle, or, for a brief moment, done nothing but watched the sunset, without another thought, then you have experienced mindfulness. That is all of mindfulness: Being present, aware, and willing to fully experience what is occurring *now*.

One can deliberately apply mindful attention to any aspect of experience, including breath, bodily sensations and movements, emotions, thoughts, or any experiences happening inside or outside one's mind and body, such as brushing one's own teeth or washing a dish or hugging a child. Mindfulness involves not only experiencing pleasant thoughts, feelings, and sensations, but also experiencing unpleasant or uncomfortable ones. You or your clients might be quite familiar with the experience of mindfully savoring and experiencing pleasant or joyful experiences, but the idea of intentionally experiencing negative emotions and thoughts with the same mindful attention may be novel. The act of mindfully observing negative experiences (e.g., emotions, thoughts), *without* trying to change them, may seem counterintuitive, and many people (including many clinicians reading this book!) may have never engaged in this activity. Most of the time, we react strongly against negative thoughts and emotions, just as we react to negative life situations. If a negative feeling emerges, we try to control it, push it away, distract ourselves, numb the feelings or thoughts with alcohol or other substances, ignore it, talk ourselves out of it, fight against it. Does this work?

Sometimes it seems to work, at least a little, for a little while. But then the unpleasant thought or feeling may come right back, big as life and twice as painful! Clients have often tried to push away negative thoughts or feelings about body image especially. But they may be able to observe that they haven't ever gone away for long: You can push them away temporarily, but they come right back.

Mindful observation offers an alternative to this exhausting process of fighting with feelings and thoughts, but it can seem counterintuitive: "You mean I should savor and experience my pain fully? Why would I want to do that?"

Clinicians should resist the urge to answer this question by telling clients that mindfulness will improve their emotions or their emotional coping. The goal of mindfully experiencing painful thoughts and emotions is *not* to improve or shrink those emotions, or eliminate the thoughts or better control them. It is important to emphasize this point both in considering mindfulness as a self-care practice and in introducing it to clients. Mindfulness has become somewhat trendy, and many people engage in it in hopes of relaxing or developing a peaceful, quiet mind. In this context, clients and clinicians should explicitly understand that relaxing or calming down is emphatically *not* the goal of mindfulness practice. It is possible, in fact, even likely, that after a client practices mindfulness on any given occasion, or perhaps even most occasions, she will feel just as badly afterwards as she did before she sat down to observe. Perhaps she will even feel worse. And *that is fine*. The goal of mindfulness is to experience *all* feelings, not to decrease negative feelings. Clients begin treatment hoping to feel *better*, with less emotional pain, especially about their bodies. Unfortunately, mindfulness will not work for that! And neither will any other tool in *the Accept Yourself!* program. Clinicians should be nakedly honest with clients: "I do not know how to make you feel better." (It is worth asking yourself as you are reading: Is this true? Do you as a clinician know how to make clients feel better in a lastingly permanent way? Do you know even how to make yourself feel better? The author of this book cannot make any such claim!) Instead, clinicians might consider offering clients a more realistically attainable goal: That after they begin a mindfulness practice and finish the *Accept Yourself!* program they will *feel* better, that is, become more skillful at feeling *whatever* it is they feel.

In any event, in engaging in mindfulness, it is neither the goal nor the assumption that after practice the mindfulness practitioner should feel better or achieve insight or be more calm and rational or accomplish any particular goal. In fact, clinicians would be wise to offer mindfulness to clients (and to practice it themselves) as an experiment in responding differently to negative thoughts and emotions. One useful metaphor to describe the goal of mindfulness is actually *mindless* television.

Have you ever watched mindless television? Have you ever been so tired at the end of a hard work day that you returned home, sat on the couch, and stared at the television, too tired even to look for the remote? You are going to watch whatever is on. If a baseball game is on, you will watch baseball. If a romantic comedy is on, you will watch the romantic comedy. If a murder mystery is on, you'll watch the mystery. If Home and Garden Television is hosting a tour of the innovations in toilets, you will be watching the toilet show.

When you have watched mindless television, what was the goal of that activity? Does this seem like a silly question? Not every activity has a goal, and mindless television is not something you engaged in expecting any particular benefit or accomplishment. However, even though all you are doing is watching whatever is on, you might still be affected by this experience. Your heart might start to pound at an exciting scene in the mystery. You might feel loving and romantic when the hero and heroine in the comedy finally kiss. However, even though these effects may occur – they might even be powerful – you still may have no particular expectation or outcome in mind from the activity of simply sitting in front of the television watching whatever is on. There's no goal except to watch. And that is precisely the goal of mindfulness: To watch whatever is on, for its own sake. If you are watching your breath, you are making the effort to watch each breath. If you are watching a sunset, you are watching the sunset. If you are watching your thoughts, you are watching whatever thoughts float through your mind as you watch. If you are watching your emotions or physical sensations, you observe them as they arise and shift and change. What is the goal of doing this? What is the goal of watching mindless television? It is to *watch whatever is on*, for its own sake, just to see and experience it.

I would caution you as a clinician against expecting any more from mindfulness than that, especially initially, either when you begin your own practice or when you offer a rationale to clients to practice. Instead, focusing on trying mindfulness as an experiment in observing for its own sake. Experiment with doing mindfulness for no other reason than simply to experience aspects of your own experience more fully and with more awareness. I generally advise clients to try a daily formal mindfulness meditation practice of any length (e.g., 5 minutes, 15 minutes, etc.), and to commit to daily practice for six weeks, before evaluating the experience either way.

The results of the mindfulness experiment, if any, do not occur immediately following a single mindfulness practice. It is possible clients will feel relaxed following a single mindfulness practice, but if this occurs, consider it a pleasant side effect, not a desirable outcome or achievement. It is also possible clients will feel worse following practice, and this should be anticipated and normalized.

Mindfulness is also an activity that clinicians should experience directly rather than recommending to clients without personal lived experience of the intervention. There is some evidence that mindfulness as a clinician self-care technique is beneficial to both clinicians and clients. Mindfulness practice appears to lead to improved therapist empathy, compassion, greater counseling skills, and decreased therapist stress, burnout, anxiety, and depression (see Davis & Hayes, 2011, for a review). There are some experimental and quasi-experimental studies that suggest that clients experience improvements in psychotherapy outcome when therapists engage in mindfulness practice (Grepmair et al., 2007; Ivanovic, Swift, Callahan, & Dunn, 2015). Interestingly, these benefits to clients appear to occur only in studies where therapists actively engage in mindfulness practice, not in studies where therapists self-report their level of mindfulness as a trait (Davis & Hayes, 2011).

### Skills for Tuning in #1: How to Practice Mindfulness

If you as a clinician would like to practice mindfulness, and if you would like to recommend this practice to clients, there are several avenues to explore. Mindfulness can be done informally, as part of daily life. You can begin by simply observing each breath you take for a short period of time, five minutes, say, or even one minute. Or you can mindfully, with full attention to every aspect of the experience, do a small task, such as walking to the mailbox, brushing your teeth, or washing three dishes. The key in both cases is to do whatever it is that you are doing with full attention. Watch each breath with your full attention. Take each step with full attention, noticing every motion of your legs, feet, and body, every sensation as your leg and foot move through space and contact the ground. Brush each tooth with full attention, tasting the toothpaste fully, noticing the sensations of brush and tongue and teeth.

However, when beginning a mindfulness practice, formal daily practice of some kind, either with a meditation group or using audio recordings, is advisable. Audio recordings for formal mindfulness meditation practice, which allow you to listen to a guided meditation for 5–30 minutes, are widely available on the internet (e.g., see www.freemindfulness.org) and most are suitable for this treatment program for either clinicians or clients. However, clients and clinicians should avoid mindfulness practices that integrate mindfulness with progressive muscle relaxation, guided imagery for relaxation, or that state that relaxation is a goal. In the case of this treatment program, there is no expectation that mindfulness will be used to relax or calm down. Indeed, experiencing unpleasant thoughts and feelings is one of the main goals of the practice.

One unpleasant experience that often emerges when both clients and clinicians do mindfulness is embarrassment or irritation at one's perceived inability to do mindfulness. While you are trying to observe your breath, you may find yourself evaluating or judging your observations or your ability to observe. For example, you may notice yourself thinking, "How can I teach my clients to accept their bodies when I still hate my body?" You may then react to that thought by thinking, "I should not be thinking bad thoughts about myself; I'm supposed to be focusing on my breathing. This is so stupid. I'm so bad at this!"

After enough of these thoughts, you may be tempted to turn off the meditation and not go back to it. (Perhaps you have already had this experience, if you were taught mindfulness as a self-care practice during your professional training!) You may have the thought "I guess I'm just no good at meditation." If this is your experience, I have empathy for you, because these types of thoughts derailed my own meditation practice for many years, even though I continued to teach mindfulness to my clients and tell them it was a good idea for them! Eventually, a patient meditation teacher helped me understand that these experiences – the judgmental thoughts about myself that might emerge, and the judgmental thoughts about mindfulness meditation that might emerge – were not a sign that I was bad at my practice. They were *the core* of my practice. Notice that all of these judgments – the judgment about your professional skills, the judgment about your body, the judgment about your mind and what it should be doing, the judgment about mindfulness – are thoughts, not facts. They are something to be observed during the practice. (And, if they are a distraction from your practice, for example, if you are observing your breath and a thought about your body or the practice arises, they are something to be observed before you turn back to observing your next breath.)

Everyone's mind wanders during mindful observation, and this should be anticipated for clients and discussed when recommending mindfulness practice. Your thoughts (as well as your clients' thoughts) may bounce around in many directions, like a monkey swinging from tree to tree. It is common to evaluate this wandering as bad, to think "I am not doing this mindfulness right." It is also common to believe that when you get better or more skillful at mindfulness, this wandering will lessen, or stop entirely. In my experience, at least, this is not true. If during your first 15-minute experience of mindfully observing your breath, your mind wanders away from breathing 100 times, when you are an expert meditator, your mind will also wander away 100 times. The expert meditator views this experience with self-compassion, holding it lightly, patiently returning his or her mind to breathing every time it wanders away. You can do this, too, even during your very first time. If your mind wanders away, notice that, and return it to the task at hand, as many times as necessary, and without judgment. A busy mind is not "cured" by mindfulness practice, and doesn't need to be.

## Types of Mindfulness Meditation to Try

A basic formal mindfulness practice might begin with mindful observation of the breath. The Free Mindfulness Project linked above has a variety of mindful breathing exercises, and they are commonly available in other locations as well. A second useful type of mindfulness to experiment with is mindfulness of thoughts. Mindfully observing thoughts is a core aspect of the *Accept Yourself!* treatment program, and will be helpful to clients as they begin to practice accepting their thoughts and acting in ways contradictory to what their thoughts suggest. The ACT exercise known as "leaves on a stream," where clients learn to imagine their thoughts as a stream covered in fallen autumn leaves, and practice attaching each thought to a leaf and watching it go by, is a particularly useful beginning mindfulness of thought meditation. You can find a recording of this meditation online at Dr. Jason Luoma's website here: www.drluoma.com/media/Leaves%20on%20the%20stream.mp3. Think Mindfully also has a computer simulation of this exercise clients can try (www.thinkmindfully.com).

Finally, it is useful to practice mindfully observing negative sensations in the body, and negative emotions. Here's a script to use in helping clients mindfully observe painful sensations and emotions, which could be used in session or audio-recorded for later use by clients or in your own practice. (I should note that my own ideas about mindfully observing emotion have been heavily shaped by the work of Zen teacher Erik Storlie and Heffner & Eifert's 2006 work with women with anorexia, and I have borrowed heavily from them in creating this meditation.) As you read the script, allow generous pauses for your listener to observe her own experiences as you progress through the meditation.

> *Begin by taking a moment to find a position that is as comfortable as possible for practice. You may want to sit in a chair, or on the floor, with your back against the wall or sitting cross-legged, or lying down on the floor or a bed. Whatever will allow you to listen and be alert for a few minutes while we explore this meditation together. Take a moment to get settled, physically. There is no hurry. There is plenty of time to get settled. You may want to loosen tight clothing, shake out the muscles of your neck, shoulders, and arms, settle the big muscles of the legs and thighs into the chair or bed or floor. Let your body find just how it wants to sit. Allow your eyes to drift gently closed.*
>
> *Now take a moment to notice your breathing. Notice the cool air at your nose and mouth, at the back of your throat, as you inhale. Notice the warm air as you exhale. Notice your belly and your chest expand as you take a breath. Then notice it draw in as you exhale. See if you can follow the entire breath as it enters through your nose, is drawn deep within your entire body, and then leaves through your nose or mouth. Take a few moments to notice each breath.*
>
> *Now, take a moment and notice any emotional discomfort you may be feeling. Name it, label it, if you can. Are you feeling sad? Scared? Anxious? Angry?*

*Resentful? Ashamed? Embarrassed? Guilty? Some other painful feeling? If you are not certain, notice that. If you are feeling nothing at all, notice that. How would you label this emotion or absence of emotion?*

*Now notice how this emotion feels physically. Where do you feel this emotion in your body? Is there tightness anywhere related to this emotion? What do you notice about this feeling in your face? What would you see of it on your face if you were looking at yourself in a mirror now? Do you notice this emotion in your neck and shoulders? In your chest? In your belly? In your pelvis or behind? In your hands or legs? What do you feel as you scan your body looking for this feeling? As you notice physical sensations of this emotion in your body, take a moment and let your attention linger on this place where you feel your feeling. Describe the sensations to yourself. Sit and watch them. As you watch, what do you notice? Do the physical sensations change as you watch? Do they get bigger? Smaller? Do you notice your attention wandering to other parts of your body?*

*Notice if the emotions or sensations have changed as you have been sitting with them. Are they bigger? Smaller? Would you use any different words to describe them to yourself now? Have any shifts occurred in them? Notice if any shifts have occurred, or if things are exactly the same.*

*Hold your own hand as you sit with these feelings and physical sensations. Sit gently with yourself, as you would with a friend who was feeling this emotion. As you notice your physical body, do you notice any other sensations of discomfort in it? Does anything itch? Are there any sore places? Take a moment and gently notice these, letting your attention linger there and watching the sensations. Notice how they change as you watch them. See if you can allow them to change, get bigger, and smaller, without doing anything about that.*

*Notice any thoughts that might be arising as you sit noticing these sensations in your body. Are there any thoughts that you can't stand these feelings any longer? Are there any urges to do anything? See if you can notice these thoughts and urges without doing anything. Notice what is happening with your emotions. Have they changed? Notice what seems to be different.*

*If your mind has wandered off and begun to think of other things, observe that experience. Notice the thoughts as they shift. Are there any shifts in your body as well? Notice these.*

*Take one more opportunity to observe your entire body. Begin at the top of your head and notice your head, face, and neck. Notice what thoughts are arising.*

*Now notice your hands and arms. How do they feel in the position they are in? Can you hold your own hands gently as you sit? Notice your shoulders and back. Notice your chest.*

*Take a moment and notice your breath in your chest and belly. Has it changed? Is it deeper or shallower? Maybe it is the same. Take a moment and notice first one breath, and then another. Notice your breath filling your belly, and then notice your belly. Notice its softness, how it feels against your clothes. Are there sensations or emotions in your belly? Notice them.*

*Notice your pelvis and bottom. Is there any emotion or sensation there? Notice exactly the shape that is made by the parts of your body that are touching the chair, or bed, or floor. Notice the support of the chair, or bed, or floor, holding you, cradling you, as you experience whatever you are experiencing now.*

*Notice your legs and feet, the nerve endings at the very tips of your toes. Take a moment to notice and appreciate the nerves that allow you to sense all the sensations and feelings you have been experiencing.*

*Now, finally, return to your breath. Notice that it is still there, constant, like the ocean, flowing in and out like tides. Watch one breath. Now watch one more. And, finally, whenever you are ready, let your eyes drift open and gently return to the room. Wrap your arms around your body and give yourself a gentle embrace. Perhaps take a moment and massage your neck and shoulders, jaws, and face, allowing yourself a little time before moving on to the rest of your day.*

After completing this mindfulness exercise, take a moment to check in with clients about what they are experiencing. Compared with mindfulness of thought and mindfulness of breath, mindfulness of emotion can be much more difficult and challenging for clients. That is often a reason specifically to spend time with this exercise, and is definitely not a reason to avoid it. Becoming skillful at feeling and experiencing painful emotions is a major goal of this phase of treatment.

### Skills for Tuning in #2: Non-Judgment

A non-judgmental stance helps clients and all people see our thoughts as thoughts, and helps us develop compassion for ourselves and others. Marsha Linehan (1993) has written about non-judgment as a skill. According to her, practicing non-judgment involves seeing but not evaluating. When we practice non-judgment, we are looking at "just the facts" of a situation. Linehan describes this as focusing on "what" is happening or being observed, not whether it is "good" or "bad," "should" or "should not." She advises clients to "unglue your opinions from the facts," from the "who, what, when, and where." What this means is that opinions may emerge, but that clients should practice looking at the facts of the situation separately from these opinions. Linehan invites clients to accept each moment, each event, as a blanket spread out on the lawn accepts rain and sun and leaves. The blanket has no opinion about the leaves, and does not reject or embrace any of them especially. They just land on the blanket and are allowed to remain there without effort or intervention. Practicing non-judgment sometimes feels restful to clients, as there is no need to bat away or get rid of unpleasant thoughts or feelings. Linehan also suggests that they feel free to acknowledge the helpful, the wholesome, but do not judge it. Similarly, they can acknowledge the harmful, the unwholesome, but also not judge it. Finally, she encourages clients that when they find themselves judging, do not judge the judging. Simply observe judging and return to observing. It can sometimes be helpful to become aware of just how often we engage in judgmental thoughts or speech, not just negative judgments, and not just body-image judgments, but all kinds of judgments. If your client wears a ring, you might suggest beginning a practice of turning the ring once around the finger when the client notices a judgment in her mind or speech. You will want to warn your clients that they may be turning their rings hundreds of times a day! The goal in turning the ring is not to stop judgments: Remember, don't judge your judging! Instead, the goal of turning the ring is to simply become aware of this judging experience and how these many judgments we make or say in a day affect us. Another way of noticing judgments is in a group. Try practicing that everyone in the group will tap their glass with a fork, or ring a bell placed in the center of the table, whenever they notice themselves or another member making a judgment (positive or negative). If you do this in a group treatment session you may be surprised how often you and your clients have to tap the glass or ring the bell, and how this derails other activities.

## Defusion: Is There a Bomb in Your Mind?

Mindfulness is one way to develop what Acceptance and Commitment Therapy (ACT) describes as *cognitive defusion* from painful thoughts about the body or the self. Defusion involves observing painful and negative thoughts for what they are – which is to say words and sounds and images produced by the mind as it engages in its endless process of chattering, evaluating, commenting on, and describing everything. Defusion can be distinguished from *believing* or *acting as if* thoughts are what they say they are, for example statements of the gospel truth, commands that must be obeyed, or perfect crystal balls that tell us about the fixed, immutable future and the objectively truthful and perfectly remembered and understood past. ACT therapists note that defusion serves to alter the undesirable functions of negative thoughts, without changing their form or frequency. For example, if a client has the thought "I'm fat and disgusting," and she responds to this thought when it occurs by feeling ashamed and avoiding going outdoors to engage in fun activities where others might see and judge her, we might say that she was fused with this thought, and this thought might be a useful target for defusion. Defusion can be a difficult concept to explain, and experiential activities may be the best means to experience defusion for both clients and clinicians. But one useful metaphor to describe defusion might be the image of a mental bomb, which can be defused. (Oddly, all of the painful thoughts clients experience as bombs are already defused, in the sense that they were always harmless, rather than dangerous. It becomes part of the work of the clinician to help the client experience this paradoxical possibility.)

Clients often feel that their painful thoughts cause depression or unhappiness, or need to be avoided. That is, they have a collection of thoughts that they may experience regularly, which they feel are actually dangerous, as if thinking them might be harmful, as if these thoughts were actually bombs that might explode and ruin everything! Are these "dangerous thoughts" actually bombs? Can your clients' most dangerous, upsetting thoughts hurt anyone? (Clinicians are often quite fearful of client thoughts, such as suicidality, and they may also be fearful of intense client emotions, feeling fearful to allow a client to go home if she seems too sad or fearful or panicky.)

To answer the question, it is worth vividly imagining, as vividly as you can, a bomb. Now that you have a vivid image, do you feel afraid? (Why or why not?) Are you willing to sit in the room with this imaginary bomb you have made? How long would you be willing to sit in the room with it? Can this bomb hurt you? No. It's harmless.

Let's see if we can make the thought more dangerous. Can you imagine actually building a bomb? Can you imagine developing the expertise to do that, constructing your bomb, placing it somewhere where it would go off and hurt or kill someone you dislike? What emotions emerge as you consider this more graphic and alarming set of thoughts? Perhaps you feel uncomfortable. Notice the resemblance to clients' "dangerous" thoughts: You certainly would conduct a detailed risk assessment, and possibly hospitalize or report to the police a client who came in discussing in detail how to make a bomb to harm someone she disliked!

But whatever has shown up, notice this: Your thoughts are harmless. An imaginary bomb – no matter how vividly imagined – cannot harm anyone. Even detailed bomb-making instructions are harmless unless someone follows them and builds a bomb with their *behavior*, not just their mind. Even the worst thoughts we or our clients may have are not actual objects of mass destruction sitting in the room – they are just sounds in our heads, just chatter, just something our minds do. Like the bomb-making instructions we envisioned, even the worst or most painful thought is not necessarily anything you have to respond to.

Perhaps we can think of these painful, "dangerous" thoughts as *defused* bombs. I like to think of defusion, and describe it to clients, as "pointing out that mental bombs are defused already." A defused bomb is a harmless hunk of metal. It may still look like a bomb, and have the shape of a bomb, but it is harmless. Would you be willing to sit in the room with a defused bomb? (If not, why not?) Thoughts, too, after we defuse them (or rather, notice that they are *already* defused, since, as we have seen, thoughts were never actually dangerous), are still there. We still think them, but we're able to notice that they are not harmful, that we need not do anything about them. Notice that defusion does not mean or imply not assessing or responding to risk of suicide or homicide when clients express dangerous or harmful urges. Instead, it means managing and decreasing the risk of client *behavior*, while noticing that thoughts and feelings *per se* do not carry any risks. You can think the most dangerous thought in the world daily for the rest of your life, and as long as you do not act on it, it remains harmless. Cognitive defusion activities allow you as well as clients to experience "dangerous" or intensely painful thoughts as thoughts, and to begin to observe that the choice of how to behave is theirs and not the thoughts'.

Defusion involves observing thoughts, observing their arbitrary nature, their harmlessness, and our ability to have these thoughts and choose to behave no matter what the thoughts say. In defusion, we thank our minds for unwanted thoughts, and go about our business pursuing the lives we want regardless of their chatter.

## Preparing for Acceptance

At this point in treatment, clients who are engaged in a regular mindfulness practice (with clinicians who are also engaged in a regular personal mindfulness practice), and who have begun to experience cognitive defusion with some previously painful, sticky or scary thoughts, are ready to begin the core of the *Accept Yourself!* program, which involves learning and practicing self- and body acceptance. Up to this point, the skills and information provided to clients have been foundational, skills and experiences that enhance clients' cognitive flexibility and help them engage in acceptance practice. Acceptance is the most difficult and challenging part of the treatment program, and a solid mindfulness practice will provide an excellent foundation and support for this more challenging work.

## References

Davis, D. M., & Hayes, J. A. (2011). What are the benefits of mindfulness? A practice review of psychotherapy-related research. *Psychotherapy*, 48(2), 198–208.

Grepmair, L., Mitterlehner, F., Loew, T., Bachler, E., Rother, W., & Nickel, M. (2007). Promoting mindfulness in psychotherapists in training influences the treatment results of their patients: A randomized, double-blind, controlled study. *Psychotherapy and Psychosomatics*, 76(6), 332–338.

Heffner, M. & Eifert, G.H. (2006). *The anorexia workbook: How to accept yourself, heal your suffering, and reclaim your life*. Oakland, CA: New Harbinger.

Ivanovic, M., Swift, J. K., Callahan, J. L., & Dunn, R. (2015). A multisite pre/post study of mindfulness training for therapists: The impact on session presence and effectiveness. *Journal of Cognitive Psychotherapy*, 29(4), 331–342.

Linehan, M. (1993). *Cognitive-behavioral treatment of borderline personality disorder*. New York: Guilford.

# 7 Building Size Acceptance, Building Self-Acceptance

What is acceptance? Many people have great difficulty with the word, as well as with engaging in the behavior. For example, imagine that today you receive an official-looking letter in the mail. You open it: It's from the city. They are claiming your home with eminent domain – your beloved family home, where you raised your children, live with your partner and pets, where you have been for 40 years, where you expected to die and be buried under the cherry tree in the backyard. But next month the city is sending a steamroller to knock your house down and put a freeway there. What's your reaction?

Certainly not acceptance! You begin with resistance. You call the city, you call your lawyer, you call the media. However: You can't fight city hall. Your efforts have come to naught. Next month, on the fifteenth, the steamrollers really are coming to knock down your house. Now your reaction may be one of passive acceptance, or perhaps "despair" is a better word. You may become so hopeless that on the appointed day, when the steamroller comes, you walk out your front door and lie down in the street to let the steamroller roll on over you. Life is over. How long does this state of passive acceptance last?

Until the steamroller runs over your big toe: Ouch! Now you are back on your feet, ready to resist and fight again. Despair is not a workable response to an unfixable situation. In this case, resistance also has not worked. What alternatives might there be? What if, on the appointed day, you came out the door, bags packed, a bouquet of flowers in your left hand, your suitcase in your right. You go up to the steamroller, hop up into the cab, kiss the driver, hip-check the driver into the passenger seat, take the wheel, and steamroll over your house yourself? What is behind this house?

That's an example of active acceptance. To be clear, this is a parable, not a workable response to the vagaries of freeway construction, but it gets at some of the core paradoxes and behavioral qualities of self-acceptance practice. Acceptance is an *active* set of *behaviors*, not a *passive* set of *feelings*. Acceptance involves willingness and bravery. Acceptance is a behavioral choice, not an emotional state. How can we develop acceptance?

## Building Acceptance by Experiencing

Self-acceptance, and size acceptance, are obviously at the core of the *Accept Yourself!* program, as the name suggests. However, acceptance is often misunderstood by both clinicians and patients. Acceptance, as the term is used in this book, does not mean liking, appreciating, loving, or wanting any particular aspect of one's experience or body. Clients often begin treatment saying "I can never love (or accept) this body," but successful self-acceptance does not mean one has to "love" yourself or "love" your body. Acceptance is also not a synonym for despair; it does not mean passively standing by and allowing unpleasantness because one feels powerless to do anything else. Some clients state that they have already "tried accepting myself," and that this just makes them feel hopeless or other bad feelings. (It's worth observing in this last case that clients are "accepting" something *so that they will feel better.* That is, they are practicing acceptance in service to non-acceptance: If I accept this properly, my bad feelings will go away so I don't have to accept them anymore.) That is not how acceptance works.

Acceptance is not love. Nor it is despair. Nor is it a trick move to eliminate bad feelings. Acceptance is not an emotion or feeling at all (and thus it is not something clients can succeed or fail at feeling). Acceptance is a *set of behaviors*, an active practice people can *choose* to engage in that is designed to help people fully experience and respond effectively to whatever painful emotions, thoughts, or sensations they have been (ineffectively) avoiding in their lives.

Acceptance can be contrasted with the Acceptance and Commitment Therapy (ACT) concept of *experiential avoidance.* Experiential avoidance is anything a person does to avoid feeling or thinking or experiencing any unpleasant internal thought, feeling, or sensation. Experiential avoidance might include any number of behaviors: It might take the form of passivity and inaction. LaToya, for example, avoided going to the doctor's office for many years, despite her diabetes, family history of breast cancer and hypertension, and need for regular screenings and preventative care, because her doctor engaged in weight-based discrimination, and she did not want to experience the feelings of shame and worthlessness she felt during doctor visits. For the same reason (to avoid feelings of shame and worthlessness), she also avoided making any complaints about the doctor. She also avoided trying to find a different provider, to avoid experiencing her fears of being judged and shamed by any provider.[1] Lori avoided going clothes shopping, instead wearing clothes that no longer fit her well, because her size had increased over the years and she did not want to experience the guilt, embarrassment, and shame she felt when she pulled a larger-than-last-time size off the rack or tried on clothes in fitting rooms with mirrors. Pauline avoided picking up the phone when she saw her mother was calling, in order to avoid the anger, disappointment, and hurt she experienced when her mother inevitably criticized her body. (Similarly, she also avoided setting limits and boundaries with her mother because of fears of being retaliated against or abandoned by her mother for setting limits.)

Experiential avoidance can also take the form of impulsivity. Jamie got on the scale, saw a number that made her feel embarrassed and ashamed, and immediately signed up for Weight Watchers in order to feel better. Bineshiinh binged on Oreos and fried dough when she felt depressed. Robin often felt lonely, and would use dating apps to find casual sex partners in the evenings to alleviate her feelings of loneliness.

Experiential avoidance can also take the form of avoidant persistence. Gretchen remained with her abusive partner, because she was afraid of living on her own, and she worried that she was unlovable. Theresa kept engaging in weight loss strategies, even though she knew these were always ineffective in the long term (and, in fact, her weight had increased over time as she engaged in them), because not engaging in weight loss strategies made her feel worthless and disgusted with her body.

Other behaviors are also possible examples of experiential avoidance. Chi tried to engage in pep talks or positive affirmations when she felt bad about her body, so she would feel better. Jennifer drank heavily in order to feel less anxious. Rachel practiced relaxation strategies and diaphragmatic breathing strategies she had learned in therapy in order to feel less panicky when she was invited to a party with an all-you-can-eat buffet. All of these are examples of experiential avoidance. The unifying feature of behaviors in service to experiential avoidance is that the goal is to avoid experiencing some internal unpleasantness.

Acceptance is the opposite of experiential avoidance. To practice acceptance, you deliberately experience whatever has been previously avoided. If previously you "pulled away," now you will "lean in." LaToya role-played with her therapist how to respond assertively to her physician's weight stigma, and made an appointment to go in for a check-up. She agreed in advance to allow herself to be tearful or panicky during the appointment (two emotions she had feared displaying), and to remain in the exam room even if these emotions emerged. She role-played asking about breast cancer screening and committed to asking about this, and also role-played giving her physician information about the Health At Every Size (HAES) approach and refusing to be weighed unless this was needed to calculate her medication dosage. She agreed to notice and mindfully experience whatever emotions emerged during this doctor visit.

Lori practiced going to both "regular" and plus-sized clothing retailers, and trying on clothes in a variety of sizes that she felt would be guilt-inducing to try on and have fit her body. Pauline role-played setting boundaries on her mother's body criticism (e.g., "Mom, if you comment about my body, I'm going to hang up the phone") with her therapist, and committed to answering the phone promptly when her mother rang and implementing these boundaries.

Jamie cancelled her Weight Watcher membership, sitting with the feelings of failure that emerged, and then practiced stepping on to the scale holding heavy objects, and sitting with the feelings of embarrassment and failure.

Bineshiinh practiced mindfully observing her depression without eating and noticing what emerged. Robin practiced mindfully observing her loneliness during a week of being alone at home in the evenings, and committed to not picking up her phone or checking the internet to avoid loneliness as she observed and experienced this feeling fully.

Gretchen practiced a variety of acceptance exercises to help her evaluate and respond effectively to her partner's abuse: She called a domestic abuse hotline and worked with a women's advocate to create a safety plan, mindfully observing the terror and uncertainty that emerged as she took this step. Then she practiced implementing various parts of the safety plan, such as saving and hiding some money of her own and looking at apartments, again mindfully observing the various emotions that arose as she did these things. Theresa engaged in the *Accept Yourself!* program and committed to six months of non-dieting, sitting with her fears of weight gain and mindfully observing these as they arose. Chi practiced mindfully observing bad feelings about her body rather than pep talking her way out of them. Jennifer experimented with a "dry January," where she committed to feeling whatever anxiety she felt for a month without alcohol or other substances. Rachel was willing to try having panic attacks without using relaxation strategies, first in her therapist's office as they practiced physical exercises (e.g., breathing through a straw) likely to induce panicky feelings, and then at the next party she attended with a buffet. In each of these cases, the therapist's role was to help the client identify what thoughts or feelings were being avoided, what situations would allow the client to experience these avoided thoughts and feelings, and to work with the client to develop willingness to approach and experience these situations without experiential avoidance.

Although acceptance practice may lead clients into more valued or more adaptive behavior (e.g., LaToya going to the doctor or Gretchen planning for safety with her abusive partner), it's important for clinicians to understand that during acceptance practice, the goal is not to be more interpersonally or behaviorally skillful, or to accomplish any other goals. Although behaving assertively with her discriminatory doctor might help LaToya get better health care, this is not the goal of an acceptance practice. The goal is for LaToya to deliberately and mindfully engage in behaviors that she expects will elicit the shame, fear, embarrassment, or guilt she has been avoiding, and to experience those emotions (and any other aspects of her experience) that emerge when she does so. Acceptance practice is aimed at mindfully and purposefully experiencing previously avoided feelings, thoughts, and sensations. That is the focus of this aspect of the work, although acceptance practice often does incidentally facilitate other valued behaviors.

### Ways to Cultivate Client Willingness to Approach Difficult Situations

Acceptance practice is often best begun as an in-session activity, where clients practice during the session experiencing a situation they have avoided because it brings up painful emotions. The idea of acceptance can be introduced as an alternative to avoidance, which clients may already be aware is unworkable for them at this point in treatment. It's important for clients to understand that acceptance is both the most difficult and also potentially the most rewarding and novel aspect of treatment. Clinicians should predict that the acceptance work will be very difficult and emotional, and should secure clients' willingness to explore and attempt this difficult work before beginning acceptance practice. The idea of experiential avoidance, active resistance, passive acceptance/despair, liking or loving something, and active acceptance can all be discussed and contrasted using clients' own experiences as examples. Clients' own experiences may also provide ideas for acceptance experiences that clinicians can help clients explore in session.

Clients should be asked to identify and brainstorm situations that they are avoiding, and to label the emotions or thoughts that are being avoided when they avoid these situations. The accompanying self-help manual to this book has a worksheet that is helpful in helping clients organize acceptance-related situations (see "My Painful Situations," Chapter 5 of the accompanying workbook). Even without a worksheet, however, clinicians can help clients create a list of situations the client has been avoiding related to food, situations avoided related to body image, forbidden or binge foods (or foods that elicit guilt, shame, or anxiety when eaten), and situations that elicit other negative emotions. A range of regularly experienced situations from each of these categories should be elicited. When clients have a list of 10–20 difficult situations with more than two from each category (food-related situations, body-image-related situations, painful foods, situations that bring up other painful emotions), they can be asked to organize these into a numbered hierarchy, with the easiest situation to approach and experience numbered one, and so on, with the highest number reserved for the most difficult or painful situation. The easiest situation should be one the client is willing to experience, and clinicians should check to make sure there is a range of distressing situations. Also, clinicians should make sure that the situations are ones that can be experienced regularly. For example, Laura wrote down "the death of my mother," as a situation that would raise substantial anxiety and sadness for her. Obviously, this situation would cause negative emotions, but it (hopefully) is not a situation that would regularly come up in therapy. For Laura, the thought of her mother dying also caused fear and sadness, and the therapist was able to ask, "What situations do you avoid because they bring up the thought of your mother dying and make you feel sad and scared?" Laura was able to identify that she avoided speaking with her mother about her will and her advance directive wishes, as well as about her long-term care needs, both topics which her mother had sought to discuss with her as part of her own planning. Speaking with her mother about her will and advance directives thus became an acceptance situation she could add to her list, as did speaking to her mother about her long-term care needs.

For each situation on the list the client brainstorms, the clinician should help the client identify and label emotion(s), sensation(s), and/or thought(s) that are being avoided when the client avoids the situation. However, clients sometimes brainstorm not a situation, but an emotion, sensation, or thought they avoid. For example, "thinking about the death of my mother," or "feeling scared," or "feeling hungry," or "feeling full," or "thinking about my disgusting body" are all examples of sensations, thoughts, and feelings clients might list as avoided. In this case, the clinician should help the client identify a regularly experienced situation that brings up the unwanted thought, feeling, or sensation. For Laura, this was discussions of her mother's will. Sueyoung, who avoided feeling scared, described several situations she avoided, such as watching scary movies with her friends, going out alone to restaurants, and online dating. Danielle, who avoided feeling hungry, described skipping a meal or not having snacks in her desk as situations that might lead her to feel hungry, whereas Christine, who avoided feeling full, noted that eating dessert after a restaurant meal or having Cheetos (a binge food for her) in the house brought up worries related to feeling full. (Note that in this case Christine is avoiding both the sensation of fullness and also fears related to having that sensation and what that sensation might mean.)

Once the client and clinician have created an ordered list, with the easiest situations first and the most difficult situations last, and that includes a variety of avoided situations and associated thoughts/emotions/sensations across a variety of domains (i.e., food-related, body image-related, negative emotion-related), the client is ready to begin to experience each situation, in order, one at a time. Experiencing these situations, both in and outside of treatment, is the major goal of the acceptance phase of treatment, and, although I know of no empirical data to support the suggestion, clinical experience has taught me that this portion of treatment is essential for treatment success. The opportunity to mindfully experience what one has always avoided is novel, and often has profound healing effects.

Acceptance practice generally has a wave or mountain-shaped quality, which should be described and predicted for clients in advance of practice. What this means is that as clients prepare to enter and actually do enter the situation, whatever emotion they have been avoiding begins to come up, and increases in intensity as the situation gets closer. For example, Amelia listed "calling contractors to get bids to work on my house" as a difficult situation that elicited anxiety for her. She agreed in session to call a contractor to get an estimate for some electrical work. She noted that she began to feel anxious when the clinician encouraged her to make the call, and that her anxiety increased when the clinician handed her the office phone, again when she began to dial the number, and peaked when the contractor answered the phone.

Clients often have an urge to avoid or escape the situation at some point as this negative emotion is increasing. Amelia wanted to hang up the phone as soon as she dialed the number but before the contractor answered. If the client obeys this urge (goes back down the mountain the way she came up it), her negative emotion will decrease. (Amelia would have immediately felt better and less anxious if she'd hung up the phone before the contractor answered.) However, going back down the mountain the way one has come up has a negative side effect: The next time one goes to climb the same mountain, it is often taller (i.e., the emotion is more daunting after avoidance and escape).

If clients do *not* obey the urge to go back down the mountain, but instead remain in the situation, what they will generally notice is that the emotion gradually (or sometimes rapidly) dissipates on its own. Amelia began to feel less anxious as she spoke with the contractor about her needs, and felt no anxiety at all when she hung up the phone after the successful call. Clients who remain and linger in the painful situation, practicing acceptance, will usually find that the next time they need to approach this situation, it is slightly easier. After several practices of the same situation, it often becomes dramatically easier, such that approaching the formerly strongly avoided situation is now not at all distressing: The mountain has become a sidewalk.

This experience can also generalize to somewhat different situations as clients learn that the fears and distress their minds anticipate for avoided situations are rarely typical of the actual experience in those situations. For this reason, gaining client willingness to engage in "easier" situations (those lower down on the list and first in acceptance practice) is generally more difficult than gaining willingness to engage in the most difficult situations on the list (which are approached last, after much previous acceptance practice and learning). Clinicians who have done any exposure treatment using cognitive behavioral therapy for anxiety may already be familiar with this mountain or wave-shaped quality to exposure work, but may not have realized that this generalizes to other avoided emotions, including shame, sadness, guilt, embarrassment, and anger. In *Accept Yourself!* any avoided emotion, thought, or sensation is fair game for acceptance practice.

Besides predicting a "climb up the mountain" for clients doing acceptance work, certain difficulties with acceptance practice should be anticipated and discussed with clients in advance. One problem is avoidance in the midst of acceptance. This is when a client agrees to enter a previously avoided situation but engages in various behaviors while in the situation in order to make it feel "safer" or more tolerable. Nevaeh, for example, listed "eating ice cream in public" as a difficult food-related situation that brought up feelings of embarrassment and shame for her. She agreed to engage in this acceptance practice by going to her local scoop shop, ordering ice cream, and eating it there, and she did do this practice. However, she ordered the "baby-size" cone, because this seemed easier and less embarrassing for a fat woman to be eating in public compared with a regular-size single or double-scoop cone. Furthermore, she took a seat in the back corner of the shop, where few people could see her, and ate and left the shop as quickly as possible. She noted that she felt extremely anxious that she would see someone she knew throughout practice, and also highly embarrassed, and she noted that these feelings got worse, rather than better, as she ate, improving only when she left the shop and was back in the privacy of her car. Both ordering a baby-size cone and hiding in a corner of the shop represented Nevaeh's efforts to avoid in the midst of her acceptance practice, and her experience (of negative emotions that worsened throughout practice and abated only when practice ended) is typical of avoidance in the midst of acceptance practice.

Clinicians should discuss the concept of "avoidance in the midst of acceptance" with clients in advance, and provide examples, helping clients troubleshoot what temptations they might have to avoid in the midst of whatever acceptance situation they are contemplating entering. For clients like Nevaeh who report difficult practices that did not improve during practice, clinicians should inquire about any avoidance in the midst of acceptance they may have engaged in. Clients who have engaged in avoidance in the midst of acceptance should repeat that practice, this second time not engaging in avoidance behavior. Nevaeh went back the following week to the scoop shop, ordered a double-scoop cone, and ate it sitting in the front window, where all the employees, customers, and passersby could see her consuming it. Going back to a practice that has previously been avoided or escaped is often more difficult the second time, as when going back down the mountain the way one has come up. This can be explained to clients and may offer an incentive to not avoid or escape on the first attempt, as well as to normalize the difficulty of a second practice.

Clients can sometimes be unwilling to enter acceptance situations. Clinicians should avoid the temptation to make a situation "easier" by adding elements of avoidance to it. Instead, clinicians can help clients explore how they usually deal with this situation and how well that is working for them, and can discuss whether acceptance is a novel approach they have not tried before, exploring for whether they have any curiosity about this approach. Clinicians can explore if there are other situations that bring up the same feeling or thought or sensation and which are avoided but which the client *is* willing to experience. Clinicians can also offer to support the client by practicing the difficult situation in session, if this is feasible, or by having the client call when she has completed her practice or if she needs coaching to enter it. Early acceptance practices (with "easier" situations) are often the most difficult, and if the first situation is one the client is not willing to experience, the clinician should try to elicit an even "easier" practice the client is willing to try. Once clients have had some acceptance practices under their belt, they are often curious enough about the properties of acceptance to try more. Later in the process, clinicians should be much more alert to avoidance in the midst of acceptance, and to encouraging clients to repeat practices where this has occurred in a non-judgmental way.

### Practicing Acceptance in Session

Mindfulness and acceptance skills can be woven together in session to help clients experience difficult situations and some of the benefits of acceptance.

While clients are working on their painful situations list at home, therapy sessions can strengthen practice by offering direct experiences of mindful acceptance in the moment. The *Scale Exercise*, for example, allows for mindful acceptance of fears related to weight gain and weight numbers. The scale exercise requires clients to hold heavy objects, and thus may need to be modified or not used with clients who have disabilities that prevent them briefly holding heavy weights in their hands.

To do this exercise, have available a scale that will accommodate the client's weight plus 40 lbs, as well as two canvas bags filled with about 10 lbs each of books or similar items, as well as a box filled with about 20 lbs of books or similar items. (Do not use items, such as dumbbells, which are labeled with precise weights, unless these labels can remain fully concealed from clients during the practice.)

Begin by asking this client if she is willing to do a difficult acceptance exercise involving body image and weight now, and letting her know that this exercise may bring up intense emotions. It is important always for the client to be fully willing to participate in acceptance. You can promote willingness by offering a strong rationale for acceptance, such as the suggestion that acceptance offers a novel way for clients to experience their distress, or an opportunity to experience something new. Another rationale might be that most people ultimately find that acceptance practice is the most useful or transformative part of the healing process. Or ask for willingness to try one acceptance practice as an experiment, to see what emerges. But if clients are not persuaded with a strong rationale, it is better to try a different activity than to press the issue. Genuine client willingness – not simply an effort to please or comply with the therapist – is essential to productive acceptance practice.

Once the client is willing to engage in the scale exercise, you begin by handing her one of the bags of books and asking her to put this on her shoulder and step on the scale. (It is important to give the client the books *before* she steps on the scale. The goal is *not* to see her current weight, but to see a number that is larger, by an unspecified amount, than her current weight.) Once the client steps on the scale, ask her to look at the number, and begin mindfully observing what comes up. You might prompt her to observe emotions, thoughts, and physical sensations, and to describe these. Have her continue to hold the books and look at the number and continue to prompt mindful observation: What shifts as she stands looking at the number? Do physical sensations become more prominent? Do emotions shift? After a few minutes, while she is still on the scale, hand her the second bag of books and have her place this on her other shoulder. Again prompt her to look at the number and to observe what arises, including emotions, sensations, and thoughts. Spend enough time that you can notice any shifts in emotions, sensations, and thoughts. Finally, hand her the box. Now she is holding about 40 lbs of books, and this is enough that the physical sensations of holding the weight may be strongly prominent in her awareness. Ask her to look over the box at the number and again mindfully observe what emerges, taking enough time to notice shifts. Be sure to have her step off the scale before removing the box or bags of books, and be sure to discuss her experience and what she observed during this practice. A variety of responses are common, and it can be interesting to notice how negative body-image thoughts related to the increasing weight numbers emerge, even though, obviously, the client is not actually gaining any weight. Nevertheless, the mind commonly generates anxiety and negative self-judgment *as if* the client had just spontaneously gained 40 lbs, and it can be interesting to observe that this mind does this even when it is obviously inaccurate.

Mindful eating acceptance exercises can also be useful in session, particularly with foods that the client considers "forbidden," on which she binges (if she struggles with binge eating), or foods that bring up shame, guilt, or fear when consumed. When engaging in mindful eating acceptance exercises in session, it is helpful if the therapist consumes food with the client, both to model mindful eating of food, and to reinforce a non-judgmental approach to food, the message that it is okay to eat all foods. Again, these exercises should begin by inquiring about the client's willingness to engage in a mindful eating acceptance exercise that will be difficult and bring up painful emotions. Because this type of exercise requires advance planning by the therapist, I generally ask at the previous session whether the client would be willing to try this next time. Clients may have detailed questions about what or how much will be eaten, and these questions are generally in service to reducing anxiety about the practice. As such, it makes sense to ask if that is how the question is serving, instead of answering it, and to encourage the client and inquire if she is willing to sit with this anxiety without knowing all the details as part of her practice.

In choosing a food, a more difficult food listed on the client's painful situations list is often a good choice, especially if the client has already had successful experiences with lower-intensity acceptance practice on her own. In choosing an amount of food to agree together to be eaten, it is useful to choose an amount that is not so large as to represent a binge, but is definitely larger than the client feels comfortable with eating, an amount large enough to bring up the shame, guilt, or fear that leads to avoidance. Both client and clinician should agree to eat the same amount. (If the clinician experiences guilt, shame, or fear at eating this quantity of a "forbidden" food, that likely represents important personal work for the clinician.)

Adiam, for example, had Krispy Kreme doughnuts listed as a difficult, forbidden food on her painful situations list. For Adiam, the clinician purchased six plain Krispy Kreme doughnuts. Eating all six would be a binge quantity – an amount definitely larger than what others might eat ordinarily. One doughnut would not necessarily be enough; Adiam, a nurse, was able to eat a single doughnut with coffee with her colleagues in the mornings, but more made her feel like "a fat, ugly glutton." Instead, Adiam and the clinician agreed to each eat three doughnuts together: Enough to raise intense discomfort, but not enough to constitute an objectively large binge. Laurie had "fast food" listed as a binge food for her, and, when queried, noted that McDonald's extra-value meals were a source of particular discomfort, especially fries. For Laurie, the clinician purchased two extra-value meals, with a quarter-pounder cheeseburger, large fries, and medium-sized regular (non-diet) cola. The clinician and Laurie each ate an extra-value meal. This is clearly not an objectively large binge – thousands of people eat this precise meal daily – but eating all of it intentionally, without binging, was enough to cause Laurie intense discomfort.

In terms of the exercise itself, the clinician should present the food and discuss with the client how much the two will eat, explaining to the client that both will eat the food together. The clinician should inquire about initial emotions, thoughts, and sensations, including their intensity. Then the pair should begin to eat mindfully. The clinician will likely have to model mindful eating, especially attending to the tastes, smells, and sensations of eating in a non-judgmental fashion. The clinician should encourage the client to focus mainly on the tastes, smells, and sensations of the food and the eating process itself. Thoughts and emotions and judgments are likely to arise for the client, and these should be briefly and occasionally inquired about and also noted if they are spontaneously mentioned, but they should not be the main focus of the exercise, and the clinician should, if necessary, continue to prompt the client to return to her experience of eating. Some clients may attempt to engage in avoidance in the midst of acceptance, either by "negotiating" the amount or what foods will be eaten, or by "nibbling" at the food or around some particularly stressful aspect of the food. For example, Jess, whose "forbidden food" was half of a Chipotle burrito, generally avoided her distress related to eating this food by ordering it with no sour cream or cheese. The clinician, of course, had ordered the burrito with all of the standard toppings. Jess responded to this by nibbling around the edge of the burrito, avoiding the cheese and dollop of sour cream in the center. The clinician, noticing this avoidance behavior, encouraged Jess to take a large bite, larger than she was comfortable with, in the center of the burrito where the feared food was visible, and to mindfully observe the tastes, sensations, and smells that occurred when she did this. The clinician should be alert both to her own mindful eating practice and to modeling this for the client, and also to the client's experience and any signs of avoidance that the clinician can prompt the client to engage with directly. Clinicians should avoid negotiations with clients about the size of the eating commitment or what is to be eaten. These can often be avoided by gaining clear, honest willingness in advance. If the client knows to anticipate a difficult food-related acceptance practice and has willingly agreed to participate, usually the clinician can successfully encourage the client to experiment with being willing and experiencing her fear and guilt. However, if the client is not willing to engage in the practice, it is better to set aside the food practice for later in the session or a different occasion than to negotiate and thus help the client avoid her experience.

The *Mindful Mirror* exercise described in Chapter 5 of the accompanying self-help workbook is another mindful acceptance exercise that can be adapted for use in session. Any painful situation on the client's painful situation list may also be a good opportunity for practice. Ishawna, for example, noted fear and shame as painful emotions that arose for her when she was tearful in front of others, and if she felt herself likely to cry, as often occurred at her stressful office job, she hid in a bathroom or sometimes left work for the day. This had led to disciplinary action against her for her unreliability and frequent absences. Ishawna was seen for therapy at the local hospital where she worked, and frequently saw colleagues in the hallways there. The clinician had asked her in advance if she would be willing to try some acceptance practice with her tears in the hospital hallways, and she agreed to this. Then, the two of them went to a hallway where there were chairs and also heavy traffic from passersby, and began to talk quietly about an issue that reliably elicited tears for Ishawna. Interestingly, even though it so happened that none of her colleagues or anyone she knew passed by while she was crying, her thoughts and emotions of embarrassment and shame still emerged and could be mindfully observed along with the grief that was related to her tearfulness.

### Promoting Acceptance at Home

Home acceptance practice begins by creating the painful situations list and organizing it into a hierarchy. But clinicians should also help enhance clients' commitment to this difficult part of treatment. One way to enhance commitment may be through the use of a self-acceptance contract. Asking clients to be bold and sign a contract that asks them to commit to various aspects of self-care and self-acceptance can be a useful way of bolstering commitment, and also can trigger a discussion about what a lifestyle of self-care and self-acceptance might look like, in contrast to a deprivation-based, stigmatizing, weight loss or weight-shaming lifestyle. Clinicians can urge clients to read the contract and then be bold, and make a leap and sign it, even if they have thoughts that they do not deserve this or are not up to the task. Clients can then be asked to hang their signed contract in a prominent location where it will support them as they do acceptance practice in and out of session. Ask clients where they will hang it, and follow up at the next session to see if they did and how they felt about this. A sample self-acceptance contract, which can be copied or tailored to fit particular clients, is on the next page.

## Commitment to Self-Acceptance

I _____,

am making a commitment to myself to practice self-acceptance with my body and moods.

- When I want to avoid unpleasant thoughts or feelings, I will practice experiencing them instead.
- I will lean in instead of pulling away.
- I will mindfully observe my thoughts and feelings on my journey.
- My body is my vehicle for living. I will treat my body with compassion and caring.
- I will give my body the gift of movement, and know that I have the right to take up space as I move through the world.
- I will eat well and nourish myself kindly, for pleasure, energy, and health.

I understand that I am a valuable human being who deserves all of the benefits my body and mind can provide.

_____     _____

Signed                                          Date

## Difficulties with Acceptance: Size Discrimination

We discussed in Chapter 2 how clinician stigma and discriminatory behavior against fat clients harms them. But fat clients experience weight discrimination in virtually every area of life. Female clients may experience body image-related gender discrimination in a variety of contexts, even if they are not fat. And both gender and weight discrimination may intersect with other oppressed aspects of clients' identities, including race, sexual identity, gender expression, disability, national origin, religion, or other aspects of identity, to intensify the discrimination clients may experience. Weight discrimination is increasing (independently of any increase in the actual prevalence of obesity; Andreyeva, Puhl, & Brownell, 2008). Weight discrimination harms clients in most domains of life, causing systemic inequities in employment, health care, education, interpersonal relationships, and in media depictions of fat people (Puhl & Heuer, 2009). There is mounting evidence that exposure to weight-based discrimination causes chronic physiological stress (Jackson, Kirschbaum, & Steptoe, 2016), with concomitant physical and mental health problems (Schafer & Ferraro, 2011), including causing weight gain and increased obesity (Jackson, Beeken, & Wardle, 2014; Sutin & Terracciano, 2013).

Because size discrimination is so prevalent and harmful, it is likely to present a barrier to acceptance practice. Size discrimination and weight stigma are likely to emerge during acceptance practice in two ways. First, *internal* fears of exposure to discrimination and shame, embarrassment, and guilt programmed as a result of past learning experiences of discrimination are likely to be some of the emotions that clients are avoiding and may need to experience during acceptance practice. In this case, it is not necessarily that clients are going to face stigma or discrimination when they engage in the practice, but rather the fear/shame/embarrassment/guilt/anger they are experiencing as a result of their past learning histories and feared futures that are leading to avoidance. Experiencing these emotions with mindfulness and self-compassion is one of the goals of acceptance practice. However, clients may also deal with *external* experiences of size discrimination and weight stigma as they engage in acceptance exercises out in the world, and even more as they begin to resume valued activities that they have given up because of avoidance of the feelings caused by stigma and discrimination experiences. Although actual experiences of weight stigma and discrimination are generally less common than clients' fears predict, they are not rare, and clinicians would do well to anticipate that they will occur and to help clients plan for how to respond to them consistent with their self-acceptance practice and values.

It is essential that clinicians do their own work to address their own fears of weight gain, lack of personal body self-acceptance, and internalized weight stigma. Clinicians should self-assess and know both their explicit and implicit anti-fat biases, and should be aware of the potential for committing microaggressions and other harms against fat clients. If clinicians cannot maintain a non-judgmental, fully accepting stance toward their clients' body weight, food, and activity choices, they may not be ready to use *Accept Yourself!* with clients, at least not without extensive supervision. Clients should be protected from weight-based discrimination by the clinician and as much as possible in the wider world.

If clients expect or have previously experienced weight stigma (or other and intersecting forms of stigma or discrimination) in a situation they plan to enter to practice acceptance (or that appears on their magic wand fantasy as a valued, desired activity), clinicians should talk with them in advance about how they wish to address this discrimination. Role-plays may be especially helpful here, but clinicians should be extremely careful to avoid perpetrating microaggressions against fat clients during role-plays. If the clinician role-plays the part of a weight-discriminatory interaction partner, there is risk that the client will feel that the clinician is expressing his or her "true" underlying feelings. It is often better to begin a role-play by having the client take the role of the discriminatory partner, having that person say whatever she most fears would be said or whatever would be most humiliating to hear. Then the clinician can play the role of the client, responding assertively to the discrimination and making it clear that it is unacceptable. Then, if it seems advisable to help the client practice, client and clinician can switch roles, with the clinician being careful to use only *the client's* language in the discriminatory role.

Michelle, for example, was a fat client whose magic wand fantasy included going rock-climbing. She feared that any climbing gym she might visit would not have equipment that would fit her body, and she anticipated a discriminatory, humiliating encounter with what she imagined would be the handsome, fit, slender young man behind the counter. Although she could have avoided this feared encounter in a variety of ways, such as calling ahead to ask about weight limits for the equipment, or renting specialized equipment in advance that would fit her, the clinician and Michelle agreed that role-playing this feared encounter and trying out the experience of actually going to the gym to find out would be worthwhile acceptance practice, "leaning in" on Michelle's fear that she did not deserve to be in the gym at her present weight.

Michelle first took on the role of the stigmatizer behind the counter, and, in that role, rudely told the clinician that he had nothing in her size, complete with elaborate eye roll. The clinician, playing the role of an assertive Michelle, asked to speak with his manager, and when Michelle-as-young-stigmatizer said he *was* the manager, the clinician smiled and said, "Wonderful! So you're the right person to tell that my money is as green as anyone's, and if you had equipment in my size, I'd be happy to spend it here climbing. I've heard your competitor downtown has made people of all sizes welcome, so I'll plan to take my business there. Thank you." Michelle was amused by this response, noting that she would not have thought of it, and that she would have "slinked out," ashamed. Then Michelle and her therapist were able to switch roles, with Michelle practicing this assertive, self-accepting response. In actuality, when Michelle got to the gym, they really did not have harnesses in her size, and it really was a handsome, fit, young man who provided this news. However, he was embarrassed and apologetic, rather than rude, promised to obtain the correct size harness, and agreed to call her when it came in and give her her first climbing lesson himself. Michelle was surprised by the mix of emotions this elicited in her, and returning for her first lesson became another opportunity for acceptance practice.

Clinicians may worry that role-playing responses to discrimination is a way of encouraging avoidance in the midst of acceptance. But role-playing these responses is not an emotion-management technique (and clients sometimes report that planning to behave assertively rather than acting ashamed actually makes them more fearful of engaging in the practice, rather than less). Instead, learning to assertively advocate for oneself in the face of discrimination is yet another self-acceptance practice. However, fat clients cannot do all the work of advocacy against fat discrimination themselves. They must have allies of all sizes. The clinician's own work addressing internalized weight stigma (regardless of the clinician's size) is essential basic work to becoming an ally against discrimination for fat clients, and clinicians must also become clear and public advocates against weight stigma as part of doing this work.

## Note

1  All case examples in this book and the accompanying workbook are composites; all client names are pseudonyms.

## References

Andreyeva, T., Puhl, R. M., & Brownell, K. D. (2008). Changes in perceived weight discrimination among Americans, 1995–1996 through 2004–2006. *Obesity, 16*(5), 1129–1134.

Jackson, S. E., Beeken, R. J., & Wardle, J. (2014). Perceived weight discrimination and changes in weight, waist circumference, and weight status. *Obesity, 22*(12), 2485–2488.

Jackson, S. E., Kirschbaum, C., & Steptoe, A. (2016, December). Perceived weight discrimination and chronic stress. Paper presented at the UK Society for Behavioural Medicine Annual Scientific Meeting.

Puhl, R. M., & Heuer, C. A. (2009). The stigma of obesity: a review and update. *Obesity, 17*(5), 941–964.

Schafer, M. H., & Ferraro, K. F. (2011). The stigma of obesity: does perceived weight discrimination affect identity and physical health? *Social Psychology Quarterly, 74*(1), 76-97.

Sutin, A. R., & Terracciano, A. (2013). Perceived weight discrimination and obesity. *PLOS ONE, 8*(7), e70048.

# 8 Identifying and Committing to the Values of Self-Nourishment

## Food Has Never Just Been Fuel: Food, Foodways, and Culture

A Buddhist teaching holds "Your body is precious. It is our vehicle for awakening" (Kornfield, 1994). Unlike other vehicles, you have no control over what make, model, or year of body you were issued, and if yours breaks down or experiences a traumatic accident, you cannot buy a new one. Your only option is a series of repairs. You may have been born with a high-quality or high-status vehicle, attractive in the eyes of others, reliable, capable, and high performing. Or you may have been born with a vehicle that in some ways, many ways, most ways, or nearly all ways falls short of what you would have chosen if bodies could be picked out like vehicles on a sales lot. And yet, regardless of how you feel about the body you were issued at birth, or how well it has performed over time, regardless of its flaws, without it you are powerless. Every aspect of your life – your ability to do things and to experience things – is mediated through your body. It is the only vehicle you have to take you wherever you want to go.

At this point in the *Accept Yourself!* program, clients have learned all of the mindfulness, defusion, and acceptance skills needed to begin more effectively driving their "vehicles" towards the lives they really want. That is the goal of the remainder of the program. Your focus as a clinician now shifts *away* from helping clients experience their avoided emotions, thoughts, and sensations related to body image and mood, and *toward* what brought clients in to treatment in the first place: Helping them pursue their values and dreams related to eating and food, mental and physical vitality, and all other important aspects of life. The next chapters focus on how to help clients pursue their values and dreams in several areas relevant to body image concerns and in general. The present chapter focuses on values and dreams related to food and eating. There are chapters to help you help clients pursue values and dreams related to appearance, image, and self-presentation, and to physical movement and enjoying the use of one's body. Finally, this section concludes with a chapter on pursuing values and dreams in general, in other areas of clients' lives.

One intriguing aspect of our own contemporary food culture, affected so severely by fat stigma and the thin ideal, is the notion that "food is fuel," that food is and should be nothing more than the minimum caloric sustenance required to get through a day. Although this may be how some animal species approach their daily diets, food has never been just fuel in any human culture. For human beings, food is rich with meaning and ritual, playing multiple roles in our lives.

Consider Stacey. Stacey is a professor of aerospace engineering, new in her career at a prestigious university. Her career is of primary importance to her, and she spends most of her time thinking about scientific and practical problems related to her research. She often forgets meals, or picks up breakfast and lunch from a coffee cart at work. She sometimes goes out for appetizers and drinks with students and colleagues after work, but more often eats a frozen dinner or some cereal with milk when she gets home from work, late at night, right before bed. She enjoys a good meal when she gets one, but she does not have either the time or inclination to make elaborate meals for herself. What does food mean to Stacey? What role does it play in Stacey's life? For Stacey, food is of little importance, and Stacey might really agree with the idea that "food is fuel." Food, for Stacey, is a necessary part of life, but not something of interest or importance to her.

Johnetta, however, thinks extensively about the food she eats. Johnetta weighs all of her food using a special scale, and records each morsel on an iPhone app, which syncs automatically to an online diet-tracking program. Johnetta strictly follows a vegan diet. Each week, Johnetta meets with professionals who measure her body fat, heart rate, and other physical indicators, and who help advise her on tweaks she should be making to her eating and movement behaviors. What does food mean to Johnetta? What role does it play in her life? Johnetta appears to see food as something that must be meticulously controlled. She may have an eating disorder. Or she may work in an industry, such as modeling or professional fitness, where prevailing cultural beliefs emphasize restriction of eating. For Johnetta, food represents risk to her body and must be carefully managed.

Kelly's relationship with food is quite different from Johnetta's. Kelly collects food from local businesses who would otherwise throw it away, and she distributes this food where she knows homeless people gather. She has a history of poverty and food insecurity herself, and she has fond memories of a bakery owner who offered her free meals during a difficult period in Kelly's life, when she was briefly homeless. She has a home and a good job now, but she makes the rounds daily to make sure others do not go hungry. She still enjoys and gets warm memories from baked goods, and she often will make pastries to donate. What does food mean to Kelly? What role does it play in her life? For Kelly, food may represent safety and security, as well as an opportunity to contribute, to "give back" and do good in the world.

Adoracion is a farmer and baker. She grows and prepares food on her organic farm, and sells it at farmer's markets. She loves the markets, because they offer a chance to meet up with and talk with her customers and others in her community. She and her husband both enjoy cooking. However, they mostly make quick meals with the garden vegetables that are on hand. What does food mean to Adoracion? What role does it play in her life? For Adoracion, food production, both for her family and her community, makes her living, and is also a source of pleasure and community for her.

Shaunika thinks of food mainly around the holidays, and in terms of Sunday dinners. Although daily meals are simple, it is a tradition in her family to go all out for an occasion. Sunday after church is definitely an occasion! When Shaunika was little, her family all got together at her grandmother's house for a large dinner. Her grandmother has since passed away, so in recent years Shaunika and her wife have hosted the clan. Shaunika is a lawyer, and her wife stays at home and does most of the cooking, but on Sundays Shaunika likes to be in the kitchen, because only she can make roast chicken and cornbread like grandma made. Christmas is even more elaborate: Shaunika's wife is of Italian heritage, and makes a traditional Feast of the Seven Fishes for Christmas eve. What role does food play in Shaunika's life? What does it mean to her? For Shaunika, food is family, community, and tradition.

As the cases of Stacey, Johnetta, Kelly, Adoracion, and Shaunika represent, food plays diverse roles in human life, and ways we eat, both how and what we eat, are often rich with meaning. Eating can express the programming we carry about food. For Johnetta, for example, ideas and beliefs she has been taught about the relationship between food and her body likely inform how she is interacting with food now. And for Shaunika, ideas and beliefs she has been taught about food, tradition, and family likely influence how she cooks and eats now. Eating can also be a way to live and express your deepest-held values. Adoracion, Kelly, and Shaunika, for example, all use food to express their values. Kelly uses cooking and collecting food to express values about giving back, about the worth of all people, and the rights of all people to access enough food. Adoracion gives her children a farmer's market allowance, and raises and processes some animals for meat and dairy products at home, to express and teach values related to animal care and treatment, community investment, and leisure time. Shaunika uses food to express family and traditional values.

It is worth exploring both clients' programming related to food, as well as their values and what they want to eat for. Exploring the meaning, messages, and values related to food in clients' lives both past and present helps in the process of defusion. In addition, it allows clients to explore whether their eating patterns reflect how they actually want to be eating and the role they want food to play in their lives, or if their eating reflects unwanted messages about food acquired through their learning history. The accompanying self-help workbook has an Identifying Food Programming worksheet (see Chapter 7 of the workbook) to help explore these issues. Alternatively, you can simply ask clients about the role food played in their lives growing up: Who made the food, what was eaten, how it was eaten, and what messages the client received about food and eating. You can also explore similar questions about how the client is eating currently, and where and how current eating patterns became established in her life.

Once clients have been able to explore and identify how food has historically and currently functioned in their lives, they may be ready to explore the idea that eating can represent not just a way to express your programming, but also a way to live your values.

## From Diets to Foodways: What Do You Want to Eat for?

Many people who struggle with weight or body image have been on many diets. The word "diet," like the word "fat," is fraught with weight stigma associations for most clients, because it often refers to a special, restricted regimen of foods one is required to eat, either for medical reasons, or, especially, to lose weight. However, the word "diet" can also be a neutral, non-judgmental word, referring to the kind of food a person habitually eats. Anthropologists use the term "foodway" to describe a culture's "diet," that is, the way people in that culture habitually eat. The word "foodway" includes not only what foods are eaten, but also the rituals and meanings and practices around food, both in everyday life and on special occasions. This chapter uses the term "foodway" as an alternative to the word "diet," both because "foodway" avoids connotations of deprivation and restriction, and also to highlight the many different functions and purposes food can serve in people lives. Here "foodway" is defined as a conscious way of eating that expresses a person's values and what is important to them.

Exploring food programming and identifying what you want to eat for is essential work for the clinician, as well as the client. The Health At Every Size (HAES) principle related to eating is called "Eating for Well-being," which means to "promote flexible, individualized eating based on hunger, satiety, nutritional needs, and pleasure, rather than any externally regulated eating plan focused on weight control." Both clients and clinicians live in an eating-disordered culture, which asserts that body size, health, and worthiness are closely correlated and that health is under one's personal control and a reward for moral behavior. Clinicians as much as clients are frequently carrying programming that suggests that eating should not be flexible or individualized, not based on personal, subjective feelings of hunger and fullness, and not in service to pleasure, particularly not if the eater is not thin. Clinicians may believe that dieting for weight control might somehow work for themselves (even when it doesn't work for clients), or be appropriate for certain body types, even if they reject it for most clients. But eating in service to weight control is not consistent with the *Accept Yourself!* program, regardless of client or clinician weight or health status, and clinicians should beware of internalized weight stigma affecting the eating-related advice they offer clients. There is no one right, empirically supported, "healthy" way of eating for everyone, no diet that unequivocally prevents acquiring or suffering from common chronic diseases or that reliably produces long-term weight loss in most people who use it, and all foods can be healthy for given individuals in given contexts. In addition, health is not the only appropriate motive for eating choices.

As a thought experiment, it is useful for clinicians, as well as clients, to ask themselves how they would choose to eat if their weight and health were completely fixed, permanent, and decided in advance, and nothing they ate made any difference. If food didn't matter to your waistline or your doctor, what would you eat? How would you choose? Some clients (and clinicians) with a long history of chronic dieting respond to this question by hungrily wishing for an unlimited quantity of previously forbidden foods. They imagine eating quarts of ice cream, entire pizzas, and sacks of fast food. Giving up dieting and restricted eating can be quite difficult for clients who experience this hunger, as they fear that they would begin an endless, unstoppable, lifelong binge if they give up the restriction they have practiced for years. And, indeed, therapist Deb Burgard has described the experience of "dieting detox," where clients give up dieting and do temporarily binge heavily on all the previously forbidden foods (www.bodypositive.com/dieting_detox.htm). However, both clinicians and clients should have faith that an experience of dieting detox is not going to last permanently. (Fears of what might happen if this experience did continue indefinitely may be a target for defusion and acceptance practice for either clients or clinicians.)

There are other reasons to eat that may emerge as you consider how you might eat if eating were unrelated to your weight or health. Perhaps you'd sustain yourself on the cheapest foods, and devote the money you spend on "healthy" food to other worthwhile endeavors. Perhaps you would only eat the most delicious or pleasurable foods – whatever you wanted. Perhaps you would eat in service to social or environmental goals. Perhaps you would eat whatever the family liked, or whatever the cook in your household wanted to serve you. Perhaps you would eat whatever was available and convenient, because food isn't really important to you. Many people are so thoroughly programmed with the idea that food, weight, and health are linked and a source of moral judgment, that they simply cannot imagine how they might eat if these factors were separated from one another.

Can you consider this question? Apart from good health and a desirable body, what do you want to eat for? What do your clients want to eat for? The answers to this question may highlight different foodways you or your clients can explore. Food can be used to pursue all kinds of values apart from weight loss. What does this mean?

Harris cared deeply about social justice. She was actively involved in her local, public, inner-city middle school (which her son attended), as well as her local parks. She worked hard for equality and economic opportunity for all people, and when she began to consider what foodway might represent her values, she realized that she was interested in eating more foods that were fairly traded, where the people who grew, made, or produced her food could be guaranteed of a living wage. Perhaps she could create a *Fair Trade* foodway. She began by purchasing fair-trade coffee and chocolate, and having a weekly neighborhood dinner party where she served only fairly traded foods.

She gradually began to realize that most of the fair-trade foods she could find or read about were made in other countries, and she also wanted her foodway to help strengthen communities and support social justice and equality closer to home. This led her to become interested in creating a *Sustainable Agriculture* foodway that might support sustainable farms in her community. She began doing her grocery shopping weekly at her local farmer's market, getting to know the farmers and asking them questions about their operations so that she would better understand how to support them. Whereas before her foodway project began, she had eaten a lot of "health conscious" diet foods that she purchased at her supermarket, she noticed that since the project began she was eating more seasonal, local vegetables (since that was what was available at the farmer's market), but also more chocolate, fancy coffee, and full-fat dairy products, including ice cream, since these things also fit her values better than the diet packaged foods she had been eating before.

Dawn, Anita, and Jo were three long-time friends who had fatness, body image concerns, and a passion for the environment in common. They had met at a local environmental organization's book club decades ago, but this shared interest had fallen out of their conversations over the years, which increasingly focused on weight loss. They had frequently challenged each other to "biggest loser"-style diet challenges, and they frequently "cheated" on their diets together, feeling guilty and also bonding over desserts at a local restaurant. Dawn felt guilty when she began *Accept Yourself!* and at first had trouble explaining it to her friends. But, ultimately, Anita and Jo followed Dawn's lead, expressing curiosity about the positive changes Dawn seemed to be making. When the three of them decided to explore foodways together, environmental issues were something all three wanted to explore. Dawn, like Harris, decided to focus on locally grown foods, which required less energy to grow and transport. She decided she would try to create a *Locavore* foodway. She spent a summer replacing her "biggest loser" challenge with an "eat local challenge," where she tried to eat only foods grown within a 200-mile radius of her home.

Anita, more interested in the environmental impact of pesticides and herbicides, decided to try an *Organic* foodway, and practice eating organic foods more frequently. She didn't change her shopping habits or set any particular rules for herself in exploring an organic foodway, but simply began adding more organic foods to her cart when she shopped and reading more about this issue.

Jo had been a serious activist on behalf of climate change, and had been vegetarian because she had read that avoiding meat was helpful in decreasing global-warming emissions. She was fascinated to discover the Eat Low Carbon website (www.eatlowcarbon.org), and used this site to inspire a *Low Carbon* foodway for herself. She decided to try to modify her family's meals so that they helped to avoid climate change. She began inviting the other women and their families over for a Wednesday night climate meal, where she served a low-carbon meal and the women worked together on environmental issues, as they had when they had first met. All three reported that talking about issues that mattered to them, instead of sharing diet talk, felt more life affirming and in line with their "true selves," and they observed, with surprise, that none of them had either gained or lost any weight as a result of these changes to their foodways.

Not everyone is interested in eating to express social justice or political values. Both Tamara and Jess had a lot of difficulty identifying what they would want to eat for if they did not "have to" diet to lose weight, and neither of them resonated with the social justice or community or environmental values that motivated Harris, Jo, Anita, and Dawn. "That sounds like just more deprivation," Tamara said. "I'm tired of depriving myself. I want to truly *enjoy* my food." For Tamara, it was the word "enjoy" that helped her identify what she wanted to eat for. She loved to cook, considered herself a "foodie," and enjoyed traveling to different cities to visit the best or most unusual restaurant in each one. She also felt guilty about these activities. She wanted to Instagram her meals but felt embarrassed: "Fat old lady taking pictures of her food. No one wants to see that!" In exploring her foodway, she realized that she could practice self-acceptance by allowing herself to eat for pleasure and enjoyment (and the aesthetic beauty of the food), and by also allowing herself to document this on social media, standing up against anti-fat stigma and her programming.

Tamara decided that she would write to the proprietors of her favorite restaurants, asking for one recipe per week, which she would try to make and document the results on Instagram. The rest of the time, she decided she would let go of all attempts to control her eating but simply try to eat what she wanted to eat, when she wanted to eat it, and stopping when she was full. She found that the restaurant recipe project led to increased mindfulness around her eating as she paid close attention to the ingredients, the process of cooking them, and their taste. She was pleased to see she could replicate many of her favorite restaurant treats at home, and she felt more connected to her community after communicating with her favorite chefs. She had had a long history of binge eating, and, at first, she had great difficulty identifying when she was full and stopping rather than feeling compelled to finish all of whatever she had started. Gradually, however, she was able to eat her favorite foods and stop when she felt full, and she noted that stopping at or just before fullness seemed to add enjoyment to her experience of eating.

Jess loved to travel, and she was inspired by the different foodways and traditions she saw on her travels, and how in many countries people seemed less concerned about body image and food. She wondered if she could create a *Multicultural* foodway to better explore the world's traditions with food. She stumbled on a blog that documented a woman's project to eat a meal from every country (http://globaltableadventure.com) and decided that she wanted to do the same. Jess lived in an urban area with groceries and markets that served immigrant communities from many different cultures, so she experimented with shopping at a different market each week. She expressed excitement at getting the opportunity to experiment with new cuisines and ingredients, and felt better able to practice self-acceptance with her body when she imagined how women in different cultures might approach food and body image.

Sapphire was Muslim, and she had no difficulty identifying what foodway she wanted to explore: "I'd like to use food to develop myself spiritually. I'd like to explore a *Halal* foodway." She found a source for contemporary Halal recipes online (http://myhalalkitchen.com) and began eating that way. "My grandmothers never worried about their body images. They just tried to create a peaceful, spiritual homelife. Food was part of that. I want to get back to that."

Devorah, similarly, was Jewish, and felt an increasing connection to Israel, where her parents had been born and raised. She was interested in the spiritual benefits of a *Kosher* foodway. She had kept kosher when living at home but not since beginning college. College was also where her eating disorder had begun, and she felt that falling away from her spiritual and community roots had been part of what led to obsessive thoughts about body image. She had kept a vegetarian diet since college, which also was related to her weight loss fears and body image concerns, but it also led her to become interested in the writing of Israeli vegetarian kosher writer Liz Steinberg (http://food.lizsteinberg.com). Intriguingly, when Devorah returned to keeping kosher, she also decided to try some kosher meats, and also to return to attending synagogue. She found that her spiritual beliefs began to evolve. Raised in the Orthodox Jewish tradition, she found that now she wanted to try a more liberal, Reform synagogue, which had a support group to discuss keeping kosher and the spiritual meaning of this practice.

Wichahpi's mother was a white woman from New York, and her father was a Lakota man from the Midwest. Her father had died when she was an infant, and she had grown up with her mother in New York City. She felt that she knew little about her Lakota heritage. She also wondered about developing more closeness with her cultural traditions via a *Traditional* foodway. For her, approaching this foodway involved making a summer trip to visit the reservation where her grandparents lived, and asking them about traditional foods. Her grandmother took her on a foraging expedition to find traditional greens, and was excited by Wichahpi's interest. This foodway helped her learn more about her father and her heritage, and also become closer to her grandparents.

Bolstering love and relationships is another value that can be explored through food. Marissa felt angry at how her long history of dieting had harmed her relationships. Always on a diet, she had skipped going out to eat, turned down birthday cake, and even missed out on an opportunity to write a book with colleagues because the writing sessions took place over pizza dinners. She found inspiration in the Andrew Zimmern TV show *Bizarre Foods*, where Zimmern is frequently shown being offered unusual (to an American palate) foods, which he then eats to ingratiate himself with his guests and build relationships. "If he can eat deep fried tarantulas to make a friend, I can eat pizza," she said. Her foodway involved *Willingly Eating*: Specifically, she began simply never turning down an opportunity to eat with others, and eating whatever she was offered. She reported an expanding sense of freedom, and also expressed surprise that her weight did not change when she began to eat this way.

Karina also resented how dieting affected her relationships, particularly with her fiancé. She was the primary cook in her household, and her fiancé disliked the diet foods Karina made for herself. She ended up cooking two meals: vegetables and chicken breast for herself, and a more complete (and delicious) meal for her fiancé. Karina began a *Giving* foodway, which for her involved simply eating the foods she cooked for her fiancé, noting that this seemed to strengthen the relationship, perhaps because Karina no longer resented the meals she made her fiancé and did not get to eat herself.

Mary's difficulties with body image began after the birth of her two children. She gained some weight after each child, and her husband began to criticize her body and withhold sexual intimacy from her. Eventually he cheated on her with her best friend, who was much thinner, and the marriage ended. Mary had not been in a relationship since then, and felt that unless she lost weight she could not have any relationship. Self-acceptance work had been difficult for her, and she was gradually coming to appreciate that her body might not change but that she was still deserving of love. In considering how she might want to express her values through food, she remembered her childhood. A Southerner who had moved as young woman to New England, she missed Southern soul foods. Large, convivial family meals full of Southern specialties were a special memory for her. Could a *Comfort Food* foodway be something she could explore? Just the idea of allowing herself comfort food from childhood seemed radical, indulgent, and even dangerous to her, and she feared gaining weight and "eating everything in sight." Still, she began cooking from a family cookbook she had been given as a wedding gift and had never used, inviting her now-grown children and their spouses. She read Southern food blogs, such as Biscuits and Such (http://biscuitsandsuch.com), and tried to put her own spin on the beloved comfort foods of her childhood. She had considered most of these foods off limits to her during and after her marriage, and she noted intense feelings of warmth, freedom, and grief as she began to eat her mother's cooking for herself.

### Identifying and Pursuing Clients' Food Values: Experiments to Try

Clinicians can guide themselves and clients to exploring foodways and values-driven eating the same way they have been exploring acceptance: via experience. Once you or your clients have articulated some non-health, non-body-image-related values you might like to explore through food, using mindful observation skills to experiment with eating using the new foodway can be interesting, fun, and transformative. As the case examples above illustrate, there is a wide range of possible foodways, associated values, and experiential exercises clinicians and clients can explore. Clients can eat in service to social change, stronger communities, equality, justice, a better environment, personal pleasure, joy, aesthetic beauty, to become closer to God, their spiritual traditions, or their cultural or ethnic identity, or to enhance their relationships, as just a sampling of possible inspirations for foodways.

Clinicians and clients should use their creativity to choose experiential activities that let clients explore new foodways, and should practice acceptance and mindfulness with body-image-related thoughts, fears, and other emotions that emerge as clients try out new ways of eating. In particular, clinicians should help clients lean in on fears of weight gain that emerge when practicing some foodways, particularly foodways that serve values of pleasure or relationship building.

Clients, as well as clinicians, may have fears that "emotional eating" or eating in service to nurturance or self-care are maladaptive, and foodways that actively encourage or permit self-care, self-nurturance, or pleasure as a value that can be served using food may therefore be challenging for the clinician or for clients. What is the difference between binging on food in service to emotional avoidance and mindfully practicing a *Comfort Food* foodway? If clients have worked through a painful situations list and learned to practice acceptance, they have probably already experienced some important alternatives to using food for emotional avoidance.

It is intriguing to notice that acceptance of painful body-and-food-related emotions sometimes involves eating foods (even eating them in uncomfortably large quantities), and other times involves not eating foods. For example, Sarah had listed bacon as a forbidden food on her painful situations list, and noted that she when she ate bacon, especially if she ate "more than my fair share," more than two or three pieces in a serving, she felt guilty, ashamed, and greedy. For Sarah, eating an entire plate of bacon was an acceptance exercise.

Alyssa, however, had listed "not be able to eat at night" as a painful situation for her. Alyssa was a critical care nurse, and worked long shifts without eating. Then she would come home and binge eat, eating a loaf of bread with butter, a box of cereal with milk, and several orders of takeout nightly as she watched television before bed. She felt ashamed about the binging, but she also felt anxious and fearful of what would emerge if she could not binge eat. For Alyssa, acceptance practice involved getting rid of all of the foods in the house for one evening, and limiting herself to one, average-sized dinner eaten in the work cafeteria before heading home. Notice that it is not the foods that are being worked with in these two examples, but the emotions. In both cases, Alyssa and Sarah are being encouraged to explore and experience uncomfortable, previously avoided feelings.

Similarly, when exploring foodways, it is the *values* that are being explored and experienced, not the foods. All cultures throughout human history have some tradition of using food for nurturance, healing, and love. Showing values of love and nurturance through food is not maladaptive, and is a human universal. Even babies eat for love: Sometimes a nursing infant is hungry when she cries for her mother's breast, but other times she is hungry only for closeness, warmth, and the physical comfort and tastes of nursing. In fact, the experiences of receiving love and being nourished in an infant are intimately intertwined and inseparable. This remains true throughout human development. If someone who loved you has ever made you chicken soup when you were sick, for example, you are probably already well aware of how food can strengthen loving ties.

Clients who wish to explore self-nurturance, self-compassion, self-soothing, and loving values through food should be encouraged and allowed to experiment with this and to notice whether it works to move the client closer to their values, as well as to observe conflicted emotions that may arise. Therapists should avoid pathologizing eating for self-nurturance values, and should take special care to avoid pathologizing this value in fat clients. All clients have the right to experience and express love, self-compassion, and self-nurturance through food, regardless of size. If clinicians are concerned that clients may be avoiding unpleasant emotions using food, rather than caring for themselves, they might wish to check in with the client about any avoidance, and to practice more acceptance before moving on to this phase of therapy. But clinicians should be extremely cautious about simply assuming that food cannot or should not be used in service to values of self-compassion and self-nurturance or love.

Exploring foodways and food-related values in service to social or environmental justice, however, can sometimes encourage clients back to unworkable, eating disordered programming. In particular, these foodways sometimes prompt clients to think of foods in terms of virtue or sin, "good" or "bad" foods, and sometimes are linked with weight loss values. Shenice, for example, stated that she was hoping to lose weight "as a bonus" as a result of her *Vegetarian* foodway in service to her animal-welfare values. When clinicians notice that clients appear to be using foodways as a justification to restrict or limit foods, this may indicate a need to return to acceptance practices related to eating "bad" foods or eating in an unrestricted way. Also, clients should be encouraged to *experiment* with all foodways, and to *experience* them, not to apply them rigidly or dogmatically. In Shenice's case, for example, the wish to lose weight "as a bonus" prompted a return to defusion of thoughts about weight loss, and some acceptance practice related to her fears of weight gain or never losing weight. When Shenice returned to wanting to explore an *Animal Welfare* foodway, her therapist assisted her in generating several experiments to explore her values. An excellent cook, she first hosted several (omnivorous, indulgent) dinner parties to raise money for her local humane society. Then she experimented with eating only meat raised humanely by her local farmers for a summer. Then she experimented with first a vegetarian diet and then a vegan diet for a week each time, with her therapist's support. After engaging in all of these exercises to serve her animal welfare values with food, Shenice noted that the dinner party fundraisers and the relationship she had developed with her local meat farmer had appeared to move her closest to her values of helping animals, whereas eating a vegan diet simply increased anxiety about her weight and feelings of restriction without actually serving her animal welfare values clearly.

Creativity and brainstorming should be employed to come up with several different experiences clients can explore to serve their values. Social media, especially Pinterest and Tumblr, as well as blogs, can be useful in helping clients collect images or examples of values-driven foodways. Experiments with new foodways should be multifaceted and time-limited, to emphasize the importance of flexibility and a non-dogmatic approach to eating, as well as to keep clients focused on what their own experience is teaching them about what helps them lead a valued life. Foodways that "cannot" be explored because of fear or shame, or those that appear to be serving an emotional avoidance goal, as well as a value, should prompt the clinician to assist the client with acceptance work related to whatever is being avoided before returning to foodway exploration. As in the example with Shenice, clinicians and clients should generate several experiments for each possible foodway, including several different ways to honor the client's value, which clients can try and compare. One-time experiments, experiments that involve others, week- or month-long challenges, experiments involving reading or research, cooking, changes in food shopping or restaurant use, all can be useful.

## Eating for Good Health

This chapter has, up to this point, deliberately avoided the value of health enhancement as a place where clients might wish to develop a new foodway. As we reviewed in Chapter 1, the evidence is limited that eating any particular diet promotes health or longevity for people in general, unless they already have or are at risk for a particular chronic disease. The evidence that certain dietary changes can promote health and disease management for people who already have or are at risk for particular chronic diseases (e.g., limiting salt for salt-sensitive hypertension, limiting saturated fats in heart disease, etc.) is more robust, but long-term experimental data are often limited, and individual variability in response to dietary interventions is generally high. Given the state of the evidence, I generally encourage healthy clients with body-image concerns to focus on non-health-related foodways, especially given the risks associated with following a restricted diet and the lack of clear benefit for physically healthy clients.

Clients who have or are at high risk for a chronic disease for which dietary changes have some evidence of benefit (e.g., hypertension, heart disease, diabetes) may wish to explore making health-related dietary changes in therapy. This should be done with caution and self-awareness by the clinician. Dietary changes to promote healing from chronic disease are unlikely to cause weight loss, and this should be made explicitly clear to clients. Because of individual variability, making health-related dietary changes *may or may not* have any benefit for individual clients, and it is essential that clinicians and clients explore the effects on clients' bodies of making any changes with an open mind. Just as with exploring foodways, the idea in exploring health-related dietary changes is to *experiment*, be flexible, and learn from what your experience teaches you, *not* to rigidly follow a diet in hopes of receiving absolution for your role in causing your disease. People have limited control over their physical health. Clients should not be shamed into continuing a dietary change that is not workable or helpful for them, even if they suffer from a chronic disease for which dietary changes have helped some individuals.

To explore health-related dietary changes, *only* with clients who actually have a specific chronic disease for which dietary changes may help, beginning by obtaining medical data about the state of their disease is helpful. Chapter 12 of this book, and Chapter 3 of the accompanying self-help manual, offer more guidance for making health-related changes.

For clients with chronic disease who also have eating-disordered behaviors, whether dietary restriction or binge eating or both, engaging in normal eating (see below) may be enough to improve laboratory values associated with chronic disease. Clinicians can also support clients in making modest dietary changes and observing whether these make a difference or not, as well as whether they are workable or not. A lack of dogmatism and judgment from the clinician, and an absolute faith that diet changes do not reflect moral worthiness or sin, is essential in exploring these changes. Clinicians must retain their scientific objectivity, and be able to observe and validate when a dietary change does *not* seem to matter (and can therefore be abandoned), as well as when it does help and therefore might be useful to continue.

Alyssa, the critical care nurse described above who did not eat during her 12-hour shifts and then binge ate a diet heavy in carbohydrates at the end of her workday, also had type II diabetes. She felt intense shame related to this diagnosis, and she had a weight-stigmatizing primary care doctor. Her clinician began by helping her to find a HAES-friendly, supportive primary care provider. Next, she encouraged her to obtain a blood glucose monitor for home use and to use it daily, as well as to take her prescribed diabetes medication, which she avoided taking because of feelings of shame. These two actions had clear, beneficial effects on her blood sugar that exceeded any benefits she attained later on through dietary change.

In exploring dietary changes, Alyssa felt intense fears related to restricting any aspect of her diet, as well as intense shame related to binge eating. As described above, acceptance work focused on experiencing these feelings, by journaling what she ate and sharing it with the clinician, and experimenting with skipping binges and seeing what emerged. Next, the clinician and Alyssa agreed to experiment with a health-related change to her diet. For Alyssa, this took the form of simply eating regularly. The therapist encouraged her to experiment with including "binge foods" in her meals throughout the day, rather than all at once, and to notice both how this felt, and if it showed up in her blood sugar measurements.

Alyssa began eating toast with cereal and milk for breakfast, a takeout lunch, an afternoon snack of two doughnuts and a latte, and a takeout dinner. She also had four slices of toast with butter before bed. She was astonished to discover that making this single change to the *timing* of her eating, not the content, had a significant impact on her blood sugar readings, particularly the morning reading, which improved dramatically once she stopped binging before bed. She could not notice any change in her physical sensations at first. However, a month or two after implementing this change, she began to notice that she felt "terrible" after her afternoon doughnut and coffee. She tried changing her order from a latte to full-fat milk, and she added a deviled egg to the snack, as she had heard a fellow diabetic saying the high-protein, high-fat snacks had helped her regulate blood sugar. This change had no effect on Alyssa's blood sugar but felt physically better to her than eating the doughnut alone.

Harriet had very high cholesterol and a family history of early heart disease. She did not like the idea of making any dietary change but was curious about replacing butter with stanol-fortified margarine. Would such a small change make a difference? For Harriet it did. She noticed no change in her bodily sensations or her enjoyment of the food, but did see a significant drop in her low-density lipoprotein (LDL) and total cholesterol after making this change for three months.

Heidi, however, cut out salt from her diet for three months to explore its impact on her hypertension. Nothing changed; she did not appear to be a salt-sensitive hypertensive. Her physician put her on an anti-hypertensive medication, and her daily reading improved. She went back to eating salt normally for her, and her readings remained low. She began to explore an *Eating for Pleasure* foodway instead, and found this was an enjoyable way to explore her values and practice acceptance.

As these case examples illustrate, making health-related changes is idiosyncratic, and clinicians should explore with clients making small changes, over brief periods of time, and assessing the change for workability and efficacy in managing clients' health. Clinicians should be prepared to support clients in dropping unworkable or ineffective health-related diet changes, and in working on other food-related values if they would prefer. There is more than one road to good health, and dietary changes are not the only, or always the most effective, change clients can make to support health.

### What if Food Is Not a Value? Normal Eating and Unconditional Permission to Eat

Some clients, like Stacey, the aerospace engineer we met at the beginning of the chapter, do not have any special values they wish to explore through food. Some clients, when asked how they would eat if their weight and health wouldn't change, express relief that they'd never have to think about food again. For clients who do not wish to express values through food, or for times when clients are not focused on expressing food-related values, there is normal eating.

What is normal eating? The nutritionist Ellyn Satter defines normal eating as follows:

> Normal eating is going to the table hungry and eating until you are satisfied. It is being able to choose food you like and eat it and truly get enough of it – not just stop eating because you think you should. Normal eating is being able to give some thought to your food selection so you get nutritious food, but not being so wary and restrictive that you miss out on enjoyable food. Normal eating is giving yourself permission to eat sometimes because you are happy, sad, or bored, or just because it feels good. Normal eating is mostly three meals a day, or four or five, or it can be choosing to munch along the way. It is leaving some cookies on the plate because you know you can have some again tomorrow, or it is eating more now because they taste so wonderful. Normal eating is overeating at times, feeling stuffed and uncomfortable. And it can be undereating at times and wishing you had more. Normal eating is trusting your body to make up for your mistakes in eating. Normal eating takes up some of your time and attention, but keeps its place as only one important area of your life. In short, normal eating is flexible. It varies in response to your hunger, your schedule, your proximity to food and your feelings.
>
> (Satter, 2008).

Notice that this definition isn't perfectionistic. There is plenty of room in this definition for many different foodways, ways of eating, and for plenty of variability in how a client eats across a day or a year or many years. Clients often find this definition surprising, because they have been programmed with the idea that "normal" eaters are eaters who are able to effortlessly and reliably restrict their diet to a perfect, consistent, "healthy" regimen. Chronic dieters conceive of normal eating as successful adherence to diets they have repeatedly failed at, and have often never imagined normal eating as something one does largely without effort or significant thought.

Another way to conceptualize normal eating is intuitive eating. Intuitive eating is associated with lower body mass index, normal, non-eating-disordered eating behaviors, and improved well-being (Van Dyke & Drinkwater, 2014). But what is "intuitive eating?" Intuitive eating, as measured by the Intuitive Eating Scale (IES-2; Tylka & Kroon Van Diest, 2013), includes several factors. One factor is "unconditional permission to eat." This means that the person has internalized unconditional permission to eat whatever she/he wants, in whatever quantity is wanted. It means honoring cravings, not having forbidden foods, and enjoying whatever food one wants to enjoy. A second factor is "eating for physical rather than emotional reasons." This means usually not using food as a tool for emotional avoidance, but eating mainly based on being hungry. A third factor is "relying on hunger and satiety cues." This means trusting your body to tell you when, how much, and what to eat. Finally, a fourth factor is "body-food choice congruence." This means usually eating and wanting to eat foods that are nutritious, make your body perform well, and give you energy and stamina. A high score on these four factors is associated with a healthy relationship with food. Clinicians can use the IES-2 for self- or client assessment, and it may suggest areas to target in developing normal eating.

Helping clients develop unconditional permission to eat often involves acceptance work related to forbidden foods, and becoming comfortable with regularly eating and having "binge" foods in the house. Simply introducing the idea of unconditional permission to eat as a positive trait can be helpful in promoting normal eating. Using hunger-fullness scales and journals can also be helpful in promoting reliance on hunger and satiety cues. Nutritionist Karin Kratina has some sample hunger-fullness scales and journals available for download on her website (www.eatingwisdom.com/eating-wisdom-products). Finally, mindful eating exercises and foodway experiments can also be helpful in helping clients notice and observe how different foods make their bodies feel and work.

Eating disorders can make developing normal eating quite difficult, and eating-disorder treatment, particularly developing a consistent pattern of eating throughout the day, with unrestricted regular meals and snacks and without binging or purging, can promote intuitive eating. Regular and consistent meals and snacks help clients observe hunger and fullness cues by ensuring that these cues are more likely to arrive on a consistent, observable schedule. Although rigidly following any meal plan is not consistent with normal eating, a brief, unrestricted, nutritionist-supervised prescribed eating plan that is not aimed at weight loss can help clients better learn normal eating skills, particularly if they have a history of eating disorders.

# References

Kornfield, J. (1994). *Buddha's little instruction book.* New York: Bantam.

Satter, E. (2008). *Secrets of feeding a healthy family: How to eat, how to raise good eaters, how to cook.* Madison, WI: Kelcy Press.

Tylka, T. L., & Kroon Van Diest, A. M. (2013). The Intuitive Eating Scale-2: Item refinement and psychometric evaluation with college women and men. *Journal of Counseling Psychology, 60*(1), 137.

Van Dyke, N., & Drinkwater, E. J. (2014). Relationships between intuitive eating and health indicators: Literature review. *Public Health Nutrition, 17*(8), 1757–1766.

# 9    Identifying, Displaying, and Committing to Values with Self-Presentation

## What Are You Allowed to Wear? Weaving Acceptance with Valued Dressing

Much of how we dress and present ourselves physically is determined by our programming – cultural messages about what to wear and how to look. All cultures prescribe norms about what men and women wear at work, during leisure activities and exercise, and for special occasions. Cultural beliefs, advertisements, media, family, and friends shape how often and how we bathe, how we smell, whether and how we wear makeup, the shoes and jewelry and outerwear and scarves and accessories we pick, the color, length, and style of our hair, and so on. Many of these extremely personal decisions occur with little conscious choice, purely as a result of cultural programming we have absorbed. Did you shave your legs or face this morning? Apply deodorant? Brush your teeth? Apply makeup? If you put on lipstick, I can take a guess (and often be correct) that you are a woman and that your lipstick was some shade of red, pink, or light brown, even though many colors of lipstick are sold, and all will apply as readily to men's lips as women's. Are you wearing underwear? Did you match your outfit to cultural expectations about how to dress for your activities today? To cultural expectations for your gender and for what it means to be "attractive" in your culture? Did you do all of these things essentially without thinking? Why did you make these specific clothing and grooming choices today? It is difficult to think of a self-presentation choice that cultural programming does not inform.

Yet self-presentation choices are highly personal, and *can* also reflect your own values and creative expression: Perhaps you deliberately chose makeup or grooming products not tested on animals because of your values related to animal rights. Perhaps you are a male therapist who carries a pink cellphone case to challenge traditional messages about gender. Perhaps you are wearing a t-shirt with a slogan for a cause you admire, or you are wearing a suit that a beloved partner gave you and that makes you think of that loving gesture, or a dress with bright colors that are your favorites because they are vibrant and cheerful. Perhaps you are wearing blue lipstick, instead of pink, to match your blue-tipped hair, which you wear because it is fun and gives you joy to have blue lips and hair. For clients who struggle with weight and body image, and for most women in the U.S. and other cultures that have adopted the thin-ideal, programming related to body image, attractiveness, and body weight and size inform and limit the choices they can make about how they present themselves and their physical appearance.

This programming is not emotionally neutral: A client who holds the programming "My stomach is disgusting," who is asked to put on a two-piece swimsuit for a mindful body observation exercise in session, may experience intense anxiety, panic, shame, grief, or other emotions, along with intense physical sensations and expression of those emotions (tears, hyperventilating, heart palpitations). This programming also leads straightforwardly to behavior: The client who has the programming "my stomach is disgusting," will often wear clothes she has been told "hide" her stomach, or may cover her stomach with a pillow when sitting in a chair in session, or may avoid moving in ways she believes highlight her stomach to others. The cultural rules clients hold about how to "hide" a part of the anatomy that is not actually invisible are also examples of programming, and, as such, you may be able to readily identify them, for example: No two-piece swimsuits. Wear black. No horizontal stripes. No clingy clothing. No crop tops.

Thus, helping clients identify and express their personal values with respect to self-presentation necessarily includes acceptance of painful emotions and defusion of programming related to how they "should" present themselves and their bodies.

This process begins with identifying self-presentation activities and choices that the client is not "allowed" to make. Are there certain types of clothes she is not "allowed" to wear? Hair styling choices? Makeup choices? Is she allowed to *not* dress up or wear makeup? Are there situations where certain choices are allowed or not allowed? Self-imposed limitations on self-presentation can become so habitual that clients do not even realize that these limitations are constricting them. Sometimes it is helpful to give examples of things some women feel they are not allowed to do or wear (e.g., tank tops, bare arms in general, swimsuits, bikini swimsuits, horizontal stripes, bright colors, short hair, gray hair, brightly colored hair, shorts, workout gear, low-cut blouses or dresses, "revealing" clothing, high heels, no makeup, bold makeup, skipping deodorant, skipping showers, not shaving your legs) to help clients identify their own self-imposed limitations. Once you have a list of self-presentation choices that clients consider off limits, they can be organized into a hierarchy like the painful situations list, with the easiest programming to defy at the bottom of the hierarchy and the most difficult choices at the top.

Piper, a thin 70-year-old artist and preacher's wife with a lifelong history of anorexia nervosa now mostly in remission except for remaining body image shame and concerns, generated the following list of things she wasn't allowed to wear or choose for self-presentation:

1. The color purple
2. Bare arms
3. Highlighter, "young women's" makeup
4. Colorful hair dye
5. Revealing or sexy clothes
6. Bikini swimsuit

Here is the list generated by Machiko, a fat 35-year-old literature professor who originally presented for help with weight loss and "emotional eating" before opting to participate in the *Accept Yourself!* program:

1. Workout wear unless I'm at the gym
2. Short hair – a pixie hair cut
3. Skinny jeans
4. Swimsuit
5. Miniskirts
6. Crop tops

It is sometimes worth exploring the programming clients have related to these lists of disallowed self-presentation choices, to better practice mindfulness and defusion of the thoughts and "rules" associated with the clothing choices, which may have become entirely habitual. Piper noted that her mother had told her that she "couldn't wear the color purple" when she was young, and that she had avoided it, even though as an artist she wore and loved lots of other bright colors, and, in fact, did a great deal of abstract art featuring the color purple. Similarly, she was attracted to modern and trendy (and artistic) makeup and hair, including rainbow-colored highlighter and neon-colored hair dye, but was able to notice in therapy that her idea that this was for "young women" and off-limits to her as an older woman arose when she noticed no marketing images of or media articles about these items featuring women her age. Sexy or revealing clothing was "off limits" because her husband had once criticized a dress she wore to a church function and asked her to be more "modest." She noted that she felt intensely ashamed by this episode, and had thrown out a large proportion of her wardrobe to try and be more "modest." Since that time, she had worn mainly t-shirts, turtlenecks, and jeans or slacks, both at church and at home, wearing no makeup and only rarely bright colors.

Machiko had criticized other women and had intensely judgmental thoughts about fat women who "think they can wear crap like that out." She noted that "no woman my size" should wear the items she considered off limits, and she noted that "all of my friends" agree. In exploring these ideas and engaging in some acceptance practice with the items of clothes she disparaged, she was able to observe how it had been for her being the "fat friend" in her peer group of women who engaged in extensive diet talk, body shaming, and critiquing of their own, others', and celebrities' bodies as a way to bond and connect. Machiko was used to being the "funny one" who was willing to respond to her friends' discrimination and negative judgment by laughing it off or co-opting the jokes at her own expense first. Short hair also appeared on Machiko's list. She noted that she had always wanted a stylish short pixie cut, but that hairstylists generally told her it would "make your face look even fatter," which embarrassed her and kept her from insisting on the cut.

For both Piper and Machiko, acceptance exercises involved wearing or experimenting with the items on their list in order (easiest items first) and in diverse environments. Piper, for example, bought a box of brightly colored hair chalks to experiment with dying her hair bright colors (including purple) using a medium that she could immediately wash out. Machiko experimented with wearing the clothes she had disparaged in limited ways first (e.g., she wore yoga pants and a tank top to the grocery store on a Tuesday morning, when she knew few people would be there to see and judge her, and she bought a pair of skinny jeans online and wore them around her house before experimenting with wearing them out in public). Therapists should explore ways to vary clothing and self-presentation choices to make them easier or more difficult, and should encourage clients to experiment with gradually more challenging acceptance practices.

Clients sometimes note that they do not want to wear clothes they are not allowed to wear. Machiko, for example, noted that she did not *want* to wear miniskirts, and she initially objected to practicing acceptance around them, especially since this meant buying an article of clothing she didn't even want. "Everyone looks stupid in them, not just fat chicks like me." In general, identifying clients' values around any issue that is also associated with emotional pain is facilitated by practicing acceptance and experiencing defusion first. Defusing the thought "everyone looks stupid in a miniskirt," either through mindful observation of this thought, or, ideally, through acceptance practice related to it, creates space in which clients can observe such thoughts as thoughts and identify valued actions apart from "programming" related to a given issue.

Thus, the therapist encouraged Machiko to buy or borrow and wear an inexpensive miniskirt in her size purely as an acceptance practice, that is, solely for the experience of fully experiencing her embarrassment, self-loathing, and fear related to engaging in this action. Both the therapist and Machiko agreed that the goal of this practice was not to wear a miniskirt or to like miniskirts or to change Machiko's fashion sense or values related to self-presentation. That is, following acceptance practice, Machiko might discover that she liked miniskirts after all, that she disliked them, or that she did not have a strong opinion of them, and that changing her mind about what to wear was not the goal of the practice.

Machiko purchased an inexpensive miniskirt in her size from Torrid, and agreed to wear it at home when it arrived, mindfully observing whatever emotions or thoughts arose. She noted intense feelings of shame and embarrassment when she put it on, and judgmental thoughts about her legs and behind, as well as feelings of anger and thoughts that the exercise was stupid and she was stupid for having "bought this ugly thing." She noted that these feelings gradually lessened in intensity as she continued to wear it around the house and go about her day, but she noted fear and unwillingness about going out wearing the miniskirt, which kept her from doing errands she needed to do (an example of avoidance in the midst of acceptance). She agreed to a second homework assignment to wear the miniskirt out on errands, and noted intense shame and an urge to change as soon as she got into her car. She noted that she began to feel better as she drove to the stores but worse again when she had to enter the stores. However, she noted feeling better as she continued to wear it, and noted with surprise that a stranger had given her an apparently sincere compliment on her skirt. Initially, she expressed to the therapist the thought, "I'm glad I did that, and I do feel a little bit differently about short skirts, I guess, but I still don't want to wear one."

However, the therapist noted a month or two later that she wore the miniskirt to her therapy appointment. When the therapist commented on this, Machiko laughed and said, "I sound pretty stupid, don't I? But it's cool in the summer, and I'm starting to think it might even look OK with ballet flats and a snarky t-shirt." Machiko's affect was brighter, and the therapist noted as she continued with her acceptance practice related to clothing that her wardrobe became more diverse and more colorful, with Machiko commenting that she felt "freer" with respect to what clothes she might choose to wear. Acceptance practice had created space for Machiko's tastes to broaden and change.

Acceptance practice related to self-presentation generally creates greater willingness to increase valued actions related to self-presentation, and (as in Machiko's case) greater clarity about what is valued and enjoyed. The remainder of this chapter focuses on increasing valued behaviors related to physical appearance and self-presentation, whereas the next chapter focuses on doing the same for physical activities.

## Fashion without Self-Hatred: What Does It Look Like?

We think of our clothing and grooming choices as personal, as very much our own. But cultural beauty standards and personal learning histories related to self-presentation interact to affect most people's programming and behavior around how we choose to dress, groom, and present ourselves. As with most other areas of life, fashion and self-presentation choices are stigmatized for fat women, and fat women are subject to discrimination in most areas related to self-presentation. They have fewer and less fashionable clothing choices. They have difficulty shopping for clothes, not only because clothes are available in few shops and of limited selection where available, but also because clothing in fat women's sizes is generally displayed on mannequins or with models who are not fat, making it difficult to imagine how the clothing will look on one's own, fat, body. (Patronizing stores that use fat models, and advocating for this with stores that do not, can be an important part of self-advocacy for clients and clinicians alike.) Model size discrimination is especially damaging because the majority of fashionable clothing options for plus-size women are available online, not in stores, and thus models are critical to imagining how a given piece of clothing will work for a person's body. Plus-size clothing is also frequently more expensive and of poorer quality, and return fees for clothes purchased online can make plus-size clothing even more expensive. Plus-size clothing may be segregated in a less-attractive area of a straight-size store, or available only online where straight sizes can be bought in stores. All of these problems intensify the larger the body you are trying to dress.

These examples of structural discrimination don't even include experiences of interpersonal discrimination related to self-presentation choices that fat women experience: Receiving judgment or criticism for clothing choices, having one's clothes used as an excuse for weight-based abuse (e.g., "she looks sloppy," said about a fat woman, but not a thin woman, wearing sweat pants), being specifically excluded based on size from clothiers' or designers' lines because the presence of your body in the store or in the clothes is perceived to devalue the brand, being treated dismissively by salespeople, and so on. And discrimination against fat women's self-presentation choices is not limited to clothing. Fat women will be criticized for wearing too much or no makeup, advised on "appropriate hairstyles," or told their self-presentation choices don't matter, since they will be ugly no matter what they do, by definition. (Note that this critique, besides being insulting and inaccurate, depends on "looking attractive" being one's self-presentational goal.) And all of these forms of discrimination may interact with other marginalized aspects of women's identities: For example, a fat disabled woman may experience discriminatory barriers to entering and using dressing rooms. A fat woman of color may experience racist and sizeist marketing designed to objectify and exoticize both her fatness and her skin color.

In this milieu of discrimination, fat and other weight-concerned female clients wearing clothing they have been told is "off limits" can be an important element of self-acceptance (even if a client is not interested in fashion), and can serve to stand up against discriminatory limits on what women may do in general. Clients' existing ways of coping with internalized and external weight-based abuse and discrimination with respect of self-presentation can be diverse.

Some fat and weight-concerned clients take meticulous care of their appearances and adhere as closely as possible to cultural beauty ideals, in terms of clothing, hair care, and makeup. This may be an extension of body image dysmorphia and eating-disordered behavior among clients who have an eating disorder, or it may serve as a strategy to avoid size-based and other forms of discrimination. Clients may groom themselves meticulously in an effort to be seen and treated as an "exceptional" fat person who does not bear all of the negative traits weight-based abusers ascribe to fatness. For these clients, self-presentation choices such as wearing sweatpants, t-shirts, not wearing makeup, or other "sloppy" self-presentation choices may be avoided or off limits, and should be explored using acceptance tools. Clients of all sizes have the right to wear all clothes and make any grooming choices they wish, not just those that conform to a particular beauty ideal.

For other clients, creative self-presentation and fashion is a valued life activity that they have not been allowed to partake in because of fears of wearing inappropriate clothing or lack of access to fashionable choices in appropriate sizes. For such clients, fashionable, revealing, clingy, colorful, or other types of boldly visible clothing may be "off limits" and may represent an area ripe for acceptance work.

Clothing purchases, whether new or thrifted, often come up as homework assignments during this phase of therapy, and clients often report that they cannot afford new clothes. Clinicians should explore this issue carefully. Some clients use the phrase "can't afford," when they mean that spending money on clothes will actually mean they must go without food, shelter, or medical care. For other clients, money for new clothes is available in some fashion but raises discomfort about spending it. This discomfort is often linked to body-image programming. Some clients may be reluctant to spend a significant amount of money on clothing in their current size, because they have been programmed to think of fatness as a transitional, temporary state, which will be ameliorated soon. If you will soon lose weight, there is no reason to buy expensive clothes for your current body size. Many women's learning histories, which include wide weight fluctuations, reinforce this idea. In addition, clients often have programming that suggests that attractive clothing should be a reward for virtuous behavior as evidenced by successful weight loss. Asking clients whether they would be willing to spend the sum of money being discussed in therapy for a clothing purchase if they had lost significant weight can help clarify this issue. If clients would "reward" themselves for attaining thinness, it is worth discussing whether they would be willing to practice kindness and self-care with their current bodies, rewarding their current bodies for faithful service, rather than weight loss.

As clients continue acceptance work related to off limits or disallowed clothing choices, and begin to shift into values-based self-presentations, where they may begin to make more affirmative, creative choices around their appearance, programming will continue to emerge. Author Lesley Kinzel was once asked by a (fat) reader how to wear the dresses and heels she longed to wear without feeling like "an elephant in drag." Kinzel's advice to the reader was to

> Embrace the elephant in drag … I know how you feel because I've felt it too, and I can tell you the only way around is through … Know that you are confronting the forces that police our bodies, and feel proud to be standing up to them.

(You can read the entire Q&A here: http://blog.twowholecakes.com/2010/01/ q-a-on-dressing-femme-being-a-bad-fat-and-changing-the-fa-blogosphere/.)

She also discussed how this relates to gender presentation, using the word "femme," rather than "feminine," to discuss how women can interrogate the cultural programming about femininity and fatness they are given, and instead choose to perform those aspects of femmeness that interest them in an idiosyncratic or political way.

## Experiments with Valued Self-Presentation: Activities and Resources

How might we help clients to do this? The accompanying self-help manual provides a variety of experiments for clients to try on different values-based self-presentations and begin to consciously "perform" their appearance in accordance with their values if they wish. The remainder of this chapter will focus on ways clinicians can support clients in developing values-based self-presentations and practicing acceptance around appearance-related programming.

Clinicians can and should serve as resources for clients in developing a more creative, values-driven self-presentation independent of size and weight-stigma-based programming. The clinician should consider his or her own rules and programming related to self-presentation and appearance, and may wish to practice acceptance activities leaning in on any rigid limitations, whether weight-related or not. Are there clothing, hair, or makeup styles you as a clinician are not "allowed" to wear, or that are so "unflattering" on you that you would not be willing to wear them? Wearing occasionally what you are not allowed to wear, whether clothing that is too "youthful," or "avant-garde," or "edgy," or "unflattering," or "revealing," or which in some other way violates cultural programming about your appearance can help enhance empathy for clients' struggles practicing acceptance, as well as help you develop your own values related to appearance.

Similarly, it is worth reflecting on your Implicit Association Test results from Chapter 2. Implicit anti-fat bias, being linked to appearance-related programming, may show up as you help clients engage in values-driven self-presentations. How might you address your own anti-fat biases? Little research has suggested effective ways of altering anti-fat bias, but altering the implicit programming and messages you as a clinician receive about weight and appearance may at least be a reasonable experiment, both to help address your implicit bias and to improve your ability to connect fat clients with role models for values-driven self-presentations. Altering your media consumption is one example. Following fat acceptance and fatshion Instagram accounts, Facebook pages, Tumblr blogs, and Twitter accounts (as well as whatever other social media you use, e.g., Pinterest) can provide a steady stream of imagery (for your own imagination and to share with clients) of fat women performing values-driven self-presentation and style. The self-help manual lists an assortment of hashtags, blogs, and influencers you can search for to begin this process. Removing from your own social media any weight loss content can also help with this process. You can also use the fat acceptance, body-positive images you find in this process as client resources, pointing you to office artwork, books for your waiting room or office, and imagery and sources for client explorations. Ask clients, too, for local recommendations of where they buy fashionable or values-driven clothes, and what personal-service providers are body affirmative as opposed to body shaming, so that you can begin to become a repository for such shared community information.

The self-help manual provides numerous activities and sources both you and your clients can draw upon as they practice acceptance and values-driven self-presentation, but there are several other considerations that may be useful as you work through those exercises and resources together. Wearing swimwear, especially bikinis, represents a feared and avoided self-presentation for many women, and yet the activities one engages in when wearing a swimsuit (swimming, sauna, hot-tubbing, sun-bathing, being at the gym, being on vacation, attending social events, hanging out with friends) represent important values-based activities for many women as well. The self-help manual has a brief bathing suit exercise in Chapter 8 to help women practice acceptance around wearing a bathing suit, but dancer Marina Wolf Ahmad's essay, "28 Days to a Bikini Mind" (available here: https://kateharding.net/2008/05/20/guest-post-28-days-to-a-bikini-mind) provides a more extensive program of acceptance exercises to help clients wear a bikini or other swimwear with courage.

When practicing acceptance and values-driven self-presentations, there is safety in numbers. *Accept Yourself!* has been researched in a group format, to take advantage of the built-in social support that a group provides for these difficult activities, and clinicians may wish to consider offering a group format to help clients engage in activities together. A beach-blanket bikini party with a group of *Accept Yourself!* participants may provide advantages in terms of avoiding or standing up to discrimination, social support, and values enhancement that an individual activity cannot provide. If you do not offer clients a group format, helping them to brainstorm and develop like-minded friends can help. Using online communities, such as the Fat Fashion discussions at the political blog Shakesville (www.shakesville.com/search/label/Fat%20 Fashion) can be one way to connect with like-minded others, and acceptance activities that focus on telling others about the self-acceptance work a client is doing may also help identify allies (as well as, unfortunately, expose the client to discrimination, which provides another opportunity for expression of values and self-acceptance).

The largest clients experience the most size-based discrimination in self-presentation. Finding any clothes at all can be difficult for the largest clients, much less creative, fashionable, or attractive clothing. Clinicians must maintain faith that such clients deserve attractive things and that the clinician will help the client find attractive things. Companies that will make affordable, custom-sized items, regardless of client size, are an important resource for clinicians to collect (e.g., eShakti, www.eshakti.com, and Love Your Peaches, www.loveyourpeaches.com/shop/default.aspx, are two examples of affordable custom clothiers who will make their designs in any size). Bold, size-neutral fashion choices can also offer an entry point for clients who have difficulty accessing plus-size fashions because of sizing out of plus-size lines, cost, or other reasons. Plus-size beauty bloggers, such as Ushshi Rashman (http://dresscarcass.com) or Gabi Fresh (http://gabifresh.com) can offer examples of how to use a size-neutral tool such as makeup to explore a different, bolder, more creative, or more values-consistent self-presentation than clients may have previously explored. Shoes, accessories, and hairstyle may offer similar opportunities.

Clients often experience intense painful emotions and avoidance related to photography. They may not allow themselves to be photographed, may avoid looking at photographs of themselves, and may carry intensely negative, judgmental chatter related to photography and selfies. Photographs may be offered as evidence of "the truth" substantiating a negative body image. Photography thus offers a powerful point of entry for acceptance work and potentially for values-driven creative expression of self and self-presentation.

Molley is a 34-year old nurse who discussed her struggles with photography in therapy. She had wanted to date but had no pictures of herself that did not make her feel ashamed or that she was willing to post on an online dating profile. She struggled with the idea that the person portrayed in the photographs she disliked was the "real her," whereas her own self-image, which was more self-compassionate and gentle, was distorted and inaccurate. Close to the conclusion of her treatment, she and her therapist discussed her desire to have attractive professional "boudoir-style" photography done. She hoped and wished for some sexy, attractive images that she could have for herself, and which she might not share with anyone else, as well as a fun, creative, affirming photoshoot session to get them. However, she thought this was an impossibility, and expected intense size discrimination even in the phase of interviewing potential photographers.

With the therapist's help, she identified a photographer in the region whose online portfolio included attractive images of fat women (www.zinfandelphotography.com). Contacting and interviewing the photographer, planning for the shoot, committing to the significant expense, purchasing clothing for the shoot, creating a Pinterest board with images similar to the ones she hoped she would be creating, and committing to a date all were therapy homework assignments that created significant emotional exploration and acceptance for Molley. In her session following the photoshoot, she reported that it had been an intensely positive experience. The hair and makeup artists who prepared her for the shoot in collaboration with the photographer had made her look "beautiful," and she had been astonished at how the photographer led her through a series of sexy poses without making her feel awkward or objectified or undesirable. However, she had not yet seen the photographs.

The photographer charged a nominal fee for the photoshoot to cover his costs, but much higher, premium prices for individual photos. She expressed fear that there would not be a single photo she would want to buy, and that she would disappoint both the photographer and herself. After seeing the photos, she reported to the therapist that she had become intensely emotional and tearful. She noted that they were "beautiful – more beautiful than I thought I could be," and she noted experiences of defusion related to thoughts about the "truth" of the camera. She was able to observe that artistic craftsmanship had created the images she enjoyed so much, and that likely artistic careless-ness was involved in unattractive images, suggesting that there was no one "truth" of how she looked in front of a camera or in the eyes of others.

Apart from supporting clients to experience a photoshoot with a body-affirming photographer, other ways to explore photography and self-presentation include taking daily selfies (perhaps documenting these or learning more about the art of self-portrait photography), and also discussing and dem-onstrating in treatment the various tools photographers can use to alter the appearance of the subjects in photographs. The use of photoshop and photo retouching is well known, but even simple camera tricks, such as changing the focal length of the shot, have an impact on how bodies appear in pictures. The same subject photographed at different focal lengths can appear dramatically different in size and weight (e.g., see this online photoset, which illustrates the effect with a first skinny, then fat cat: https://petapixel.com/2013/01/11/how-focal-length-affects-your-subjects-apparent-weight-as-seen-with-a-cat).

Exploring the various ways people alter their appearance *other than weight change* can aid in body image defusion and open up self-presentation options for clients. For example, the anonymous blogger at the Tumblr blog *Whatever, Etc.* describes a friend's anecdote about how celebrities manage to look chic. The blogger's friend, a fat woman, won a style consultation with Clinton Kelly, of the makeover show *What Not To Wear*. The friend's first question was about how celebrities always look terrific, even in jeans and a t-shirt. His answer: Everything a celebrity wears, right down to their t-shirts and camisoles, is tailored to fit. Celebrity stylists don't buy their clients' clothes based on size. They ignore the number on the tag, and find clothes that fit the celebrity's body at its widest point. Then the rest of the garment is tailored to fit, which is how jeans or t-shirts magically fit celebrities smoothly all over. (You can read the entire story, as well as the blogger's reaction, here: http://inkdot.tumblr.com/post/7243925631/no-shit.) The realization that size numbers are not a reflection of your virtue or worth, that larger sizes tailored to fit will look more polished than smaller ones, and that a celebrity's self-presentation is not the magical product of perfect fitness and dietary behaviors can all help with clients' defusion of self-presentation-related judgment. Some clients are moved to experiment with tailoring as a form of self-care and self-compassion.

Helping clients develop values-driven self-presentation is not, how-ever, about making them look as attractive as possible. Instead, the goal is to develop defusion from cultural programming around attractiveness (including body shape and weight), mindful, self-compassionate acceptance related to one's own feelings of unattractiveness and body discomfort, and then to consider what values or creative counterprogramming the client would like to express through her appearance, if any. Supporting political and social causes, expressing personal artistic creativity, pushing back against negative body image programming, identifying more strongly with your culture, or simply bravely living visibly in a fat body are all possibilities the clinician can help clients explore (with the accompanying self-help manual as a guide).

# 10 Embodying Values

## Physical Activity and Weight Concerns: Common Barriers to Acceptance

At this point in treatment (after substantial acceptance and defusion of negative body image experiences, and after beginning to explore valued living in various domains, such as food or self-presentation), clinicians may want to revisit with clients the magic wand fantasy that they developed at the beginning of treatment (see Chapter 4) to identify any physical activities that seem impossible for clients to do at their current size. Hiking, kayaking, surfing, swimming, skiing, rock climbing, sexual activities, travel, horseback riding, or other activities that require the body's function and help are all activities clients may include. Clients should be encouraged to brainstorm what they would do with their bodies if their bodies had no limitations in terms of either appearance or function: The sky is the limit.

This list of "impossible" activities is a useful resource for both acceptance work and clarification of valued life activities. Helping clients move towards the "impossible" activities on the list is the main goal of this phase of treatment. Both internal and external barriers arise, in both clients and clinicians, as clients begin to move toward these "impossible" activities. Before considering client barriers and how to cope with them, we must first address clinician barriers. When I conduct continuing education seminars training clinicians in the *Accept Yourself!* approach, and when I discuss the magic wand fantasy and the goal of treatment being to help clients obtain all the elements of this fantasy, invariably I am stopped by at least one clinician during or after the training to discuss a case for whom attaining one or another aspect of her fantasy is "impossible." The clinician asks me how to work with the client's unrealistic dream within the *Accept Yourself!* framework. Consider some examples: Bonnie was an elderly, nursing-home-bound, disabled client who dreamed of having a romantic and sexual relationship. Maeko had once wanted to do a triathlon, but now was so extremely deconditioned that she could scarcely leave her home for appointments, and used a wheelchair to attend sessions with her clinician. Natalie was a 64-year-old breast cancer patient currently receiving chemotherapy who dreamed of being a trapeze artist. Terri was a middle-aged former mountain climber with a degenerative neuromuscular disease who dreamed of returning to climbing mountains. Each woman felt foolish and in some cases ashamed for having such "unrealistic" dreams and, in some cases, these women's clinicians also had difficulty imagining how to help her attain or move toward these wishes, or wondered whether encouraging such wishes would "do more harm than good." These examples also illustrate how disabilism or ageism intersect with weight stigma and healthism to negatively affect both clients' and clinicians' faith that the client could do the "impossible."

To be effective in this phase of treatment, clinicians need to unequivocally maintain the stance that clients can and are welcome to do the full range of human activities, including those activities that are often restricted or denied to people with various disabilities, ages, sizes, or levels of fitness. Clinicians need to consider the ways that oppression against fat, disabled, and old people (as well as other groups of people) affect their own programming about what is "realistic" for themselves and others, and affect access to opportunities and adaptations for enjoyable, valued, physical activities. Clinicians need to maintain this stance of possibility and welcome toward clients' magic wand fantasies with this awareness in mind, and to be imaginative and resourceful in helping clients advocate for needed resources and adaptations to do a given activity.

Bonnie discussed her romantic relationship history with the clinician, and found helpful the clinician's aphorism, "There's no expiration date on love." The clinician also shared research with Bonnie that even the oldest women commonly engage in sex if they have an available partner (Lindau et al., 2007), which challenged Bonnie's stereotypes about aging and sexuality. Bonnie committed to engaging in social activities sponsored by her nursing home (which she had previously avoided out of depression and embarrassment, as well as ageist stereotypes about the quality and vitality of other people she might meet there), and began attending a weekly yoga class and a choir. She made new female friends at these activities, and agreed as a homework assignment to tell her new friends she was interested in dating, although she felt intense fear of being judged "foolish" and "silly," if she shared this wish. One of her friends introduced her to her recently widowed brother, and Bonnie dated him briefly. Although the relationship did not continue, Bonnie noted that she felt more confident and engaged because she had been able to pursue her goal of dating, and she felt connected to a broader community of friends.

Maeko's clinician, in supervision, was absolutely convinced that it was "madness" to encourage her toward a triathlon. Maeko weighed nearly 500 lbs, was 5'4" inches tall, and had great difficulty with walking. She could walk short distances with a cane, but otherwise used a wheelchair or scooter. She had chronic knee and back pain, and spent most of her time at home in bed or on her couch watching television. She also had binge eating disorder. She had described her dream of becoming a triathlete with a sad, rueful smile, noting that this wish must seem ridiculous, to look at her "disgusting" body now. Furthermore, Maeko had shown little motivation to sustain an exercise program of any kind: Her doctors recommended resistance training at home with exercise bands, and brief walks, but Maeko felt stupid and ashamed when she tried these, and hated going outdoors where others could see her. She was also fearful of falling during exercise, since she could not rise without help, and many people couldn't help her, because of her size. In supervision, her clinician was able to clarify his values related to helping clients achieve their dreams, and he agreed to commit to exploring the behaviors that might make up a triathlon with Maeko.

She began with swimming, which seemed easiest for her to try, and her clinician was able to locate a Health At Every Size (HAES)-friendly physical therapist (PT) who could help her practice swimming skills at their hospital pool. Maeko did not have a swimsuit, and felt certain she couldn't find one at all at her size. She ultimately had a custom suit made by Love Your Peaches (www.loveyourpeaches.com/shop/default.aspx), and she noted that shopping for and receiving the suit made her feel "a little bit" encouraged that swimming, at least, might be possible for her. Getting into and out of the pool was her biggest challenge. Her clinician encouraged her to practice going slowly down the stairs, making others wait behind her, and asking for help, all of which brought up anxiety and shame, as acceptance exercises. Once in the water, she found she could move with ease and comfort, and she readily recovered her good swimming form from childhood involvement in swimming as a sport, although her fitness was limited and she could swim only for short distances. She began to swim regularly, and for some time reported that this was "enough" for her.

Her clinician suspected that running and biking brought up additional avoidance of anxiety and shame, and eventually he encouraged her to experiment with both of these sports as acceptance exercises, if not valued activities. Her fitness level had improved with the swimming, and she could walk more easily, although she still experienced knee and back pain. Her PT suggested working up to walking an hour a day as preparation for running, which Maeko found discouraging and embarrassing, but the hospital had a gym for cardiac rehabilitation, which she obtained permission to use after regular hours. The gym had one treadmill that would accommodate her size, so she began walking before her early-morning swimming appointments and her therapy appointments, about four times a week. Eventually she was able to walk without her cane on the treadmill, especially with strength and stretching exercises prescribed by the PT. Maeko gradually experimented with walking outdoors in workout wear as acceptance practice, and became more comfortable with this. With her PT's approval, Maeko began adding brief runs (about 30 seconds) interspersed with her walks. Her clinician suggested she follow Ragen Chastain's Iron Fat blog, which follows Chastain's progress toward completing a Iron Man triathlon (https://ironfatblog.wordpress.com/blog), and that she join the Fit Fatties facebook and online support group (www.facebook.com/groups/fitfatties). Although Maeko noted that most of the people in both groups were "much smaller and healthier than me," she still felt a sense of solidarity and encouragement from this. Ultimately, she signed up for a 5 K run, which she was able to walk and run to complete, which astonished her. She told her therapist that receiving her 5 K t-shirt was "all I needed" to satisfy her triathlon dream, along with becoming a proficient swimmer, but her clinician encouraged her to experiment with bicycling, again as an acceptance practice.

She rented a vintage bike from a local bike shop. She expressed concern that the bike was not rated for her size, and that she might damage it, but she noted that the bike shop owner who helped her pick it out was surprisingly helpful, discussing features that made the bike suitable for her and giving her the impression that she helped riders her size pick out bikes frequently. (You can find a similar, detailed discussion of features that make a bike suitable for fat riders here: http://chicargobike.blogspot.com/2013/05/youre-not-too-heavy-to-ride-bike.html.) The bike shop also noted that they were insured against rental damage, and that she needn't worry about hurting the bike they had chosen with her. She experienced some shame and embarrassment as she began to ride, as well as knee discomfort, but noted that as with her other acceptance exercises, this passed and she became more quickly comfortable. However, she discovered that she did not especially enjoy cycling compared with running, walking, and swimming, and she did not end up pursuing a triathlon or serious bike training as she had initially hoped. However, she noted that she no longer felt her weight would stop her from athletic pursuits, and she began training for a 10 K, with the goal of eventually completing a marathon.

For Natalie, the therapist's difficulty imagining someone of her health and age and weight engaging in trapeze may have been the biggest barrier. The clinician simply avoided discussing this "unrealistic" dream with Natalie for some time. Once the therapist was willing to discuss it, she was surprised to learn that Natalie had, in fact, already taken several trapeze classes and was able, even with her chemotherapy, age, and weight, to perform well in these. Natalie noted that she had initially been very uncomfortable, but as she began to realize that she could do trapeze, albeit at a somewhat slower pace than others in the class, she had grown to love the sport. However, she had avoided performing, out of anxiety about performing without a coach onstage, fears about how she looked on the trapeze as a fat woman, and general performance anxiety.

She discussed how as a teenager she had loved to sing and had always been in the choir, but had always been "sick" on performance days. She reported that as a very little girl she had done ballet, and she reported that she used to enjoy her ballet recitals until one day, when she was eight years old, getting ready for her recital in her tutu and leotard, and her alcoholic father had said she looked like "a fat slut" in the outfit. She had not understood the word "slut," but her mother had kept her home from the performance, and she felt deeply ashamed of and confused about how she must have looked in her dance costume. She did not continue with ballet and avoided any type of performance after this.

The therapist had to re-evaluate her stigmatizing assumptions about the barriers to trapeze performance for Natalie, and reconceptualize how to help. The therapist looked with Natalie at fat women aerialist performances by searching the Instagram hashtag #plussizeaerialist, and Natalie began her acceptance practice by purchasing a dance costume she found especially attractive on one of the aerialists she saw in the Instagram videos. Wearing this costume, first at home with mindful observation in front of the mirror, and then to trapeze class, was the next acceptance practice Natalie worked on with her therapist. Next she confided in her trapeze instructor both her wishes to perform publicly and her fears related to this, and her instructor agreed to help her practice a routine that she could complete independently without coaching or spotting at her skill level. The instructor also created a slot for her routine in her school's upcoming circus showcase. Intensifying cancer treatment slowed Natalie's progress, and she had to reschedule this showcase, but ultimately was able to perform in the same week she learned her cancer was in remission. She noted an intense sense of pride and an "adrenaline rush" from successfully performing, taking her fears along, and she noted that she wanted to continue and to increase performing. For her therapist, too, Natalie's case was an experience of examining her own implicit biases related to age, illness, and weight.

Terri had been a mountain climber and avid skiier a decade ago, but a progressive degenerative disease that attacked both muscles and joints left her unable to exercise at an athlete's pace. She felt tremendous anger at the medical profession for being unable to better preserve her athletic ability, which she felt had "caused the onset of obesity." She also felt intensely angry with herself for being unable to push through the intense pain and increasing disability caused by her disease, and being unable to lose weight. When she began treatment, she had numerous medical appointments and was actively engaged in several sessions of weekly swimming (even though she had always disliked swimming) and personal training in an effort to "at least preserve my function, keep my job, and keep walking." However, all of this effort had not seemed to slow the progression of her disease. Terri was depressed, anxious, and working a 60-hour workweek, because, as she said, "work is the only thing left I can do." She was intensely bitter at the therapist's suggestion that she might return to skiing and climbing, noting correctly that the therapist did not have a disability: "You don't know what you're talking about."

For Terri, internalized disablism, fears of being unproductive, "weak," and useless were all important foci for acceptance practice. Negotiating for a more manageable work schedule that left her with some energy for leisure or rest, setting boundaries on her work time, and asking others for help with household chores and medical appointments were some of the initial acceptance exercises she and her therapist identified that she thought would intensify her feelings of "weakness" and worthlessness, and thus provide a useful point of entry for acceptance practice.

Even if Terri had been able to easily ski or climb, at the outset of treatment she neither had time nor energy to do it. When Terri had mindfully experienced her feelings of worthlessness and weakness, while also expanding her time and support network adequately that she had some weekend time and energy available for physical activities she valued, the therapist inquired whether she might like to explore skiing. Terri remained adamant that this was impossible for her, that she had no ski gear anymore that fit her. It was difficult for her to commit to buying ski clothing that would fit: "It's expensive, and I'll never use it again," but eventually she was willing to buy a pair of ski pants.

Interestingly, then, without discussing it with the therapist, she went on her own to try skiing again. She noted that in some ways she enjoyed being back on skis and was able to ski, although not with the same skill as when she was younger. However, she noted intense pain during the ski and afterwards, and noted that she had missed two days of work trying to recover. "See?" she said to the therapist, "I told you I can't do this, and you didn't listen to me. You don't get it: I'm disabled. I'm not an athlete anymore." The therapist was experienced working with disabled athletes, and encouraged Terri to explore her disablist programming related to the opposition between "disability" and "athlete." Terri noted that she had "powered through" the pain on the ski hill, gone alone, and that she was fearful of injuring herself if she continued. The therapist suggested working with an adaptive ski program in her state, and provided information about local programs, including a coupon for a free adaptive ski coaching session. Terri initially insisted that she "didn't fit in" to this program, as she could walk, was not a wheelchair user, and only sometimes used a cane. She expressed fears of diverting resources from "really disabled" people if she used the program. The therapist was able to work with Terri to identify avoidance of anxiety and embarrassment that these thoughts were in service to, and to explore applying for the program, discussing her fears with program staff, and ultimately making an appointment to ski. With adaptive equipment and coaching, Terri was surprised at how much she enjoyed her day of skiing. She noted that it was more social because she skied with a coach, and also that the adaptive equipment and techniques he taught her allowed her to be nearly pain free at the end of the day. She continued to ski occasionally throughout the winter with the program, although she had ongoing difficulty allowing herself the "expense" of the sport in her "diminished" condition.

In all of these examples, the therapist's faith and resources (or absence of these) strongly affected the client's ability to practice acceptance and move toward valued activities. Both internalized and institutionalized weight bias, disablism, ageism, and other biases strongly affected the work as well, but in each case, the therapist could serve either as a model and resource or a barrier in helping the client navigate these forms of oppression. Therapists may not always have or know of resources immediately that clients will need to navigate institutionalized oppression. However, the clinician's faith that such resources must exist (or at least *should* exist, and will be advocated for by the clinician and the client if they do not exist as part of treatment) is essential to helping clients move forward on their magic wand fantasies. The clinician must be willing to exercise imagination in service to helping the client achieve bodily dreams that are implicitly restricted by institutionalized oppression and cultural programming to certain privileged groups. The clinician should practice flexibility in encountering the client's barriers to their dreams, holding on to the awareness that it is as a result of moving toward valued actions that barriers emerge. In addition, moving toward valued action often brings up thoughts that require defusion and emotions that require mindful acceptance practice.

In Terri's case, for example, the clinician could have simply encouraged Terri to go skiing. In fact, this was Terri's idea, in part in service to "proving" to the clinician that she was too disabled to ski. Instead, the clinician was required to be sensitive and flexible enough to identify and defuse thoughts related to Terri's internalized disablism: That she was worthless or weak because of her disability; that only excessive work redeemed her status as a disabled, single woman; that she was not "really" disabled and entitled to adaptive services for the disabled; that using such services made her "weak" or not really an athlete; that disability caused fatness and worthlessness; that disability and athleticism were mutually exclusive or only compatible if the disabled athlete was "strong," "inspirational," and worked through, rather than with, pain. Thus, working toward skiing and mountain climbing did *not* involve Terri practicing acceptance of physical pain. (Terri was already experienced at ignoring her pain and "pushing through," sometimes causing worsened physical health, in service to avoiding feelings of weakness.) Instead, the first steps involved experiencing and accepting feelings of weakness, embarrassment, humiliation, and shame related to publicly having and acknowledging her disability and receiving adaptive support for her athletic activities.

In Natalie and Maeko's cases, however, the clinician was required to willingly embrace the possibility that their bodies could do the physical activities they wished to do, with help and support as needed. Identifying the client's internal barriers and acceptance needs accurately (and distinguishing these from the therapist's assumptions) is important: For Terri, pushing through her fears and pain, while ignoring her body's physical needs, was an avoidance strategy. For Natalie, taking her fears along onstage, while the therapist practiced accepting her *own* doubts about Natalie's physical capacity, represented acceptance and a route to valued action.

Social support and therapy groups are both important options to enhance clients' willingness and ability to engage in valued physical activities. The *Accept Yourself!* program was pilot tested in a group format, and the group format has unique benefits for clients (see Chapter 13). In particular, when considering physical activities, having other fat women working on self-acceptance and/or more experienced with self-acceptance as "partners in crime" can promote greater participation in valued activities. Social support should not be used in service to avoidance (i.e., if a patient is willing to go to the beach with friends but unwilling to go alone for fears of being humiliated or embarrassed, then the feelings of being humiliated and embarrassed alone at the beach should also be targeted for later acceptance practice, even though going initially with friends may be highly beneficial and powerful). Social support offers unique opportunities for fat women to model challenging activities for one another, as well as to experience greater physical safety and solidarity when entering spaces where anti-fat discrimination has been experienced in the past or where it is suspected.

Commitment is also helpful in supporting valued physical activities and the related, often challenging, acceptance experiences and transition of barriers that go along with engaging in previously avoided valued activities. Clinicians should ask clients to commit to specific activities in between sessions as homework, and should have clients verbally commit to specific days, times, and locations for activities. Making this specific verbal commitment helps clients and clinicians visualize and troubleshoot possible barriers to engagement in the activity in advance, as well as increasing clients' intention to follow through with the commitment (Mahrer, Gagnon, Fairweather, Boulet, & Herring, 1994). Clinicians should also ask clients to write down and formalize these verbal commitments, either by writing them into a planner or smartphone calendar, or simply writing them down on note paper, as this extra step also enhances commitment and compliance (Levy, 1977; Scheel, Hanson, & Razzhavaikina, 2004). Finally, rituals and strategies to enhance the general commitment to behave with acceptance and in line with values in situations that formerly evoked avoidance can also be helpful. For example, clients might make a "commitment to self-acceptance" to hang in a prominent location at home (see Chapter 7). Or they might buy, create, or wear a token of their self-acceptance practice or their pursuit of values.

One common barrier for clinicians and clients in engaging in valued physical activity and movement is failing to distinguish between valued physical activity or valued movements and physical exercise. Exercise is fraught for fat women and women of all sizes with body image concerns. Exercise regimens are often in service to weight loss, avoidance of feelings of shame, embarrassment, worthlessness, or fear related to body size, avoidance of fears of aging or "letting oneself go." Clients have often been coerced into exercise regimens by family members, lovers, or healthcare professionals as part of weight-based abuse and discrimination. Clients may refuse to do any exercise or refuse to stop doing exercise, may express shame at not doing the exercises they "should" do or fear and anger at any suggestion that they engage in anything that resembles exercise. Compulsive exercise or behaviors characteristic of exercise addiction (e.g., unwillingness to take a break from exercise regimens, exercising for emotion change, increasing exercise quantity or conflicts with others over exercise, rigid adherence to exercise as a component of identity) are associated with poor interoceptive awareness and greater risk of injury (Lichtenstein, Christiansen, Elklit, Bilenberg., & Støving, 2014). The goal of *Accept Yourself!* therefore is explicitly *not* to encourage clients to engage in rigid physical exercise regimens. Instead, *Accept Yourself!* attempts to teach and support clients' involvement in valued physical and movement activities, those activities that allow clients to experience the full intensity and vibrancy of life that their bodies have to offer. In addition, *Accept Yourself!* seeks to help clients increase their interoceptive awareness and to support clients to honor their bodies' signals for movement, rest, and other elements of wellness.

A metaphor might help illustrate the distinction between valued physical activity and movement versus rigid exercise: Consider your dog (or any dog you know, if you've never owned a dog yourself). How does your dog feel about taking a walk? Take a moment and imagine asking your dog (or the dog you know best) if she/he'd like to go for a walk? What is the response? I feel confident in asserting that your dog does not say, "Wait, wait, let me get my Fitbit first, so it counts!" On the contrary, most of the time, a walk is so precious and exciting an experience to a dog that the dog will learn the word "walk." You can probably picture the whole-body excitement visible in your dog at the mere mention of the word. For a dog, the chance to go out in the world, explore it, run, walk, experience things, is inherently joyful. The same is true for small children. Why isn't it true for some adults? Adults are encouraged to "take responsibility for their health" (which, in fact, is ultimately out of everyone's control) and to be morally good via exercise programs, which are described as inherently unpleasant or even hurtful, but necessary: "No pain, no gain." This is not the way your dog experiences movement and physical activity. And in fact, even though usually your dog is very excited to go for a walk, and finds an easy, evident pleasure in using his or her body, it is not the case that a dog *always* wants to go for a walk. If you invite Fido for a walk and she sits on the couch, staring at you with baleful eyes, it is because something about moving does not feel good to her at the moment. Perhaps she is exhausted, or in pain, or ill. She does not guiltily strap on her Fitbit and come for a walk, or berate herself for lying on the couch. Your dog is an expert in joyful, vibrant, life-enhancing physical activity and movement, and also an expert at listening to his or her body and honoring its cues. It is this straightforward relationship between movement and the body that we want to encourage in our clients: where the body is allowed and invited to move in all the ways it wants, in service to values and dreams, and limited only by its own needs for rest, relaxation, care, quiet, and stillness.

Clinicians need to be careful to make this distinction between exercise and movement/physical activity. It's not that *Accept Yourself!* always discourages specific athletic training regimens. In fact, Natalie and Maeko, described above, both engaged in relatively rigorous and structured athletic training in service to their dreams of performing flying trapeze and participating in a triathlon, as is appropriate and typical for involvement in these sports. However, in both cases, the structured training was in service to a specific dream articulated by each woman, with concomitant underlying values (for Maeko, values to achieve and provide role modeling for others; for Natalie, values of artistic expression and enjoyment of her body's capacity). Clients might even engage in structured physical activity in service to a health goal (e.g., walking

30 minutes a day to help reduce hypertension). However, clinicians need to be extremely cautious about encouraging or supporting exercise goals. Implicit weight stigma may lead clinicians to tacitly or actively place moral value on physical movement, blame clients' fitness level for their physical health, or offer preferential support to fat clients who engage in fitness or athletics. None of these stances are consistent with *Accept Yourself!* Instead, clinicians should model for clients and actively teach and support movement and activity as enjoyable opportunities to pursue values and dreams.

Clinicians should also model and support attending to interoceptive cues about the body's needs for movement. Fat clients have often been told to actively ignore their body's cues and needs in service to weight loss. This is often most noticeable with food, where many fat clients are made to feel guilty and ashamed of feelings of hunger, and to ignore these no matter how insistent, until a binge inevitably occurs, when the client may ignore feelings of fullness and keep eating a binge food in order to "hide the evidence," or avoid future binges by getting rid of all the food. However, it also occurs routinely with exercise, where cultural programming related to exercise as moral atonement for fatness, as well as the idea that exercise is more beneficial the more intense or painful it is, leads to clients following these rules even to the point of injury or self-harm. Some fat women may also lead their lives as detached from their bodies as possible, trying to live life exclusively in their heads and thinking of their bodies only in terms of how they compare to others' or to social standards, an experience blogger Kate Harding has described as living in a "floating head." (You can see her essay on this topic here: https://kateharding. net/2007/02/27/youre-not-fat.) Being a "floating head" often means ignoring basic bodily cues of pain, hunger, need for rest, and even medical symptoms – an experience that intersects with the fear of medical care engendered by experiencing weight bias at the doctor's office.

Jana, for example, was a public defender who drove long distances to meet with clients in their homes and worked extremely long hours. She identified strongly with the "floating head" metaphor, and noted that she had often had urine and even stool accidents while driving, because she did not listen to any bodily cues, including those about needs to relieve herself, instead throwing herself into her work at all costs, trying to avoid and ignore thinking about her "disgusting" body. In this phase of *Accept Yourself!*, when discussing the importance of listening to and honoring your body's cues during movement and at rest, she announced an intention to begin to take "pit stops" when driving as soon as she noticed any urge to relieve herself. She described in therapy group how much better her body felt simply from this small change.

Barbara, however, had a history of episodes of overactivity and compulsive exercise in service to weight loss mixed with periods of total inactivity. She had attended intense gyms and fitness programs that encouraged her to work through pain, and she noted that she believed that "pain is weakness leaving the body." Interestingly, she also presented on disability from work and having recently had surgery for an injury to her hand from overwork.

She listened to the therapist tell an anecdote about stopping to do yoga during the workday when her body gave her signals that it felt stiff and tired, and responded with some intensity: "Really, you're that in touch with what your body wants? You stopped to do exercise right in the middle of work because your body told you it wanted that?" She returned several times in group to discuss this idea, that her body might provide signals for its physical needs, and incorporating this idea into her life was a turning point in treatment for her. She noted that she had joined a regular walk with friends which she usually avoided, because the friends were both thinner and fitter and she had difficulty keeping up with them. She noted that this time she had simply encouraged them to go at their own pace and meet up with her at the coffee shop where walks concluded, and that she had enjoyed walking at her own pace, sometimes with friends and sometimes alone. She described refashioning a favorite shirt she had outgrown so that she could wear it comfortably during her walks. She returned to running, which she had once done as part of her compulsive exercise, but noted that this time she simply ran to enjoy the sensations of running, such as the wind in her hair or the feeling of her heart pumping. She noted that her runs had become shorter than before, interspersed with walks, and she described how she was running "just for fun now. It feels more sustainable, like I can run as much or as little as I want." She began to consider returning to weight lifting, which she had initially enjoyed, but which she had given up when the intensity of her former training program had become intolerably painful to her. "This time, I'm planning to take it easy, really work on form, and see how it feels. I'll go as long as it feels good, and then stop!"

Mindfulness exercises can be used during movement activities with clients, and clients can also be prompted in session with questions such as "What does your body want now?" or "What would feel good to your body now?" to attend and respond to interoceptive cues. The clinician can also model noticing and responding to interoceptive cues as a form of self-care: "I'm noticing I need to use the restroom now. Will you excuse me for a moment?" "I'm noticing that I'm restless from sitting, would you like to take a walk with me for our session today?" "I'm noticing that I need a stretch. Would you like to stretch with me?" When experimenting with movement in or outside of session, clinicians should encourage clients to mindfully attend to, describe, and respond to how different activities feel inside their bodies.

## Experiments with Embodied Values: Activities

As in the case examples above, clients' magic wand fantasies and lists of impossible activities should be mined for specific activities clinicians can support clients to experiment with inside and outside of session. And, also as in the case examples above, even if the clinician is fully willing and committed to helping the client explore, both internal and external barriers will arise for the clinician to help the client troubleshoot.

As a younger, thinner woman, Ebony had enjoyed surfing. She still enjoyed sailing and being on the water, but since she lived in Northern New England, surfing was not possible without a wetsuit. Ebony insisted that wetsuits were not available in her size. The clinician was able to help her locate appropriate sized wetsuits in a range of options and price points (iSnorkel carries Henderson wetsuits for women (front and back zip styles) up to size 24, with petite and tall options, $130–150, www.isnorkel.com. Tommy D Sports carries women's wetsuits up to size 6X, for less than $100, www.tommydsports.com. Wetsuitrental.com offers an inexpensive plus-sized rental option for wetsuits: www.wetsuitrental.com. Custom wetsuits in any size are available from: www.wetsuitwearhouse.com/wetsuits/category/custom-wetsuits.html). Once Ebony realized a wetsuit in her size was available to her, an internal barrier emerged: "If I put that on and try and go surf, I'm going to look like a whale." The clinician worked with Ebony to develop willingness to "look like a whale," and eventually Ebony was able to embrace this idea: "Doesn't bother the *actual* whales!" She rented a large-sized wetsuit to check fit, went on a one-day surfing excursion with her boyfriend, and noted with pride the feeling of empowerment and joy that emerged for her returning to this beloved sport. She came to her next session wearing a pendant of an Orca whale, to symbolize returning to the activity she loved.

Natalia did not have any physical activities or sensual experiences on her magic wand fantasy list, and, in fact, never having to worry about exercise again and being free to draw and paint and read as much as she wanted without guilt was the central element of her fantasy. She identified strongly with the idea of living as a "floating head" and noted that she could not imagine ever doing anything other than hating and trying to forget she had a body. Her therapist inquired if she might be willing to explore some dance experiences to begin to at least experience her body and learn more about its cues, and she was willing to do this. The therapist used Ragen Chastain's dance videos (available to purchase and download immediately here: https://danceforeverybody.com/download-the-classes) in session to practice beginning dance routines, warm up, and cool down with Natalia. The therapist and Natalia tried the classes together, and the therapist stopped the video after each segment to explore Natalia's observations about her experiences. Natalia reported that she felt "stupid, ridiculous" doing the videos, and initially wanted to stop: "I look terrible." The therapist encouraged her to notice and mindfully observe what physical sensations she noticed in her body while it moved, and Natalia was able to do this, and gradually shift her attention from what she thought her body might look like (and what Ragen and the other teacher's bodies looked like) to how it felt. She expressed willingness to continue progressing through the video series on her own, exploring as a mindfulness exercise the physical sensations involved. Although Natalia ultimately was able to better notice when her body needed and wanted to move, dance and other physical activities never became valued actions for her. Instead, she was able to accept and experience feelings of shame and anxiety related to not being "a good fattie" and not caring about exercise, and focus on behaviors that served the values most important to her: art and education. Clinicians should mindfully observe without acting on (possibly weight-stigma driven) thoughts that clients should or must exercise or move their bodies. People differ in how and how much they want to move their bodies as they pursue a valued life, and all levels of movement are acceptable in this program.

Sharon had listed "kayak comfortably" on her magic wand fantasy. She enjoyed regular kayaks with her husband, but her size had increased over time, and she noticed that she did not fit comfortably into the kayak cockpit any-more. During her paddles, she was distracted by the sensation of the edges of the cockpit digging into her sides. Getting into and out of the kayak had become more difficult, and she had mostly stopped going, because they put the kayak in at a public dock, and she feared being embarrassed as she tried to get in and out. The therapist explored with Sharon the idea of purchasing a kayak that could fit her body comfortably and was easy to enter and exit. Sharon initially resisted this idea on the basis of cost. Cost is a frequent barrier to valued activities, and it is worth exploring with clients whether cost is a significant barrier in the sense that they would have to do without basic needs if they spent the money on this valued activity, or whether cost is a proxy for how much the client believes she deserves. In this case, Sharon acknowledged that it was not the case that if she purchased the kayak, she would be unable to pay her mortgage or purchase food, but instead that she felt ashamed of having to spend a significant chunk of money on a piece of equipment that "if I lost weight like I am supposed to, I wouldn't need." She expressed willingness to at least shop for a kayak and determine if one was available that might be comfortable. She found a sit-on-top kayak style that easily accommodated her body and was easy to get in and out of, and noted that she could sell the old kayak, thus ameliorating some of the cost.

Sulani, like Natalia, did not focus on physical movement on her magic wand fantasy, but going to the gym, running, biking, and swimming were all on her lists of impossible activities. She noted that her doctor had suggested that regular aerobic exercise of some kind would likely help with her hypertension, but that she felt such intense shame about being seen in her body in public she scarcely knew where to begin. In the *Accept Yourself!* group, the ther-apist arranged an introduction to the gym for participants, including Sulani. Participants were able to go with the therapist and a HAES-friendly physical trainer to a local hospital's cardiac rehabilitation gym (hospitals may provide a more readily available partnership for clinicians, or consider if you have access to workplace gyms or local non-profit recreation centers for a similar activity), where the trainer introduced them to the equipment, demonstrated modifications, and helped participants, including Sulani, try out the machines without any pressure to have a "workout." Once Sulani felt more comfortable with how to work the machines, which ones were more accommodating to her body, and how to adapt exercises so her body was comfortable and effective in the machines, she was willing to try out her workplace gym, albeit very early in the morning when she felt she would risk fewer embarrassing interactions. (Note that this avoidance represents an area for later acceptance work.)

Swimming was a second area Sulani explored in group. Initially, she reported that she was willing to go to the pool with the group, therapist, and trainer, and agreed to bring her swimsuit, but she noted that she was not certain the suit fit her and was not willing to actually change into it or get in the water, but would sit and observe the group's activities near by. Once at the pool and observing, other group members encouraged her to at least try changing into her suit, and one got out of the pool to go to the locker room with her and change. Sulani found that her suit, while not of optimal fit, was sufficient for the circumstances, and she entered the pool with her comrades and found she enjoyed the remainder of the movements and activities the trainer had planned for them. She noted that her most intense feelings of anxiety and shame had been in the car on the way to the pool, and sitting by the pool fully clothed, which surprised her.

For Kati, hiking with her husband and grandchildren was part of her magic wand fantasy. She had fears of being unable to keep up, slowing the party down with her weight, and being laughed at or judged by her companions or by strangers when she was visibly winded or having a difficult time. She expressed willingness to go on an "easy" hike up a local mountain with her husband, and agreed to mindfully observe and honor bodily sensations that emerged, practicing acceptance with feelings of shame, embarrassment, worthlessness, and anxiety rather than pushing herself to keep up. She reported that she had done this, and that the hike had been a good opportunity for acceptance in the sense that it was a busy Saturday, with many people hiking the trail her husband chose for them, and "all of them" apparently young, healthy, and fit. She noted that several times she had held up her own party and other parties behind her on the single file trail as she stopped for rest, and she did note feelings of embarrassment and shame. She expressed surprise that no one was rude to her, but simply walked around them and exchanged pleasantries as if going at various paces on a hike was something everyone was accustomed to accommodating. She noted that in the end she had mostly enjoyed the hike, even though she had had to go much more slowly than was comfortable for her, and she reported that her usually taciturn husband had expressed intense gratitude for her joining him. "He worries about my health, and I think he doesn't like it that I'm fat, but he really did seem glad I'd come, and he said he felt lonely hiking on weekends without me." She began to hike regularly with her husband after this, noting that she was becoming more comfortable with moving at her own pace during their hike.

## Resources for Valued Movement

Resources for joyful movement and sensual experiences at any size are constantly evolving. But here are some resources you may find helpful in facilitating your clients' magic wand fantasies at every size and with varying abilities.

### Sexuality

> Book: *Big, Big Love: A Sex and Relationships Guide for People of Size (And Those Who Love Them)*, by Hanne Blank.
>
> Web Articles: How to have sex while fat: A short guide to sexy fun for fatties and people who f#&@ them, by Marianne Kirby. www.xojane.com/sex/sex-with-a-fat-person

F*ck me, I'm fat: A hot guide to fat sex, by Kitty Stryker. www.blogher. com/fck-me-i'm-fat-hot-guide-fat-sex (Stryker is a queer, fat sex worker who blogs and writes at her own domain as well: http:// kittystryker.com.)

Fat sex: What everyone wants to know but is afraid to ask, by a blogger writing under the pseudonym of "Ms. Vagina Science" at *Persephone Magazine*. http://persephonemagazine.com/2012/03/ fat-sex-what-everyone-wants-to-know-but-is-afraid-to-ask

### Bicycling

Web Article: You're not too heavy to ride a bike, at Chicargo Bikes. http://chicargobike.blogspot.com/2013/05/youre-not-too-heavy-to-ride-bike.html

Worksman Cycles sells bikes for bigger people: www.worksmancycles. com/big-bikes.html

Bikes for folks with disabilities: Creative Mobility: http://thebikerack. com/articles/about-creative-mobility-pg396.htm

### Swimming/Surfing/Kayaking

Web Articles: I wore a bikini and nothing happened, by Jenny Trout. www.huffingtonpost.com/jenny-trout/i-wore-a-bikini-and-nothing-happened_b_5546206.html

28 days to a bikini-ready mind, by Marina Wolf-Ahmad. www. huffingtonpost.com/jenny-trout/i-wore-a-bikini-and-nothing-happened_b_5546206.html

Wetsuits: iSnorkel carries Henderson wetsuits for women (front- and back-zip styles) up to size 24, with petite and tall options, $130–150, www.isnorkel.com

Tommy D Sports carries women's wetsuits up to size 6X, for less than $100, www.tommydsports.com

Wetsuitrental.com offers an inexpensive plus-sized rental option for wetsuits: hwww.wetsuitrental.com

Custom wetsuits in any size are available from: www.wetsuitwearhouse. com/wetsuits/category/custom-wetsuits.html

Sit-On-Top Kayaks for Larger Paddlers: FatYak Kayaks: https://fatyak-kayaks.co.uk/kayak-for-larger-paddlers

### Aerial/Trapeze/Circus

Web Articles: Nine things I learnt as a plus-size aerialist, by Natasha Puszczynska. www.verticalwise.com/en/plus-size-aerialist

Instagram hashtags to search: #plussizeaerialist
#curvyaerialist

## Running

Blogs: Ragen Chastain's IronFat blog, which chronicles her progress toward an IronMan triathlon. https://ironfatblog.wordpress.com/blog

Fat Girl Running, by Mirna Valerio. http://fatgirlrunning-fatrunner.blogspot.com

## Yoga

DVDs: Sally Pugh's *Grateful Spirit Yoga* series. www.sallypugh.org

Websites and Online Tutorials: The Body Positive Yoga website. http://bodypositiveyoga.com

Yoga for All online yoga teacher training program. http://yogaforalltraining.com

Book: *Yoga XXL: A Journey to Health For Larger Bodies*, by Ingrid Kollak.

## Dance

Blog: Ragen Chastain's dance blog, Dances With Fat. https://danceswithfat.wordpress.com/blog

DVDs and downloadable dance classes: www.danceforeverybody.com

Dance Troupes and In-Person Classes: Big Moves (Boston). www.bigmoves.org

Fat Kid Dance Party (Los Angeles). http://queerfatfemme.com/2017/06/12/fatkiddanceparty

## General Fitness and Movement

Book: *The Fat Girl's Guide to Exercise and Other Incendiary Acts*, by Hanne Blank.

Online Communities: The Fit Fatties Forum. http://fitfatties.ning.com and on Facebook: www.facebook.com/groups/fitfatties

Movement-Based, HAES-friendly Gym (Los Angeles): Everybody. www.everybodylosangeles.com

## References

Levy, R. L. (1977). Relationship of an overt commitment to task compliance in behavior therapy. *Journal of Behavior Therapy and Experimental Psychiatry*, 8(1), 25–29.

Lichtenstein, M. B., Christiansen, E., Elklit, A., Bilenberg, N., & Støving, R. K. (2014). Exercise addiction: A study of eating disorder symptoms, quality of life, personality traits and attachment styles. *Psychiatry Research*, 215(2), 410–416.

Lindau, S. T., Schumm, L. P., Laumann, E. O., Levinson, W., O'Muircheartaigh, C. A., & Waite, L. J. (2007). A study of sexuality and health among older adults in the United States. *New England Journal of Medicine*, 357(8), 762–774.

Mahrer, A. R., Gagnon, R., Fairweather, D. R., Boulet, D. B., & Herring, C. B. (1994). Client commitment and resolve to carry out postsession behaviors. *Journal of Counseling Psychology, 41*(3), 407–414.

Scheel, M. J., Hanson, W. E., & Razzhavaikina, T. I. (2004). The process of recommending homework in psychotherapy: A review of therapist delivery methods, client acceptability, and factors that affect compliance. *Psychotherapy: Theory, Research, Practice, Training, 41*(1), 38–55.

# 11 Values and Barriers

## Identifying and Pursuing Values

Because body image and weight concerns are so pervasive and can be so central to identity, they may affect the expression of and movement towards most values and goals in women's lives. Previous chapters have discussed how to identify and pursue values and dreams related to food, self-presentation and image, and movement and physicality. In this chapter, we will discuss values and dream identification and pursuit in general, in other areas of client's lives.

Constructing a values narrative and completing a values assessment are both useful places to begin in helping to clarify clients' values. Kelly Wilson and colleagues' Valued Living Questionnaire-2 (VLQ-2; Wilson & Dufrene, 2009) offers 12 domains of life valued by many people that can serve as a jumping-off point to discussion. These domains include family (other than marriage or parenting); marriage, couples, or intimate relations; parenting; friends and social life; work; education and training; recreation and fun; spirituality; community life; physical self-care and wellness; the environment (caring for the planet); and aesthetics (art, literature, music, beauty). The Acceptance and Commitment Therapy (ACT) manual (Hayes, Strohsahl, & Wilson, 2011), which also includes the VLQ-2, offers a Values Narrative Form (p. 313) and interview questions to help clients describe their values in each of these domains. (A similar exercise is available online here: http://thehappinesstrap.com/upimages/Values_Questionnaire.pdf, but the book's version is more updated and useful.) You can also develop a values narrative for each domain in session, as a whiteboard exercise, where you and your client collaborate to construct a description of the client's values in each domain, or clients can be asked to create an art project, collage, or scrapbook visual representation of their domains in each area. Clients can also be asked about their goals and dreams in each area, and this can be added to the narrative as well.

When developing the values narrative and discussing clients' dreams, it is important to continue to use the imagery of the magic wand, and to ask clients to imagine their values as if anything were possible and attainable for them. In other words, in a perfect world, what would they value in each of these domains? What kind of a family member, partner, worker, member of a community, person who enjoyed fun, person who cared about the environment, and so on, would they like to be? Remind clients that we will discuss and work with possibilities and barriers to their values throughout treatment, but when clarifying values, it's important to dream big.

In addition, it's important for the clinician to assess values narrative statements for the presence of social rules about what a person "should" care about, rather than this individual client's authentic values. This is especially important for the physical wellness and self-care domain among clients with body-image concerns, and also comes up with most of the other valued domains. Clients may tell you, for example, that they value exercise and eating healthily, when this is merely a learned social rule about how they should live or appear, rather than a deeply held personal value. To clarify the difference, clients can be asked how their narrative might change if no one knew they held these values or no one could ever tell they cared about this. What if they had to, for some reason, pursue the value in complete secrecy? Would eating healthy and exercising still be important if no one other than themselves knew or could tell that they did this? What if, every time they acted on or expressed the value, people they knew saw them as expressing the opposite value – would the value still be important? So, for example, would eating healthily and exercising still be important to them if every time they ate a "healthy" food and exercised, somehow, by magic, a trick occurred whereby everyone they knew saw them and judged them as eating "unhealthy" foods and sitting "lazily" around doing nothing? What if people in their lives actively disapproved of them behaving in line with this value, would it still be important? If their mother, partner, therapist (or whomever might be the source of the "rule" the client may be following in pursuing the value) disapproved of their eating healthily or exercising, or felt they were doing this incorrectly, would it still be important? Such questions can help distinguish values from learned social rules.

For example, it is important to me to be a loving and generous parent. If no one but me knew or could tell that I was trying to be a loving and generous parent, if I had to keep it a secret, I would likely feel unseen, invisible, perhaps lonely, but it would still be important to me. If, by magic, it appeared to people in my life that my behavior in service to being a loving and generous parent was actually its opposite – if people thought I was a cruel, unkind, self-centered parent instead, even though in reality I was acting with love and generosity to my son – I would probably have all sorts of negative feelings and fears, even self-doubt, but I would still do my best to move forward on this value. It would still be important to me, even if no one knew or approved, or thought I was doing it "right."

Once you and the client have developed a clear picture of what the client's values are in these various important domains of life, the VLQ-2 can be used to clarify a variety of clinically important aspects of the client's relationship with her values. For example, the VLQ-2 helps the clinician and client to assess how possible the client feels it is to pursue the value currently (and thus prompts the clinician to discuss barriers with the client), how important it is to her currently and in general, how much action the client is currently taking toward this value, and how satisfied she is with her actions. Using the results, clinicians can help conceptualize clients' perceived barriers to valued action, and also how much discrepancy there is between the client's values and her current behaviors or lived priorities.

Another important way to both investigate values and explore progress in treatment thus far is to return to the Magic Wand fantasy that clients generated near the beginning of treatment, and review this with the client. Clinicians should explore with clients their progress toward the fantasy. Have they achieved in treatment any of these dreams that they originally thought were predicated on weight loss? After the acceptance work and the valued activities pursued thus far, clients typically report that they have already attained many aspects of their fantasy, and they often express surprise and pleasure at this fact.

What has changed? Have their wishes changed or evolved any since experiencing acceptance, mindfulness, and defusion? Some element of the fantasy may now seem less important, because of the decreased attachment to programming related to body image, weight, and shape. Are there things in the fantasy that still feel desirable but impossible in their current bodies? There may be remaining aspects of the fantasy that represent valued life activities and directions to be explored.

When clients began treatment, they generally imagined that weight loss was a prerequisite to living the life elucidated in their magic wand fantasy. Now is the time to revisit this belief. In the *Accept Yourself!* group, we complete a collage activity to support this process, where clients have the opportunity to imagine the lives they'd like to be living *now*, in their current bodies, with their current minds, by visualizing this in a collage art piece. To do this activity with your clients, it is important to offer the right collage materials. Stacks of pictures of fat women of diverse ages, ethnicities, and presentations wearing a variety of attractive, sensual, revealing, fashionable, and other clothing, as well as engaged in a variety of exciting activities, should be provided in lieu of the usual magazines. (This collage activity should *not* be completed with standard women's magazines as collage material.) In addition, other magazines that feature photography of other valued life activities without people can also be included, such as travel, art, and food magazines, as well as art supplies, glitter, markers, and so on, and various sized and colored sheets of paper. Once the collage is created, it can be taken home and hung in a place of honor. Siri made her collage in an *Accept Yourself!* group with pictures of women swimming ("My new happy place!"), pictures of a variety of travel destinations, and luscious foods, as she was a gourmet cook. She also drew henna-inspired designs on the poster in glitter paint, as women in her community hennaed their hands before a wedding and their bellies before pregnancy: This was a symbol of her hopes to find a loving partner and have children. She expressed hope that these dreams were attainable now, in her current fat body, and noted with pride and surprise that she was enjoying dating a new partner she'd met online, swimming regularly, and planning a trip to the Azores, where she had always wanted to visit.

Siri came back to group the following week and said that she had hung her collage in a special place. Ever since the age of 16, her pair of "goal shorts" had hung over her bed. This was a beloved pair of "Daisy Duke"-style denim cutoffs that she had worn her sophomore year of high school, before gaining too much weight to fit into them her junior year. She had kept them, hoping to fit into them again, but although her weight fluctuated with diets, she had never again fit these teenage jeans. In her twenties, she had hung them up on the wall above her bed as a goal for diet and fitness motivation, and they had stayed there. She was now 37 years old, and wore a size 3X in jeans. She had taken down those size-five jeans, which were thickly caked with dust, and thrown them out, noting a sense of freedom and liberation in doing this: "Those jeans aren't even my style any more. They were worn out and ratty and no longer cute. I wouldn't have worn them if I could." And in their place she had hung her collage, as a symbol of the life she intended to live now, with the energy she had freed up from dieting and weight loss.

## Navigating Internal and External Barriers

In previous chapters we've discussed the various barriers clients face as they begin to move toward living a life in line with their values and dreams. Many of these variables are internal – the fears, shame, self-doubt, depression, negative thoughts, and unpleasant physical sensations that clients conjure up as soon as they contemplate or begin to move towards a valued but previously avoided activity. Some may be external, including the weight-based (and other forms of) discrimination clients face as they live a valued life in the world, as well as other concrete limitations (e.g., lack of money, rejection by others, lack of resources).

Clinicians often find the barriers that clients offer up as blocking their path forward exhausting. "Yes, but" can be a difficult client statement to respond to, especially when the barriers to forward progress are concrete, or when the client appears especially fused to them. And yet the emergence of barriers is the natural, inevitable outcome of doing any valued activity in life.

Consider this in your own life. When was the last time you achieved an important life dream or wish? What was the path you took to obtain this dream? When did the dream first emerge? When did you begin to want this? Was it a childhood dream, or was it in adolescence, or adulthood? Did you take any initial steps toward achieving your dream, back when it first emerged? What happened then? Did you experience any internal barriers, such as self-doubt, lack of motivation, perceptions of limited time or energy, fear, or shame? Did these stop you from moving forward? Did they lead you to even abandon your dream at any point? Did you follow any unhelpful arbitrary social rules or programming that led you astray from your dream? (Perhaps a mentor or a parent discouraged you, or gave you unhelpful advice, or perhaps you had been taught something about how to achieve such dreams, or whether such dreams were realistic or attainable for you, that took you off course.) What about external barriers? Did you experience rejection? Were there concrete barriers of money or resources or physical limitations that emerged?

For most people, progress toward a lifelong dream does not consist of ease and linear motion. In fact, you may discover that you faced numerous barriers along the way, both internal (self-doubt, lack of motivation, fear) and external (rejection, losses and lacks of various kinds). Even worse, whenever you made a significant step forward toward your dream, you may have encountered new, discouraging barriers. It is as if the act of moving toward the thing you wanted most brought up barriers, both internally in your mind and externally in the world.

And indeed, this is exactly how valued living works. You pursue a dream, a goal, or a value, and you hit a wall. If you do not want to hit that wall, this is easy: Pursue nothing. Stay home. Do as little as possible. You will face few external barriers to your dreams if you do not pursue them! (Unfairly, there is no way at all to avoid internal variables. Even if you stay home, do nothing and "give up" your values and dreams, your ever-busy, ever-chattering mind will continue to dog you with thoughts: Wishes to move forward, recriminations that you have not, and predictions of your ultimate failure at anything that matters to you. Thank you, mind, for these thoughts!) Don't believe me? Consider: Is this how it is in your own life? Was your progress toward the last dream you attained smooth and untroubled? Or was it rich with self-doubt, fear, and external problems you were forced to transcend as you persevered toward your dream?

Most things worth having come with difficult barriers along the way. How can you and your clients cope with all these barriers? Steven Hayes, Kirk Strohsahl, and Kelly Wilson, creators of ACT, suggest that clients cope with barriers, particularly internal barriers such as doubt or negative thoughts that steer us off course, like a soap bubble. Here is how they describe doing this:

> Imagine that you are a soap bubble. Have you ever seen how big soap bubbles can collide with smaller ones and the little ones are absorbed into the bigger one? Well, imagine that you are a soap bubble like that and you are moving down a path you have chosen. Suddenly, another bubble appears in front of you and says, "Stop!" You stand there for a few seconds. When you move to get around, over, or under the bubble, it moves just as quickly to block your path. Now you have only two choices. You can stop moving in your valued direction, or you can collide with the other soap bubble and continue on with it inside you. This second move is what we mean by "willingness." Your barriers are largely feelings, thoughts, memories, and so on. They are really inside you, but they seem to be outside ... "Willingness" is not a feeling

or a thought – it is an action that answers the question the barrier asks: "Will you have me inside you by choice, or will you not?" In order for you to take a valued direction and create a new behavioral pattern, you must answer yes, but only *you* can *choose* that answer'.

(Hayes et al., 2011, p. 338)

With internal barriers, such as thoughts, memories, or visions of the future, efforts to talk back to them, to get rid of them, to be "rational" about them, to "psych yourself up" by making your fears go away, often go nowhere. The thoughts return, more powerful than ever. Because you are the one thinking your thoughts, it is difficult to ever defeat them or make them go away.

You (or your clients) can try a concrete example of the mind at work in this way. Stand in front of a mirror and try giving yourself an affirmation about your appearance. Choose an affirmation about an aspect of your appearance you really do genuinely like. Perhaps, "Wow, I have pretty eyes!" or "I look sexy," or whatever else you believe to be true about yourself that is positive. As you do this, notice what your mind provides. What is its initial reaction? Now amp up the affirmation a little. Out loud, talk about the same good aspect of yourself, but make it even more positive. "I have *gorgeous* eyes! They are the most limpid, radiant brown. Everyone thinks they are beautiful." What does your mind give you now? Now take the affirmation right over the top, as you stand talking in front of the mirror: "I have the most gorgeous eyes of anyone! Famous models would kill for my eyes. Men and women alike are transfixed by them. I've never seen anyone with such beautiful eyes, anywhere." Now what does your mind give you? At some point in this process – probably with the very first self-compliment, but definitely by the end, your mind provided you with the affirmation's opposite – a reminder that your eyes are not *that* pretty, exceptions or details about how your eyes are not that pretty, reminders of people with prettier eyes than yours, and perhaps criticism that you were ever so stupid or vain as to think your eyes were pretty at all! ACT therapists call this tendency for the mind to pull for its opposite "mental polarity," and (besides providing a rationale for never prescribing affirmations in treatment) this property of our minds helps illustrate why talking yourself out of your thoughts rarely works. Your mind is a skilled courtroom lawyer for both sides of any given argument, and since there's no judge to arbitrate the dispute, the arguments never end: In the meantime, you or your clients are engaged in a fruitless struggle to "feel better" before you or they can act.

Instead, you might encourage your clients to bring their fears along with them, willingly holding them inside of themselves as they move towards what really matters. Acceptance exercises have already provided clients with experience doing this, as they have already taken negative feelings about their bodies and fears of being judged with them as they engaged in feared activities, wore shame-inducing clothing, or ate in ways that felt frightening or shameful to practice acceptance. Now it is time to consider where else they could go if they could easily bring these thoughts and feelings along for the ride?

Randy Pausch, the Carnegie-Mellon professor of computer science who gave his famed *Last Lecture* when he was dying of cancer, was another expert at navigating barriers, and he provides an excellent metaphor for navigating external barriers. Even after clients are able to effectively bring their internal fears, doubts, and other negative thoughts, feelings, or sensations along for the ride, they will, as you have no doubt already experienced numerous times, encounter external barriers. External barriers are even more difficult for clinicians than internal barriers, because they represent *real* barriers that clinicians often cannot directly help clients transcend. What can you say to a client who has bravely applied for a job or asked for a date she really wanted and been rejected? What if this has happened multiple times? Is it right to encourage a client toward a dream that will be difficult, or even impossible to obtain?

Pausch's work provides a metaphor that is useful in considering this question. *The Last Lecture* was actually entitled "Achieving Your Childhood Dreams," and used Professor Pausch's own life experiences achieving what he truly dreamed of as a case example. Professor Pausch had big dreams as a kid: He wanted to play for the NFL, be an astronaut, and work as a Disney Imagineer, among other things. He also had big brick walls standing in his way: He wasn't strong enough or fast enough to play a decent game of football; he didn't see well enough to be an astronaut; and when he applied to work for Disney they sent him a nice rejection letter. But this is what Professor Pausch said about the brick walls created by external barriers:

> The brick walls are there for a reason. The brick walls are not there to keep us out. The brick walls are there to give us a chance to show how badly we want something. Because the brick walls are there to stop the people who don't want it badly enough.

(If you'd like to learn more, Randy Pausch's homepage, where you can access a video and a transcript of *The Last Lecture*, is here: www.cs.cmu.edu/~pausch)

What are your clients' brick walls, the external barriers that stand in their way? Instead of avoiding them, struggling with them, looking for ways around them, are there ways clients can use them creatively? Can they go over them, through them? Can they use them as forums for their values, as demonstrations of their commitment to what really matters to them? This is the goal of working with external barriers. One of the aspects I find most intriguing about working with client goals and dreams and the external barriers that get in the way is that I need not become attached to the ultimate outcome of their struggle with and transcendence of their brick walls. (Although Pausch did fly in a zero-gravity simulator with astronauts, he did not ultimately go to space as a NASA astronaut.) The clinician does not need to be clairvoyant, and help the client choose only "realistic" or "attainable" goals. In fact, in ACT, we acknowledge that such thoughts are just thoughts, and that they do not reflect any objective reality one way or the other. Instead, the clinician helps the client move toward her dreams by acting on her values, holding the faith that dreams, in general, are attainable and that the client is worthy of the pursuit of her deepest dreams, and with the awareness that acting in line with your values is worthwhile whether you ultimately attain any particular goal or not. If dreams are the X's on clients' personal treasure maps, then values are the compass headings that provide direction along the way. There may or may not be treasure at any given point on the map. Any given point on the map may or may not, in reality, be accessible to the client. But whether the client achieves any given dream or not, her values still provide direction, both at the high points of life and at its low points.

When discussing this issue with clients and predicting that barriers will emerge, clinicians can help clients brainstorm how they will demonstrate their commitment to their values and dreams when barriers arise. What small, committed actions can clients take when brick walls show up to demonstrate how they will transcend them? As with any homework assignment, committing to these actions is most helpful if clinicians help clients make a specific, concrete, behavioral plan for when, how, and with what support they will demonstrate their commitment in the face of barriers.

## Valued Living and Self-Acceptance for the Clinician

Clinicians may or may not share the body image and weight concerns that are the main topic of this book, and that clients bring to *Accept Yourself!* treatment. (If clinicians do struggle with these concerns, the ideas contained in this book and the accompanying self-help volume, as well as therapy and supervision with a Health At Every Size (HAES) and ACT-knowledgeable clinician, are likely to be helpful, and perhaps essential before engaging in client work.) However, the pursuit of valued living is something that all human beings share and can benefit from enhancing. Clinicians who are clear about their personal values and dreams and who are engaged in pursuing these actively and navigating barriers with commitment and grace are likely to experience several benefits.

Commitment to values and valued living may help prevent burnout among mental health clinicians. Lack of values commitment was more strongly associated with burnout than several more commonly researched work site factors, such as co-worker and supervisor support, and salary, in one study of addiction counselors (Vilardaga et al., 2011). The values-commitment component of ACT helped university employees experience less interference in their work and social lives from distress, and less impact from their stressors, compared with a version of ACT treatment without the values commitment component (Hermann, 2008). Living a life guided by your values and moving toward your most deeply held dreams is likely to enhance personal life satisfaction and clarity, making work and life decisions more straightforward and enriching your life by adding more of what you most value to it.

In addition, pursuing your own dreams and values, and navigating barriers as they arise using acceptance and mindfulness, will help develop your empathy for clients' experiences as they also walk this path. Greeting one's own thoughts and beliefs with flexibility and defusion, leaning in to accept painful sensations, emotions, and thoughts, and bravely striding forward toward the life you most deeply want to live is rewarding and challenging in nearly equal parts. If you are doing this on a daily basis yourself, you are better poised to assist clients to do it.

The same values-clarification and values-commitment exercises already described and delineated in Chapter 9 of the accompanying self-help book are likely to be as helpful to you as to clients in identifying, clarifying, and committing to your values. Determining a framework and structure through which you will pursue valued directions and dreams may be a more personal process. As a personal example, I've explored several ways of incorporating my values into daily life and thus giving myself the opportunity to live a life with a high degree of correspondence between my values and my daily activities.

Valued living was not my initial focus as I learned how to incorporate ACT and HAES principles into my own personal life. HAES Principles had been an intuitive outgrowth of my lifelong involvement in feminism, and I was privileged and lucky to have avoided a struggle with body-image concerns in my youth and young adulthood. ACT was less intuitive, and my own personal integration of ACT principles into my own life began with developing a mindfulness practice and beginning to use active acceptance to experience previously avoided negative sensations, feelings, and thoughts. Although ACT as a therapy and life philosophy can be pursued flexibly, beginning with any aspect, I suspect either clinicians or clients who start with values clarification and commitment will discover rapidly that acceptance and mindfulness strategies quickly become relevant in coping with barriers if they are not previously learned. Thus, clinicians may want to develop their personal mindfulness, defusion, and acceptance skills before working on values clarification and commitment.

For my own personal commitment to valued living, I experimented with several structures. One was to make a list of my values and to devote each day to one of them. I would post the word describing the value where I could see it each day, and try to think about it and infuse my day with it, and also try to do something small in line with that value each day. For example, if the word representing my values was "kindness," I might add a grocery trip for the local foodbank, and purchase especially nice treats, like real maple syrup or expensive chocolate, which usually do not get donated. This was an enjoyable, low-key way to infuse my values into my daily life, but I also found that it did not seem to move me closer to any of my deeply held dreams, which was also important to me.

Another structure I experimented with (and continue to use) was more effective at infusing values and dreams into my daily life. Here, I made a list of 11 core, valued domains in my life. (My domains were: Parenting, romantic relationships, pleasure and adventure, art, writing, environmental justice, social justice, beautiful surroundings, gratitude, friendship, and rest and relaxation. A life rich in these domains represents a life well lived to me. Obviously, your valued domains would differ based on what is important to you.) Under each domain, I listed a huge variety of goals and dreams. These included large and small things I wanted to do, have, or experience in my life related to that domain. Some of the experiences are one-time events you could cross off the list and have achieved (e.g., writing a book or visiting Japan), and others are events I want to do regularly, on an ongoing basis (e.g., being intimate with my partner). The list is long, and although some domains have many items listed underneath them, others have only a few. Effectively, this created 11 "bucket lists" of things I would like to do, experience, create, or have in my life, all of which would enhance my core values. Then, I began devoting my weekends, initially, to moving toward an item on one of the lists. Initially, I did this in an arbitrary way: I had collected the items on the lists as I thought of them, and I continue to add to the lists as I think of new things I want to include. I simply started with the first domain (parenting), and did the first item on that domain's list (helping my son enroll in an archery class – one of his dreams). When I finished the first item on the first list, I moved to the first item on the second list.

Some of the items were completed in an afternoon, like enrolling a child in a class. Others were significant, months-long projects. In some cases I experienced no internal or external barriers in accomplishing a (usually small) dream. In other cases, the barriers were significant. I committed to practicing acceptance and honoring my commitment with internal barriers that arose. For example, learning printmaking and letterpress printing was one item on my list for art. I enrolled in a local, free letterpress class to set a chapbook of poetry, and chose some of my own poetry to typeset. The process was long and somewhat difficult for me, and brought up feelings of embarrassment, inadequacy, and boredom. I had urges to quit the class before completing it. However, in the spirit of acceptance and commitment, I completed the class and the edition of chapbooks, mindfully observing my experience and learning from it.

In the case of external barriers, when I encountered a significant barrier in my path after a significant amount of work in one area, I gave myself permission, if I wanted, to set that dream aside and go on to the next dream in the next domain. My commitment to myself was that I would leave the dream on the list in its same position, and when I returned to that valued domain again, I could reconsider how to attack the external barrier that had arisen, or consider whether that dream remained important to me.

I have tweaked this system for valued living pursuit in the six years that I have used it. I add to or remove items from lists regularly, and have sometimes removed or changed valued domains. I added a seasonal structure to the lists as well, so that projects can be slotted into times of year when they work best for me (e.g., as an academic, certain writing and travel projects are more accessible to me during the summer), and also so that I can work on small, enjoyable dreams during the weekdays, as well as the weekends. For example, small, ongoing, enjoyable dreams show up at the end of my workday, whereas bigger projects wait for better times. My experience with this system has been very rewarding and reinforcing: Since I implemented it, my life has caught fire. Things I have wanted for some time have come to fruition, and I am more solidly and definitely who I want to be. I have also learned more about how commitment works in the face of a changing emotional landscape: Even the most desirable and wanted dreams can temporarily or permanently lose their luster in the face of internal and external barriers, a change of heart, or the difference between my mind's prediction about what an experience will be like versus the reality of that lived experience. However, the overall picture – what has happened to my life and emotions as a whole by centering a commitment to valued living in my life – is rosy. There is much more of what I want and enjoy and value and am proud of now than there was before.

How could you implement a similar system? You might begin by making a list of your own personal valued domains – five to 15 areas where, if your life was rich in them, you would feel you were living well. And you might also create your own "bucket list." What are all the things you would do, experience, have, pursue, if you had all the resources (money, support, etc.) in the world and no limitations on what you could do? Include big and small things, things you would do regularly, and things you would do only rarely. Now compare the two lists. Do any of your dreams map on to your values? Add the dreams to the valued domains where they match.

Now consider what it would mean if you began pursuing these dreams. What if, this weekend, you worked towards the first dream under the first valued domain on your list? (Notice that this is chosen somewhat arbitrarily.) What shows up? Do you find you'd rather work on a different domain or list instead? What shows up if you arbitrarily commit to this first dream and domain for this weekend? What would you do? Are there internal barriers that emerge? External barriers to plan for? Try committing to pursuing the first two or three dreams under the first two or three domains for the next month of weekends. What do you notice if you implement this experiment?

I encourage you to experiment with this process and experience as an exercise in willingness and commitment, if nothing else. However, although this system has been workable and deeply rewarding for me, it may not be the most effective way to center your values and dreams in your life for you. If, after experimenting and mindfully observing the results, this process does not seem to bring you closer to a valued life or help support your dreams, you should consider what other kind of structure might work for you in committing to valued living and in bringing your stated values in line with your daily lives and behaviors. Brainstorm several structures and experiment with them, noticing what your experience tells you about how they work for you. Be careful of socially mediated rules about what you "should" value or what are "realistic" or "attainable" dreams: Values are deeply held and personal. A good structure or list that you might use to prompt you toward your values and dreams should feel exciting and satisfying, although it may also feel daunting and intimidating. Being willing around implementing your own values and achieving your own dreams, and recommitting to them over and over again, is a process that will match the one you engage in with your clients.

## References

Hayes, S. C., Strosahl, K. D., & Wilson, K. G. (2011). *Acceptance and commitment therapy: The process and practice of mindful change*. New York: Guilford Press.

Hermann, B.A. (2008). *Dismantling an ACT-based intervention for work stress: Do values really matter?* (Doctoral dissertation). (2008). Retrieved from http://digitalcommons.library.umaine.edu/etd/23

Vilardaga, R., Luoma, J. B., Hayes, S. C., Pistorello, J., Levin, M. E., Hildebrandt, M. J., … & Bond, F. (2011). Burnout among the addiction counseling workforce: The differential roles of mindfulness and values-based processes and work-site factors. *Journal of Substance Abuse Treatment, 40*(4), 323–335.

Wilson, K. G., & DuFrene, T. (2009). *Mindfulness for two: An acceptance and commitment therapy approach to mindfulness in psychotherapy*. Oakland, CA: New Harbinger.

# Part 3

# Special Situations in Treatment

## 12  Acceptance-Based Approaches When Clients Have Weight-Related Physical Health Concerns

### A Challenge for the Clinician?

What if my client has an weight-related health concern? How can I tell a client to give up weight loss, if her weight is adversely affecting her health? As we've discussed in previous chapters, obesity *is* associated with a variety of health problems, including hypertension, type II diabetes, obstructive sleep apnea, certain cancers, and cardiovascular diseases (Lavie, McAuley, Church, Milani, & Blair, 2014). Not only that, there is evidence that successful intentional long-term weight loss is associated with improvements in some obesity-associated diseases, such as hypertension (Horvath et al., 2008; Neter, Stam, Kok, Grobbee, & Geleijnse, 2003) and type II diabetes (Diabetes Prevention Program Research Group, 2009; Norris et al., 2004), although the benefits are modest and inconsistent, especially when the weight losses are modest (as they typically are) or when medications are used as part of the weight loss intervention strategy.

It's difficult for many clinicians to give up prescribing weight loss and to stop stigmatizing obesity when clients appear to be unhealthy because of their excess weight. But let's consider a little thought experiment, an entirely imaginary case example intended to help you as a clinician contextualize how your clients' health intersects with their weight (and perhaps other aspects of their identity, such as gender or race or disability or gender identity or sexuality).

Picture this: You're a fat person with worrying symptoms. You avoid going to the doctor, because you're ashamed and fearful that the symptoms will be blamed on your weight. But the symptoms don't go away, so eventually you go in. Sure enough, the doctor spends five minutes with you, doesn't examine you, says you need to lose weight, and charges you $300 for the office visit. (You have the high-deductible health plan, which is all you can afford, because your employer only offers "discounts" on health insurance to people with a "normal" body mass index (BMI).) But the symptoms don't go away, so you eventually go back to a different doctor. (That's another payment toward your deductible, which you don't have.) That second doctor examines you, at least, orders tests, and ultimately diagnoses you with an obesity-associated cancer, and sends you off to the oncologist.

The oncologist would like to help you with chemotherapy, but no research has been done to determine whether your chemotherapy dose should be based on lean body mass, total body weight, or whether dosage need doesn't vary based on weight. She makes her best guess, but your cancer doesn't respond to the chemotherapy. She doesn't know if that's because your cancer didn't respond or because the chemotherapy dose was wrong. Also, your cancer was staged higher because it took you months to get diagnosed. The oncologist would like to get a better look at your tumor, but you don't fit into the CT or MRI machines, even at this top-notch cancer center. Nowhere that takes your insurance has a machine that can scan you. The oncologist recommends surgery to remove the tumor, but the surgeon says your body weight puts you at too high a risk of complications – none of his equipment is suited to your body, and he had no training working with someone of your size and shape.

You die, and become a statistic useful to epidemiological researchers, who dutifully report a correlation between adipose tissue and premature death from your cancer type. Your legacy becomes a stigmatizing news item about this correlation and how terrible and unhealthy it is to have too many fat cells. Someone "helpfully" shows this newspaper article to their "normal"-weight teenage daughter, because they perceive her as "overweight," even though she is not, at least according to government BMI guidelines. Alarmed, she goes on a diet, first loses and then gains weight, and suddenly starts avoiding her doctor.

What do you make of this mental experiment? Is this situation plausible? (*New York Times* journalist Gina Kolata wrote an interesting article exploring these various contributors to poor health outcomes for fat people. You can read her article here: https://mobile.nytimes.com/2016/09/26/health/obese-patients-health-care.html). Reducing the problem of obesity-associated diseases to a demand that fat people lose weight in hopes that this will make their risks resemble those of thin people presents an individual solution to a fundamentally systemic problem. Clinicians who work with weight-concerned clients around health issues must be aware of the diversity of factors that interfere with their care, most of which are beyond their control.

Still, you may be thinking, if successful intentional weight loss is associated with improvements in obesity-related disease, shouldn't we prescribe weight loss to our clients who have such diseases? Perhaps, but *only if it is likely that they will achieve it.* The likelihood that the average client will achieve successful long-term weight loss, particularly of enough weight that they can expect to experience health benefits, is low. As we discussed in Chapter 1, even the most optimistic meta-analyses of non-surgical weight loss interventions conclude that the average participant can expect only a 3–6 percent long-term loss of body weight (Franz et al., 2007). There is little evidence for any health benefit from a weight loss below 5 percent (Blackburn, 1995). One large cohort study of more than 175,000 obese British men and women followed over nine years found that the annual probability of attaining normal body weight was 1 in

210 for mildly obese men and 1 in 124 for mildly obese women. The probability was even lower for more obese men and women: 1 in 1,290 men and 1 in 677 women with BMIs between 40 and 45. More obese men and women achieved a 5 percent body weight loss (i.e., enough to obtain health benefits) at some point during the study, but the majority who achieved 5 percent weight loss (78 percent) had regained that weight and then some five years later (Fildes et al., 2015).

Long-term weight gain as a result of weight loss efforts is obviously not beneficial, and there is some evidence that weight cycling (repeated cycles of gaining and losing weight) is itself harmful. Compared with weight stability, both weight gain over time and weight cycling independently increased risk of cancer in women (Welti et al., 2017), and weight cycling is a risk factor for worsened cardiovascular disease and death in patients both with and without pre-existing cardiovascular disease (Bangalore et al., 2017; Montani, Schultz, & Dulloo, 2015). Thus, while it may be tempting to prescribe weight loss for clients suffering from obesity-associated diseases, there are clear and present health risks to doing so without substantial evidence that the client is capable of significant, sustained weight loss. A client with any previous history of unsuccessful dieting and/or weight cycling is already presenting evidence that she is not likely to benefit from renewed weight loss efforts now.

In any event, the benefits of weight loss for managing chronic obesity-associated diseases may have in some cases been overstated. A systematic review of the long-term effects of intentional weight loss on hypertension among overweight and obese participants found that both surgical and non-surgical weight loss interventions were associated with little long-term improvement in blood pressure, even when substantial weight losses were achieved (Aucott et al., 2005). Similarly, as described in Chapter 1, the Look AHEAD trial found no benefits for cardiovascular disease with successful intentional weight loss among type II diabetics, although some diabetes indicators did improve with weight loss (Look AHEAD Research Group, 2013; Unick et al., 2013). Even bariatric surgery, commonly recommended to treat diabetes via weight loss, is of uncertain long-term benefit for this disease among the mildly obese (BMI < 35; Maggard-Gibbons et al., 2013). Globally, people who successfully lost weight using weight loss interventions evaluated in randomized controlled trials (RCTs) experienced no improvements in mental health, and no or modest benefits for physical health, compared with control participants who did not lose weight (Warkentin, Das, Majumdar, Johnson, & Padwal, 2014). Based on these modest health outcomes, some researchers have concluded that weight loss interventions tested in RCTs have little applicability to clinical practice, given the modest weight losses, unclear health benefits, and high attrition rates of weight loss interventions (Douketis, Macie, Thabane, & Williamson, 2005).

Clinicians may also overestimate the risks of fatness on the outcomes of obesity-associated disease. Researchers have long known about and described the "obesity paradox," briefly described in Chapter 1, which is the common finding in research on obesity-associated diseases that, although obesity is a risk factor for the development of these diseases, once you have the disease, obesity is actually a protective factor against disease morbidity and mortality. The obesity paradox has been demonstrated for many forms of cardiovascular disease, hypertension, stroke, diabetes, chronic obstructive pulmonary disease, surgical, intensive care and critical care outcomes, hemodialysis outcomes, and osteoporosis (Hainer & Aldhoon-Hainerová, 2013). The obesity paradox appears strongest for those in the "overweight" and "mildly obese" categories, as well as for those with at least moderate cardiovascular fitness, but even non-fit and moderately to extremely obese participants show some protective effects of obesity on chronic disease (Lavie, De Schutter, & Milani, 2015). Why obesity is a risk factor for disease acquisition but a protective factor for morbidity and mortality is unknown, and it is likely that the stigma of obesity has limited research in this area. However, body fat reserves have served over our evolutionary history as a resource in times of stress, and they may continue to do this when facing the stress of disease.

One intriguing line of research for the clinician wondering how to advise weight-concerned patients who have obesity-associated diseases concerns the role of cardiovascular fitness in mortality. Researchers have long suspected that both cardiovascular fitness and obesity contribute to mortality risk. However, which aspect is more important (cardiovascular fitness or weight) has been controversial. Recent meta-analytic research, however, suggests that people who have good cardiovascular fitness (as measured by a maximal or $VO_2$ peak exercise test) are at similar risk of death whether they are normal weight, "overweight," or obese, as assessed by BMI. Normal-weight, fit individuals are not at lower risk of death than overweight or obese fit individuals. Interestingly, among the unfit, increased BMI (especially for those in the "overweight" range) showed a protective effect against the risk of death; that is, the normal-weight unfit were more likely to die than overweight or obese unfit individuals. Among fit individuals, weight showed little effect on mortality (Barry et al., 2014). Researchers in this study concluded that clinicians and public health officials should focus on physical activity and fitness-based interventions rather than weight-loss driven approaches to reduce mortality risk.

## Dealing with Medical Professionals

Clinicians should be mindful of the possibility that implicit weight stigma may emerge for them and that they may engage in microaggressions or other stigmatizing behaviors, especially with fat clients who have obesity-associated diseases. Clients with such diseases are also likely to be at increased risk of discrimination and stigmatizing interactions with other health professionals, because their illnesses may make their weight a target.

Clinicians should ask clients – regardless of weight status – about their physical health concerns, and should do this as a matter of course, in a fashion that makes clear to clients that such questions are not being asked because of the client's weight. For example, clinicians could offer an intake checklist that includes a list of physical ailments and ask all clients to indicate which problems they have, or could ask all clients at intake about medications, including their purpose for the client. Clinicians should also ask all clients (again, regardless of weight) about their healthcare providers, including whether clients have a regular primary care provider or specialty providers, how those relationships are for clients, and how frequently they are seen. Clinicians should also consider reassessing these questions as treatment continues, because clients may not be forthcoming about problems with healthcare providers before they have established trust with the clinician that they will not be exposed to more weight-based shame. Even clients who present asking for help with weight loss and with substantial self-stigma may nevertheless struggle with stigmatizing medical professionals and the avoidance of medical care due to shame.

Clinicians should validate any experiences of healthcare provider weight discrimination and weight-based abuse that clients report, and should state unequivocally that this behavior is discrimination or abuse, that the client does not deserve it, and that it is not good or appropriate or ethical medical care. Hearing a health professional condemn discriminatory behavior from a fellow professional can be a powerful experience for clients and may help empower them to seek out or return for better medical care.

Because weight-based discrimination is widespread in medical care (see Chapter 2), clients may have difficulty accessing appropriate, non-stigmatizing care. Chapter 7 discusses ways clinicians might help clients cope with weight-based discrimination in various settings, and many of these strategies are likely to be useful in coping with healthcare professional weight discrimination.

However, because of the intensity of weight-based shame linked to health, as well as the power differential between physician and patient, where the client may depend upon a discriminatory or abusive provider for her ongoing physical well-being or survival, these interactions may be especially fraught and emotionally intense for clients. A detailed understanding on the part of the clinician about how the client feels about her healthcare provider, and that provider's strengths and weaknesses, as well as the history of the relationship, is essential. Clients may value their doctors, even when they are highly discriminatory and stigmatizing, and they may continue to blame themselves for their poor health and echo the doctor's advice, even after much self-acceptance work has been done with apparent success.

Clinicians can discuss a variety of strategies clients can use to remove weight as a topic of discussion in the doctor's office and to help the provider shift to a more productive discussion of how to enhance the client's health independent of her weight. The clinician can offer him or herself as a resource, or to play the "bad guy" with the physician. For example, clients can tell their stigmatizing healthcare provider, "I am working on weight management with Dr. *Accept Yourself!* We have weekly sessions and are making great progress, so I'd like to use our visit today to talk about _____ instead. I can sign a release if you'd like to talk to Dr. *Accept Yourself!* about my treatment."

If clients find that seeing their weight worsens eating-disorder symptoms or body-image concerns, or engenders weight stigma from physicians or their staff, they can practice asking not to be weighed in the doctor's office, or to ask why weight is needed. (Sometimes patient weight *is* needed medically, for example to calculate a medication dose for those medications that are dosed by weight, or to monitor the metabolic side effects of a medication. More commonly weight is collected automatically as a vital sign. Refusing to be weighed can be an opportunity for clients to practice asserting and negotiating their needs with the doctor.)

Clients can also bring written materials to help them talk with providers about the Health At Every Size (HAES) and *Accept Yourself!* approaches to physical wellness. Size acceptance activist Ragen Chastain has published a set of "How to Talk To Your Doctor" cards that include research and talking points both for clients and their providers; they are available for download here: https://danceswithfat.wordpress.com/2013/04/01/what-to-say-at-the-doctors-office. HAES expert Linda Bacon has a message for healthcare providers that patients can print off and bring to their appointment for discussion here: https://lindabacon.org/HAESbook/pdf_files/HAES_Providing%20Sensitive%20Care.pdf (Dr. Bacon has many more relevant resources on her website: https://lindabacon.org/_resources).

Many physicians can be educated by their patients to provide more appropriate care. However, patients should not have to do the work of protecting themselves against weight-based discrimination and abuse at the doctor's office. It may be worth affirming your client's right to a size-inclusive, nonstigmatizing healthcare professional. (Note that even if your client can obtain such a provider, this does not ameliorate the effects of size-based stigma on her health, since this pervasive stigma affects the evidence base used to make treatment decisions for her, the equipment and training physicians are provided to treat her with, and sometimes the financial resources she has available to access care.) Nevertheless, a size-accepting or HAES-practicing healthcare provider can go a long way toward helping your clients get appropriate health care. The HAES Community and the Association for Size Diversity and Health both maintain lists of HAES-friendly providers. The HAES Community list is here: https://haescommunity.com/search; and the ASDAH provider search function is here: www.sizediversityandhealth.org/content.asp?id=32.

If no local providers are available in your community, or if available providers are inaccessible because of financial or other reasons, then assisting clients to advocate for their needs and to stand up to discrimination using role-plays and written materials may still help your client get effective medical care, despite the presence of discrimination. An advocate of any kind is helpful; you can be that advocate for your clients.

## HAES Approaches to Diabetes and Cardiovascular Health

If you're not going to prescribe weight loss to clients with chronic, obesity-associated diseases, how can you help them? The first question to ask is whether your help with physical health concerns is even being sought. Clients with weight concerns and obesity-associated chronic diseases may or may not want help from you as a clinician in addressing their physical health. Other concerns may be more relevant. If you are aware that a client has a physical health problem, but their magic wand fantasy focuses on other concerns, such as self-esteem or romantic relationships or leisure pursuits, then it may be more appropriate to focus on their dreams, goals, and values, rather than the clinician's concerns. This is a place to check for implicit weight stigma: Is your urge to help a thin client with physical health problems as intense as with a fat client?

If clients do include better physical health as part of their magic wand fantasy, then it may be an appropriate focus of treatment. (Clients may insist that this is one area that cannot improve without weight loss, and may include it as a way of testing whether the clinician plans to stick to the HAES approach.) In this section, several common obesity-associated chronic health concerns that may benefit from lifestyle modification are discussed, including diabetes, hypertension, and cardiovascular disease risk.

A focus on physical health concerns in *Accept Yourself!* treatment necessarily involves discussing healthism, weight stigma, and the shame clients may feel about having a disease that is associated with obesity. It's important to help clients understand that their diseases are not their fault, regardless of their size, activity level, eating habits, or other lifestyle factors. Diseases are multiply determined; in the case of diabetes and cardiovascular disease, genetic factors likely contribute the most explanatory power in understanding why any given person developed a chronic disease. (It can be worth asking clients what diseases run in their families, and noting the diversity of life experiences among various family members that nonetheless share these diseases.) Clients should also know that people of all sizes, including thin people, get obesity-associated diseases. Health is individualized, and does not perfectly correlate with size. (HAES expert Linda Bacon has a useful handout to share with patients who have diseases blamed on their body size, which is available here: https://lindabacon. org/HAESbook/pdf_files/HAES_Message%20for%20People%20with%20 Disease.pdf.)

The first step in helping clients manage chronic obesity-associated diseases is to make sure they have ready access to appropriate medical care and are able to use it without engaging in avoidance. Clients with significant shame related to having diabetes or hypertension or heart disease may avoid their physicians, be stigmatized by their physicians when they do go, may avoid taking medications or monitoring blood pressure or blood sugar at home to avoid shame or stigma from family members, or may avoid taking medications (e.g., insulin) that must be taken during the workday out of fear that their illness will be discovered and shamed by others.

Because the focus in *Accept Yourself!* is on helping clients access resources to support their health, and on developing an individualized interoceptive awareness of behaviors to enhance good health, clients must be able to both access and use medical care and engage in physical health-related self-monitoring to get benefit out of any behavioral interventions. In *Accept Yourself!* physical and mental health and the behaviors that will support them are all conceptualized as individualized. There is no one healthful diet or healthful exercise regimen that clients should all implement in the *Accept Yourself!* framework, so to learn what is healthful for their bodies, clients need to develop their mindfulness, acceptance, and interoceptive awareness skills. When learning to attend to the subtle or sometimes invisible body cues associated with chronic disease, clients may also benefit from outside feedback (other than weight change) to help increase interoceptive awareness and monitor whether a behavior change really is or is not helpful for their physical health. Therefore, first steps in helping clients with chronic diseases often involve helping clients establish self-monitoring of their disease, and practice acceptance related to emotions, such as shame or fear, that emerge when they take a closer look at their health in an ongoing way.

For example, a client with hypertension might obtain a home sphegnometer and begin monitoring her blood pressure daily or weekly. A client with diabetes might begin regular blood glucose monitoring. Clients at risk for cardiovascular disease might want to partner with their physicians to discuss tests they could use to monitor whether or not behavioral health changes made any difference to their cardiac health: Should they monitor their blood lipids? Should they get a $VO_2$ max test or do a six-minute walk test or another test of cardiovascular fitness? (As an aside, it is worth observing that modifying cardiovascular disease risk factors, such as lipids, does not always lower the risk of acquiring a disease or reduce its mortality and morbidity. Clinicians should familiarize themselves primarily with experimental research on modifiable risk factors as they affect actual diseases, not other risk factors. As we discussed in Chapter 1, for many diseases there is surprisingly little evidence that any lifestyle factor affects actual disease risk, or morbidity and mortality, but this varies depending on disease.)

Once clients have some data about their bodies that is not linked to weight, it becomes possible to experiment with making behavioral changes. However, behavioral changes should be based on three factors: (1) Clients should address problems they actually have (or are at clearly defined risk for), rather than "eating healthy" or "developing an exercise routine" for its own sake; (2) clinicians should use relevant research to make recommendations about specific, high-priority behavioral changes to experiment with, rather than encouraging broad health changes; and (3) clients should be taught to self-monitor and self-assess to see whether changes are helping. Clinicians should allow clients to admit when a change isn't helping, and to discard it without shame.

Why should clinicians not encourage "healthy eating" or "an exercise routine" in healthy clients in general? The goal in *Accept Yourself!*, of course, is to help clients develop a healthy relationship with food, to eat nutritiously, and in a way that supports physical health, and to enjoy the physical vitality involved in moving our bodies. However, standard recommendations for healthy eating and exercise are restrictive, related to weight loss, and often encourage clients with a history of unsuccessful dieting or eating-disordered behaviors back into that unhelpful cycle. In *Accept Yourself!* the goal is for clients to become more self-aware about what their bodies need, ask for, and what feels good to their bodies to receive. To support that goal, research-based recommendations specific to problems clients actually have, coupled with self-monitoring of changes as they are implemented, helps clients develop greater self-awareness of how their health does or does not respond to their behavior.

## Helping Clients Pursue Health Goals

What health changes should clients attempt? For hypertension, there is reasonable evidence that for some people engaging in regular physical activity, following the DASH diet (a heart-healthy eating plan that is not necessarily aimed at weight loss), eating less salt and decreasing sodium in the diet, and decreasing alcohol consumption all may help. The National Heart, Lung, and Blood Institute has a detailed guide, including information about the DASH diet, here: https://www.nhlbi.nih.gov/files/docs/public/heart/hbp_low.pdf. However, this brochure recommends weight loss and does not take a HAES approach, so clinicians should modify it for use with clients to focus on the other recommendations.

For diabetes and impaired fasting glucose, besides regular medical attention, an *Accept Yourself!* approach to diabetes might involve taking frequent blood glucose readings using a home glucometer available in drug stores, and beginning to pay better attention to how food tastes and feels when clients eat it, afterwards, and how it seems to affect their blood glucose. The time of day when your clients eat, eating regular meals, eating in low-stress situations, and specific types and amounts of food all may affect your blood glucose. HAES expert Linda Bacon has an article about this approach to managing diabetes here: https://lindabacon.org/pdf/BaconMatz_Diabetes_EnjoyingFood.pdf. Michelle May, M.D., and Megrette Fletcher, a dietician, have developed a HAES-based plan for eating well with diabetes; information about their program is available here: http://amihungry.com/programs/mindful-eating-for-diabetes/how-it-works; and a meal planning handout based on their program is available here: http://amihungry.com/pdf/Eat-What-You-Love-with-Diabetes-Plate-and-Tips.pdf.

In terms of improving lipid profiles, the most important step clients can take to lower LDL (low-density lipoprotein) and total cholesterol is to quit smoking. The next priority is to limit saturated fats. Avoiding trans fats and eating foods fortified with plant sterols/stanols also has some research support to suggest they might be helpful. Lower priority changes that might also help include limiting dietary cholesterol and eating more foods high in soluble fiber. To lower triglycerides and increase HDL (high-density lipoprotein) cholesterol, again the highest priority is to quit smoking. The next highest priority is physical activity: 30 minutes of at-least-moderate-intensity physical activity 6–7 days a week, all at once or broken up into 10-minute intervals, are all thought to be helpful. Other changes with some research support include eating more omega-3 fatty acids, eating more monounsaturated fatty acids, and drinking 1–2 standard drinks per day of wine or beer among clients who are already drinking.

With any of these lifestyle changes, however, you will want to research the latest findings with respect to efficacy, particularly for disease, not just risk factors. For example, although limiting saturated fats does, indeed, improve lipid profiles, recent meta-analyses have suggested that this makes little difference in whether one actually acquires cardiovascular disease (Siri-Torino, Sun, Hu, & Krauss, 2010). In addition, you'll want to encourage clients to make *just one* change at a time, to commit to sticking with it for a specified period of time, and to carefully evaluate how that change works, feels, and whether it has any impact on a health indicator the client is actually monitoring. Clinicians should help clients develop specific, behavioral, measurable goals, and should use mindfulness techniques to help clients explore how the change affects them in terms of taste, physical and body sensations, both immediately and over time. If a change does not make a difference, clients should be allowed to discard it without judgment. Lifestyle changes do not help all clients with obesity-associated diseases, and they should not be coerced into staying with an ineffective strategy because it satisfies the cultural rule that fat people should be hard-working and repentant about their fat. Clinicians should also be careful to help and encourage clients to integrate health behavior change with non-stigmatizing medical care. If the client discovers, for example, that avoiding saturated fat makes little difference in her very high cholesterol levels, with her family history of premature heart disease, having a physician prescribe a statin, if clinically indicated, which she then is able to observe does successfully lower her cholesterol, serves to enhance both her health and her self-awareness about body changes that benefit her.

Chapter 3 of the accompanying self-help manual features additional guidelines to help clients make and evaluate a health change. Clinicians can help most by fostering a curious spirit, wherein the client is encouraged to look to her own bodily experiences and test results, rather than arbitrary social rules about healthy eating and exercise and fatness, to evaluate the benefits of health changes she chooses to make.

# References

Aucott, L., Poobalan, A., Smith, W. C. S., Avenell, A., Jung, R., & Broom, J. (2005). Effects of weight loss in overweight/obese individuals and long-term hypertension outcomes. *Hypertension, 45*(6), 1035–1041.

Bangalore, S., Fayyad, R., Laskey, R., DeMicco, D. A., Messerli, F. H., & Waters, D. D. (2017). Body-weight fluctuations and outcomes in coronary disease. *New England Journal of Medicine, 376*(14), 1332–40.

Barry, V. W., Baruth, M., Beets, M. W., Durstine, J. L., Liu, J., & Blair, S. N. (2014). Fitness vs. fatness on all-cause mortality: A meta-analysis. *Progress in Cardiovascular Diseases, 56*(4), 382–390.

Blackburn, G. (1995). Effect of degree of weight loss on health benefits. *Obesity, 3*(S2).

Diabetes Prevention Program Research Group. (2009). 10-year follow-up of diabetes incidence and weight loss in the Diabetes Prevention Program Outcomes Study. *The Lancet, 374*(9702), 1677–1686.

Douketis, J. D., Macie, C., Thabane, L., & Williamson, D. F. (2005). Systematic review of long-term weight loss studies in obese adults: Clinical significance and applicability to clinical practice. *International Journal of Obesity, 29*(10), 1153–1167.

Fildes, A., Charlton, J., Rudisill, C., Littlejohns, P., Prevost, A. T., & Gulliford, M. C. (2015). Probability of an obese person attaining normal body weight: Cohort study using electronic health records. *American Journal of Public Health, 105*(9), e54-e59.

Franz, M. J., VanWormer, J. J., Crain, A. L., Boucher, J. L., Histon, T., Caplan, W., ... & Pronk, N. P. (2007). Weight-loss outcomes: A systematic review and meta-analysis of weight-loss clinical trials with a minimum 1-year follow-up. *Journal of the American Dietetic Association, 107*, 1755–1767.

Hainer, V., & Aldhoon-Hainerová, I. (2013). Obesity paradox does exist. *Diabetes Care, 36* (Supplement 2), S276–S281.

Horvath, K., Jeitler, K., Siering, U., Stich, A. K., Skipka, G., Gratzer, T. W., & Siebenhofer, A. (2008). Long-term effects of weight-reducing interventions in hypertensive patients: systematic review and meta-analysis. *Archives of Internal Medicine, 168*(6), 571–580.

Lavie, C. J., McAuley, P. A., Church, T. S., Milani, R. V., & Blair, S. N. (2014). Obesity and cardiovascular diseases: implications regarding fitness, fatness, and severity in the obesity paradox. *Journal of the American College of Cardiology, 63*(14), 1345–1354.

Lavie, C.J., De Schutter, A., & Milani, R.V. (2015). Body composition and the obesity paradox in coronary heart disease: Can heavier really be healthier? *Heart, 101*, 1610–1611.

Look AHEAD Research Group (2013). Cardiovascular effects of intensive lifestyle intervention in type 2 diabetes. *The New England Journal of Medicine, 369*(2), 145–152.

Maggard-Gibbons, M., Maglione, M., Livhits, M., Ewing, B., Maher, A. R., Hu, J., ... & Shekelle, P. G. (2013). Bariatric surgery for weight loss and glycemic control in nonmorbidly obese adults with diabetes: A systematic review. *Journal of the American Medical Association, 309*(21), 2250–2261.

Montani, J. P., Schutz, Y., & Dulloo, A. G. (2015). Dieting and weight cycling as risk factors for cardiometabolic diseases: Who is really at risk? *Obesity Reviews, 16*(S1), 7–18.

Neter, J. E., Stam, B. E., Kok, F. J., Grobbee, D. E., & Geleijnse, J. M. (2003). Influence of weight reduction on blood pressure. *Hypertension, 42*(5), 878–884.

Norris, S. L., Zhang, X., Avenell, A., Gregg, E., Schmid, C. H., Kim, C., & Lau, J. (2004). Efficacy of pharmacotherapy for weight loss in adults with type 2 diabetes mellitus: a meta-analysis. *Archives of Internal Medicine, 164*(13), 1395–1404.

Siri-Tarino, P. W., Sun, Q., Hu, F. B., & Krauss, R. M. (2010). Meta-analysis of prospective cohort studies evaluating the association of saturated fat with cardiovascular disease. *The American Journal of Clinical Nutrition, 91*(3), 535–546.

Unick, J. L., Beavers, D., Bond, D. S., Clark, J. M., Jakicic, J. M., Kitabchi, A. E., ... & Look AHEAD Research Group (2013). The long-term effectiveness of a lifestyle intervention in severely obese individuals. *The American Journal of Medicine, 126*(3), 236–242.

Warkentin, L. M., Das, D., Majumdar, S. R., Johnson, J. A., & Padwal, R. S. (2014). The effect of weight loss on health-related quality of life: Systematic review and meta-analysis of randomized trials. *Obesity Reviews, 15*(3), 169–182.

Welti, L. M., Beavers, D. P., Caan, B. J., Sangi-Haghpeykar, H., Vitolins, M. Z., & Beavers, K. M. (2017). Weight fluctuation and cancer risk in postmenopausal women: The Women's Health Initiative. *Cancer Epidemiology and Prevention Biomarkers, 26*(5), 779–786.

# 13 Special Topics in Self-Acceptance-Based Treatment

## Beginning Treatment: Informed Consent for Acceptance-Based Weight Management and Clarifying the Clinician's Stance and Limits

How do you go about introducing the *Accept Yourself!* approach to clients who present for help with weight management? Although body positivity is increasing as a social movement thanks to the hard work of size-acceptance activists for many years, I have yet to have a client present to treatment with me asking for help with self-acceptance or learning to love her body as it is. In general, clients who ultimately complete the *Accept Yourself!* program initially present asking for help with weight loss, and also acknowledging a variety of co-occuring concerns, such as depression, body image problems, disordered or "emotional" eating, and other mental health issues.

Ethical treatment includes informed consent: Clients who present requesting weight loss cannot be offered *Accept Yourself!* instead without a clear understanding and willingness around the reality that weight loss is neither the goal nor the likely outcome of the program. In addition, because of the differing goals and strategies for treatment held by *Accept Yourself!* clinicians and weight-loss-seeking clients at treatment outset, clients and clinicians are unlikely to be in a state of goal consensus about treatment (i.e., unlikely to agree on goals, strategies, and tasks for client and clinician). Psychotherapy research has demonstrated that goal consensus is an effective element of the empirically supported psychotherapy relationship, and important for good client outcomes (Tryon & Winograd, 2011). The informed consent process is thus essential to beginning *Accept Yourself!* treatment successfully, in order to help clients and clinicians achieve goal consensus and to discharge the clinician's ethical obligation to make certain that clients understand and are choosing to engage in this approach in lieu of weight loss.

Treatment should begin with a comprehensive intake and clinical interview, as the clinician might do for any type of treatment and client concern. Clinicians should consider if they want to use outcome measures for treatment, and what those outcome measures should be, whether a standard battery given to all clients or an individualized set of measures based on the client's concerns. Collecting client feedback about outcomes of psychotherapy is also a demonstrated effective element of the empirically supported psychotherapy relationship, and helps the clinician identify if treatment is helpful, or stalled and requires modification to be effective (Lambert & Shimokawa, 2011). Collecting outcome data regularly prior to treatment, during the informed consent process, and during and after treatment also allows clinicians to investigate empirically whether *Accept Yourself!* treatment is effective for the client, which may be especially important to assure both client and clinician that this novel treatment is appropriate. Free statistical packages and guidance are available to clinicians who wish to use outcome measures to test hypotheses about the efficacy of treatment in single-case designs (e.g., Borckardt et al., 2008).

What outcome measures might be appropriate in this treatment? Although in the pilot research on *Accept Yourself!* we collected client weight data, as a safety outcome, primarily to assure funders and others that the approach did not cause substantial weight *gain*, in clinical practice I do not generally collect client weight data when using *Accept Yourself!* There is one exception: I collect client weight blind (without showing the client) at every session for underweight clients or those that meet criteria for anorexia nervosa (for whom *Accept Yourself!* is not appropriate as a standalone treatment), unless that client is also receiving concurrent weekly or biweekly medical follow-up, as a rough means of ensuring that I refer underweight clients to a higher level of care if they are losing weight or may be at risk of becoming medically unstable. However, client weight is not a target in *Accept Yourself!* treatment, and it is important that both clients and clinicians understand that it is not considered relevant to the treatment's efficacy. If clients ask me whether they will gain or lose weight in *Accept Yourself!* I generally respond that most clients experience little weight change, whereas some gain a little or lose a little, and that all of these outcomes are acceptable in effective treatment. Thus, weight is not a useful outcome measure.

Other measures of physical health could be considered, however. The clinician may want to monitor the client's blood pressure, lipids, or fasting blood glucose periodically through treatment, or collect a measure of cardiovascular fitness, such as $VO_2$ max, performance on a six-minute walk test, or a self-report measure of physical activity. Mental health measures should also be considered, such as measures of depression, obesity self-stigma, obesity-related quality of life, or eating-disorder measures. Finally, a measure of general psychotherapy outcome, such as the Outcome Questionnaire (OQ-45; Lambert & Finch, 1999), or of health-related functioning or quality of life in general, might also be a useful outcome measure for clients. Having outcome data available from the beginning to end of treatment can be very powerful for clients, especially in bolstering their self-acceptance. Being able to observe that regardless of weight, mood, self-image, physical health, and wellness improved in concrete ways in treatment is a powerful gift clinicians can offer clients at treatment termination.

Once clinicians have completed their intake process and collected any initial baseline outcome data, clinicians should provide their case formulation (and diagnoses, if any) to the client. The client's goals for treatment can be elicited at this point, and this is often the point in therapy where clients discuss in detail their weight loss goals. Be certain to *ask* why the client is hoping to achieve weight loss: These are the real goals of treatment, and knowing them helps the clinician to explain how *Accept Yourself!* can be helpful, even though it will not be using the strategy the client expects.

Once the client understands the clinician's diagnoses and formulation of her problem, and has stated her goals, the gap between the clinician's and the client's goals may have become evident. It is at this point that the clinician can begin to make treatment recommendations. I explain to clients at the outset that although I have expertise in eating behavior, eating disorders, and weight management, I do not engage in behavioral weight loss with clients, because I do not believe the research literature supports its efficacy. I tell the client that I instead use an alternative approach that I believe offers better outcomes for weight-concerned clients, but which does not focus on or cause weight loss. I never present *Accept Yourself!* as the only option for clients, and, indeed, I always leave open the possibility of referring clients for behavioral weight loss if, at the end of a discussion about why I do not do this type of treatment, they are still interested in pursuing a weight-loss-focused approach. I may present other treatment options as well, if they appear indicated. For example, if a client has severe generalized anxiety, as well as weight and body-image concerns I might offer as an option a treatment primarily focused on her anxiety rather than *Accept Yourself!* Providing clients with choices for their treatment helps to create goal consensus and enhances their commitment to the *Accept Yourself!* approach if they choose it.

Having briefly discussed options for treatment, I then present to clients the reasons why I personally do not offer behavioral weight loss as a service. This means a somewhat formal presentation of much of the information presented in Chapter 1, and in Chapter 2 of the accompanying self-help manual. This research is surprising for clients (as it may have been surprising for you), and it is wise to have copies of research articles and lists of citations available for clients who want verification of the data presented. Once these data are presented, by way of explaining why I do not offer behavioral weight loss or even consider it ethical to offer to my clients, I then offer a caveat.

Medical and psychological research is conducted on the average patient (and, in some ways, on an average *exceptional* patient – one with the set of unique characteristics that matches the inclusion and exclusion criteria for a given randomized controlled trial). I have never met – and neither have you – the average patient. Every person who walks into my practice presenting for care is not at all average. She is an individual, who varies in a myriad of ways we cannot possibly know from the "average" patient on whom we do research and for whom we make treatment recommendations. So when I tell clients that the average patient, for example, does not lose weight and often gains weight in behavioral weight loss interventions, it is reasonable to assume that my client is like this average patient. However, even though this is a reasonable assumption and a useful basis on which to make initial treatment decisions, my client may be unusual or exceptional compared with the average. Weight loss interventions might be as unhelpful for her as for most people, even more unhelpful and harmful, or more helpful than they are for most. Once the client understand this, the clinician can invite her to explore her own personal history with weight loss in order to make a treatment recommendation with the best combination of research data on average patients and data specific to her. The creative hopelessness techniques described in Chapter 4 of this volume and Chapter 1 of the accompanying self-help manual serve a dual purpose. Not only do they help clients identify and collect data on how weight loss strategies have really worked for them, they also bolster commitment to an alternative approach.

At some point, either after presenting the research data on the poor efficacy of weight loss strategies, in general, or after a detailed exploration of the likelihood of weight loss strategy efficacy for this particular client using a creative hopelessness approach, I return to enquire and be certain that the client would like to use the *Accept Yourself!* approach rather than any of the alternatives presented. If clients absolutely insist on behavioral weight loss at this point, I advise them to seek out that service, paying careful attention to the short- and long-term impacts on their physical and emotional well-being. However, I have rarely had to make that recommendation. The combination of research data and personal experience, carefully and honestly presented, is usually damning in the eyes of the client to a weight loss approach, and she is usually willing and curious to try a different alternative. When a client insists on weight loss, I invite her to come back in the future if she finds that it is not effective, and I wish her well in her journey. It is important for clinicians to remember that weight loss outcomes are highly idiosyncratic and variable, and that clients are the best determiners of their needs and outcomes. An openness to allowing clients' experiences to teach them and you will help them choose the best approach for their needs in the moment.

Clients who insist on it – who cannot be dissuaded from it even after a full informed consent process describing the risks of weight loss – may seek out weight loss. However, clinicians should not offer both behavioral weight loss and *Accept Yourself!* to their clients. Clients who insist on behavioral weight loss should not be treated by the *Accept Yourself!* clinician. As discussed in Chapter 2, clinicians who are committed to evidence-based practice should not be offering behavioral weight loss to clients in any event, and there are serious ethical concerns with offering behavioral weight loss under the best of circumstances. In addition, there are no benefits that come with weight loss that cannot be pursued through *Accept Yourself!* or another approach. Clinicians who have difficulty giving up behavioral weight loss should consider their own weight-stigma and their own relationship with body image and body size: Are you able to practice self-acceptance with your own body? With all bodies of all sizes you may encounter in practice? If not, you might consider working through the exercises in this book and in the accompanying self-help manual, both to enhance your self-reflection and to learn if this approach is right for you as a clinician. If after that experience you still feel that behavioral weight loss is an essential part of your practice, you might consider specializing exclusively in that, rather than using *Accept Yourself!*

## Ending Self-Acceptance-Based Treatments

*Accept Yourself!* is a relatively structured treatment. The group-based version that we evaluated in pilot research and continue to study (as described in Chapter 3) has a published session-by-session protocol (Berman, Morton, & Hegel, 2016). And, as is true for Acceptance and Commitment Therapies in general, *Accept Yourself!* can also be implemented flexibly, as the clinician sees fit, as long as the processes of creative hopelessness, defusion, mindfulness, acceptance, values clarification, and commitment are included, and the Acceptance and Commitment and Health At Every Size (HAES) Principles described herein are consistently taught. However, it is clear that whether implemented as a treatment manual with a specified number of sessions in a specified order or implemented more flexibly, this approach is a time-limited treatment, with specific content to be taught and experienced by clients over some definable period of time. (In the pilot research, the treatment was delivered in 11 two- or three-hour group sessions.) Therefore, *Accept Yourself!* treatment will have an endpoint, and it is important to consider termination concerns, as well as plan for termination from the outset of treatment.

Clients are ready for termination when they have a regular mindfulness practice of some kind; are able to take their thoughts about weight and shape and self-image lightly, without seeing them as the truth or requiring a response one way or the other; are no longer focused on weight loss or weight gain as an outcome to be attained or avoided; have begun to engage in activities that formerly they avoided because of body image, mood, or eating concerns; express willingness to continue to engage in acceptance in situations that once prompted avoidance; have explored and clarified their values related to food, self-presentation, movement, and other important aspects of life; and have begun acting on their valued commitments in these areas. It is likely, if these therapeutic goals are attained, that they will have experienced clinically significant improvements on outcome measures as well.

Termination should include helping clients to generalize their therapy experiences, although, in general, by the time termination is being considered, this process has already begun, both because clients are accustomed to doing acceptance and valued living practice as homework, and they have had the opportunity to experience the benefits of these activities directly and been reinforced by them. One client expressed this idea by noting, toward the end of treatment, that "I realize my brain can't be trusted – it says to avoid or else, but when I lean in, it's almost always so much better and easier. It's gotten so I just do whatever is the opposite of what my avoiding brain suggests!" Clinicians may want to taper treatment, moving from weekly to biweekly or monthly sessions, before ending treatment. When a tapering schedule is used, clients often benefit from scheduling a self-therapy session on the off weeks, making time during their usual appointment time to sit down with themselves, review their progress toward acceptance and valued living for the week, and set their own homework.

One of the most important issues for termination involves helping clients locate other sources of size-acceptance support. The clinician may have been the first (and may still be the only) person in her life to accept her size and not urge her to change it or treat her with weight-based abuse and discrimination. Other important people in the client's life, including family, spouses, health professionals, and friends, may still believe she should lose weight, or that she intends to, and they may see her treatment as a failure and disparage her investment in it. In a fat-hating culture, having allies beyond the therapist can be an essential form of support. Therefore, a major focus of termination should be on helping clients identify and connect with endogenous sources of size acceptance support. This book and the accompanying self-help manual are full of online and publication resources that clients can use to find support. Online communities like those at Shakesville (www.shakesville.com/search?q=fat+fashion), the HAES Community (https://haescommunity.com), the Association for Size Diversity and Health (ASDAH; www.sizediversityandhealth.org), and the Fit Fatties Forum (http://fitfatties.ning.com), as well as Instagram/Twitter/Facebook hashtags like #effyourbeautystandards, can all help clients find sources of support. Online communities can also help clients link up with local supporters, such as by finding HAES-friendly providers at the HAES Community or ASDAH. Clinicians should discuss with clients who can serve as a source of size acceptance support in their lives, and a topic for self-therapy during treatment tapering should be researching online and face-to-face (if available) communities of support. Clients may wish, toward the end of treatment, to practice being more public in their size acceptance and to practice standing up assertively to any discrimination that they encounter as they stand up in public. Some clients choose to keep their size acceptance private, sometimes out of atonement for weight loss evangelizing they may have done in the past. One client said, "I've learned I can't tell other people how to live in their bodies, I can only live my best in mine." However, for clients who want to support women in similar struggles, being more public with size acceptance experiences and ideas, by posting on social media, or speaking assertively to discriminatory family members or through other actions, can be a powerful mix of acceptance and valued action that helps clients continue on their independent journey.

Clients who continue to have significant psychological symptoms after *Accept Yourself!* should be re-evaluated for co-occuring concerns and current goals. Some common issues that may not be fully resolved after *Accept Yourself!*

include eating disorders (including binge eating disorder), depression (particularly if there are unrelated stressors or other prompting events), and anxiety disorders and post-traumatic stress disorder (because these are relatively common but not targeted specifically by *Accept Yourself!*). Clients may require additional treatment using a different treatment modality or referral to address these concerns. If making a referral, ideally, clinicians should refer to other HAES-friendly providers.

Clinicians should also give some thought to and discuss with clients how they might like to mark their progress in treatment and celebrate the accomplishment that termination represents. Perhaps the client would like to wear an outfit she previously thought was off limits for her to the final session, or would like to share some celebratory foods with the clinician, or perhaps she would like to do a movement activity with the clinician if this has been part of treatment which she has valued.

In a group setting, participants are encouraged to bring something meaningful to share – a food from their cultural tradition, an activity, or a gift. Clients have developed creative gifts to share at this final group celebration. One client brought her "proposal chicken" to share – a dish she had invented that was so delicious she'd been given marriage proposals by two different men to whom she had served it. One brought giant-sized whoopie pies, an indulgence she had once forbidden herself. Another brought framed collages of body-accepting affirmations for each participant, complete with a sprig of rosemary in each collage, to symbolize remembrance. One brought shell leis she had gotten on the beach in Hawaii, where she had finally developed the courage to travel in her current body, rather than waiting for weight loss. One Pilates instructor led her peers in some gentle Pilates movements.

In individual treatment, the clinician may wish to consider if she/he wishes to share a token gift of some kind with the client for her to take on her journey. If the clinician chooses to provide a gift, a size-acceptance book is a good choice. If the clinician has collected outcome data, a graph of client's progress in treatment can be a meaningful gift at the end of treatment, and it can also help plan for future treatment needs.

## Coping with Common Problems in Practice

A variety of clinical problems may emerge in offering *Accept Yourself!* treatment, in both individual and group formats. Although this is not an exhaustive list, these are some of the clinical problems commonly observed, and how clinicians can begin to address them. Some of these problems we have previously described in another publication (Berman, Morton, & Hegel, 2016).

### Binge Eating Disorder and Other Eating Disorders

It is not unusual for *Accept Yourself!* clients to have some co-occuring eating pathology. If a weight-concerned client meets criteria for full or subclinical anorexia nervosa or bulimia nervosa, referral for specialty treatment for those disorders is probably indicated before or instead of *Accept Yourself!* Anorexia and bulimia are both associated with high morbidity and mortality (Chesney, Goodwin, & Fazel, 2014; Crow et al., 2009), and because *Accept Yourself!* does not directly target these disorders, it may represent inadequate treatment for them. Similarly, *Accept Yourself!* is not empirically supported as a treatment for binge eating disorder (BED). However, given that the mortality risk in BED is lower than in the other eating disorders, and given that body image and weight concerns are common in BED, it may be appropriate to offer *Accept Yourself!* concurrently with another, more evidence-based treatment, such as cognitive behavioral therapy (CBT) for BED, and the two treatments may support each other. Treating a client with BED exclusively with *Accept Yourself!* can lead to clinical problems, as the chaotic eating patterns, restriction, and binging that BED sufferers engage in may draw clinical attention away from other concerns. I have no empirical data to offer, but can report that clinically I have treated women with BED using the two modalities (CBT and *Accept Yourself!*) concurrently in twice-weekly individual sessions to apparently good outcome.

### The Body Disparagement-Free Zone in a Group Setting

In group treatment, clients are encouraged to create a body disparagement-free zone (see Chapter 5). Participants are asked to notice that even though their minds may produce negatively judgmental "chatter" about their own and others' weight, shape, eating, and movements, it is possible to witness these thoughts without acting on them by voicing them aloud. Participants are given the body disparagement-free zone doorhangers described in Chapter 5 and are asked to hang them at home, and a similar doorhanger is hung on the group door during sessions. However, participants do make body-disparaging comments about themselves and others during group. This is mostly either self-directed or directed at photographs displayed during group, but can include invalidating comments about other participants, as well. For example, a larger participant may comment disparagingly about a smaller participant's "feelings of fatness." When any form of this occurs, the clinician should point it out, stop the behavior, and ask participants to observe these thoughts as thoughts without acting on them, creating a norm within the group that such comments are not acceptable, although the thoughts that give rise to them are to be expected (and accepted). In addition, when such comments are directed at peers or photographs, they represent an opportunity to discuss how participants wish to approach size diversity within the group, and what their values are related to making comments about other women's appearance. Therapist comments about these participant comments can be experienced as embarrassing, an emotion that participants can be encouraged to experience and tolerate in service to their values. For example, one participant in our pilot research described this as follows ("P" refers to participant; "T" to therapist; comments are derived from qualitative interviews described below):

P: This was exactly what I needed: A little slap on my hand to sometimes close my mouth and not to say something that really might have been hurtful to other women there. I thought about it at home a lot. This was when you were showing women, fat women, some of them just with their underwear and they looked kind of … you know … not too aesthetic. You know. But I thought that at that time; now I don't.

T: Sounds like you were hurt at that time.

P: Yeah. I think I may have offended other people and I didn't think about it.

### Waiting for a Control Strategy That Never Comes

Despite the informed consent process, weight-concerned clients expect to be prescribed weight loss, and they may consider weight loss a prerequisite for mental and physical health. Clients may not believe that weight loss is not an aim of the program, nor that engaging in treatment will not cause weight loss, and they may continue to hold these beliefs regardless of informed consent or how many times this is discussed in treatment. Some clients may remain fused with the idea that weight loss is necessary to achieve health, and this belief should be a target of defusion and valued living experiments. For example, when asked about unhelpful or detrimental aspects of the *Accept Yourself!* group in our pilot research program, one participant responded:

P: Um. I wouldn't say detrimental. I think the acceptance, that you're not gonna change, you're not gonna get thin, this is not about losing weight. That's the hardest one to take, and you, you think you're there, and then you get knocked back down. … Um, it, it's not detrimental, but it was the hardest part, is the actual acceptance, like, oh, this is how I am, and this is fine, and I don't need to work so hard to try to change it because it's not gonna change.

T: Uh huh. Well, sounds like that was a really difficult mental shift to make.

P: Well, I never … I don't remember hearing you say that it wasn't about weight loss. I, the whole time, was thinking, okay, where's the trick?

Ongoing creative hopelessness strategies, enthusiastic support for body diversity and display of a variety of images of fat women engaging in valued health behaviors during treatment and throughout the treatment context (e.g., in waiting rooms and offices), as well as repeated, clear communication about the aims of treatment may help to address this problem. Fat female clinicians may have an advantage over other clinicians in communicating this message. If you are not a fat woman, including and privileging the perspectives of your fat female colleagues as group co-facilitators or members of a group practice may also make this message more persuasive and enhance the practice's or group's efficacy.

### Depressing Stressors

Clients are often coping with depressogenic life events unrelated to body image. Caregiving for elderly family members, family drug addiction, financial limitations, relationship conflicts, loneliness, and other stressors unrelated to body image were all issues raised in our pilot groups. Such stressors contribute to participants' pain, and yet the nature of treatment means there is little focus on them, especially in a group format. For example, one pilot group participant, when asked what might have helped her more in the group stated:

P:  Maybe talking more about what was, you know, what the main issues were. And less about weight.
T:  So that sounds like, for you, if you could have talked more about what was going on with your [family member] and some of those other issues and gotten some support earlier that might have helped more.
P:  I think, yeah.

In individual treatment, clinicians can make time to talk about these concerns and use ACT strategies related to values, acceptance, mindfulness, committed action, and defusion to address them, while remaining mindful not to veer off course into unrelated treatment on a permanent basis. In a group, participants can be encouraged to use one another for social support around stressors, as well as use these same ACT strategies to address them.

### "Comforting"

A common pitfall for beginning ACT therapists that also emerges among participants in a group context occurs when a client's emotion arises and is made visible to the clinician and/or group members. In ACT, all emotions are permissible, and clinicians must develop acceptance around both their own and their clients' emotions. Actions taken to contain or suppress client (or clinician) emotions in session, as opposed to mindfully experiencing them, are contrary to the spirit of ACT. Clinicians can trust that client (and their own) emotions will ebb and flow during the session, and that no matter how intense a given emotional experience may be, it is sure to pass or change somewhat within a few minutes. Thus, appropriate interventions in the face of client emotion (as well as appropriate management of intense clinician emotion on the rare instance it arises in session) include a warm, quiet receptivity, and perhaps encouragement of the client to observe what she is noticing in her mind, body, and in the room (or similar inward encouragement of the clinician to him or herself). Although I keep tissues ready and within reach of clients in my office, I do not offer them myself to clients unless asked, as I do not want to communicate the message that clients need to "dry up" and stop crying. Emotion experienced by the clinician during a treatment session (e.g., crying at a moving client story) can be used to model a mindful acceptance of emotion. Clinicians can draw attention to their emotional expression gently, and note the interpersonal connection this represents with the client (e.g., "See? Your story has moved me to tears"). Clinicians should be mindful of their reaction to clients' or their own emotions in session, and note if any personal acceptance practice is needed to tolerate this effectively without encouraging the client to "bottle up."

Similarly, when emotion arises during group treatment, participants sometimes seek to control their own distress about this by encouraging peers to stop displaying emotion, for example by speaking to them, "comforting" them, passing tissues, and so on. This behavior can be gently noted and stopped by the clinician, and used as an opportunity for everyone to observe and experience the difficult emotions that arise when we witness pain.

## *Accept Yourself!* in Group versus Individual versus Self-Help Format

*Accept Yourself!* has been researched only in a group format, although it has been used in an individual format clinically, and perhaps more frequently. With the publication of the accompanying self-help manual, it is now also available for independent client use. How can a clinician choose which format to offer and recommend to clients?

Although we have no comparative data to make a definitive statement, group delivery of the intervention may be optimal. Clients experience the self-acceptance message of the treatment as novel, even countercultural. A group of peers who have faced (and sometimes conquered) similar struggles helps participants undertake acceptance and committed action behaviors. For example, one participant in our pilot research noted that her magic wand fantasy included getting a massage but that she had never done this, because she did not want to subject the massage therapist to her "disgusting" body. A second participant responded by giving her the card for her massage therapist, explaining that she had gotten massages regularly, and the therapist had never shamed her body. This kind of peer-to-peer support for valued behavior is highly compelling. In addition, the creative hopelessness intervention is more powerful when experienced in a group. Participants who are fused with the idea that *they* remain fat and depressed because of their inherent laziness and lack of motivation are able observe that *others'* lists of ineffective strategies to lose weight and feel better represent substantial, even Herculean, effort, and that if these strategies have not worked for anyone in the group, perhaps it is the strategies and not the participants who are to blame.

However, individual and self-help treatment modalities, although no data exist to support their efficacy, may be useful as well, and more practical for many applications than group treatment. In individual treatment (and guided self-help), the clinician must take special care to help the client facilitate a community of support around her self-acceptance. The clinician and/or the self-help book may be the only ally the client has supporting a self-acceptance message, against a life context that may be rich with weight-based abuse and discrimination. Helping the client expand that network of support beyond the therapy office is a primary clinical goal in individual *Accept Yourself!* treatment.

## Clients (and Clinicians) of Different Sizes

*Accept Yourself!* was pilot tested as a treatment for obese, depressed women. However, clinically it can be and has been used with women of diverse body sizes and types who experience weight concerns. Body image and weight concerns span the weight spectrum: People of all sizes believe they need to lose weight in order to be acceptable. Dieters are often normal or underweight (de Ridder, Adriaanse, Evers, & Verhoeven, 2014). People of all sizes even experience weight-based stigma, abuse, and discrimination. Looking at the comments section on any celebrity magazine website which profiles professionally thin and beautiful actors and models will reveal that the word "fat" is used to attempt to shame, hurt, and control women of all sizes, races, and levels of wealth and prestige. Clients often describe a history of being called "fat" (as an epithet) and experiencing weight-based discrimination and abuse from peers and family members, at weights that a body mass index (BMI) calculator will tell you are "normal." However, the issues clients face and the language that is appropriate to discuss their concerns varies for women of different sizes. In addition, even among women who meet BMI criteria for obesity, sizes vary significantly, and some clinical issues vary based on size.

Experiences of weight-based discrimination are associated with BMI (Puhl & Brownell, 2006). Heavier clients experience more weight-based abuse and stigma. In addition, normal-weight or underweight clients who struggle with body image and present asking for help with weight loss may have greater thin-ideal internalization than obese women with similar concerns. In other words, while clients of all sizes may have experienced weight-based abuse and discrimination, and may endorse a thin-ideal, the relative balance of these problems as foci of treatment may vary based on client body size.

Clinicians should be prepared to help clients of all sizes navigate the external barrier of weight-based discrimination, with the awareness that institutionalized oppression is more severe for clients of the largest sizes. Difficulty finding fashionable, attractive clothing (or any clothing at all), sports equipment, adaptive equipment, medical equipment, furniture, and suitable spaces to exist in public life all increase for clients of larger body sizes. These brick walls represent substantial barriers to clients engaging in valued living: It is difficult to obtain medical care if equipment and medicine is not sized or studied to fit. It is difficult to go places and do things if appropriate attire is not available. The most basic aspects of dignified life may be inaccessible to your fattest clients, even if somehow they do not experience any verbal or direct interpersonal size-based discrimination. However, for the largest clients, interpersonal discrimination and abuse based on weight and intersecting or interacting with other oppressed aspects of their identity, such as race, gender, disability, or sexual orientation, is likely to be common if not frequent.

A clinician stance of appropriate anger and social justice advocacy in the face of this discrimination can be validating for clients and helpful in engaging them to move mindfully through self-blame and shame. In addition, it is essential that clinicians screen their offices for structural discrimination against the fattest clients, as well as clients who experience intersecting oppression along multiple dimensions of identity. Are there comfortable, visibly solid and sturdy places to sit in your waiting room and office for clients of all sizes and heights? (Sofas can be particularly helpful.) Is there space to maneuver a wheelchair, cane, or other adaptive tools easily? If you have or use medical equipment (blood pressure cuff, scale), do you have options to smoothly accommodate all different-sized clients without undue fuss? Does artwork display clients of all sizes and other dimensions of human identity positively? Asking clients how to make your practice more accommodating may reveal unexamined examples of structural discrimination in the space.

In addition to creating as accommodating a space as possible in the clinician's office, clinicians should be prepared to model advocacy on behalf of clients of all sizes, particularly the largest sizes, out in the wider world. Exploring your own implicit biases, especially as they relate to the fattest clients and/or to clients with multiple oppressed identities, as well as allowing clients to see you advocating for social justice on their behalf in public and private spaces, can both be helpful here. For example, clinicians can help clients locate inexpensive custom clothiers, or advocate within hospitals and with medical professional colleagues for appropriate care for clients, or can network to help clients locate HAES-friendly professionals across disciplines to help them get better health care or access to other opportunities. A clinician stance that clients *deserve* all the tools and resources for a rich, valued life at any size, whether these tools are readily obtainable or not, can be helpful, as can creativity in locating resources.

For thin clients with weight concerns, the fear of becoming fat, and the idea of "feeling fat," may be a prominent aspect of treatment. Fat is not an emotion; one cannot "feel fat." Clinicians can help clients mindfully explore and experience what is being felt when the client "feels fat," and can help clients practice acceptance around these feelings. Clients can practice wearing clothes that make them "look" or "feel fat," and notice what arises. Deliberately wearing "unflattering" clothing can be a useful acceptance exercise for thin clients, and can result in liberation, as the client begins to have the opportunity to choose clothing based on her wishes, rather than on programming related to what "looks good" or "minimizes flaws." Similarly, the fear of becoming fat is a worthy target for defusion and acceptance. Clients can experiment with engaging in activities that they fear will lead to fatness, such as overeating "fattening" foods or avoiding exercise, and notice what emerges in mind and body when engaging in these behaviors mindfully. HAES clinicians do not value one body size over another, and should not collude with clients in calming fears of gaining weight. People do sometimes gain weight for all sorts of reasons; the client may gain weight at some point in her life. Rather than reassuring the client that this is unlikely to happen in treatment or if she gives up weight loss, the clinician should work on accepting and defusing this fear and helping the client live out her values with respect to being non-judgmental and supportive of other women in her life.

Clinicians should also be aware of the dynamic between clients of different sizes that may emerge in an *Accept Yourself!* group. Larger clients may be judgmental and disparaging of smaller clients' concerns, whereas smaller clients may express fear of becoming like the larger clients in body size, or relief that they are not "so fat." This same dynamic can emerge, often implicitly, as the client contemplates the clinician's body and compares it with her own (while possibly using the clinician's body size as a potential metric of the validity of the approach). HAES clinicians believe in the inherent, equivalent worth and value of bodies of all sizes and abilities. Judgments like the ones just described represent cultural programming to be observed as programming without engagement. A body disparagement-free zone may help highlight valued responses to such thoughts, while clinicians can work one-on-one to defuse thoughts of inferiority or superiority based on body size or capacity.

## Keeping in Contact and Learning More

At this point, you may be ready to experiment with using the *Accept Yourself!* approach, particularly in combination with the accompanying self-help manual. Involvement in ACT and HAES clinician communities may be especially helpful to you in seeking peer consultation and support as you begin. The Facebook group Health At Every Size Therapists and Nutritionists may be one source of support, as well as the Association for Size Diversity and Health (ASDAH) and the Association for Contextual Behavior Science. Because this approach is new, I am eager to hear your experiences in implementing it. I am grateful to you for doing this important work, and invite you to reach out to me at margit.i.berman@dartmouth.edu or at https://margitberman.com/ to provide feedback, share resources, or ask questions.

### Additional Readings

This is a by-no-means-exhaustive list of additional readings and resources you may wish to explore on your *Accept Yourself!* treatment development journey.

> *Get Out of Your Mind and Into Your Life*, by Steven C. Hayes, 2005.
> *Health At Every Size: The Surprising Truth About Your Weight*, by Linda Bacon, 2010.
> *Lessons from the Fat-O-Sphere: Quit Dieting and Declare a Truce with Your Body*, by Kate Harding and Marianne Kirby, 2009.

*Shadow on a Tightrope: Writings by Women on Fat Oppression*, edited by Lisa Schoenfielder and Barb Wieser, 1995.

*An Unapologetic Fat Girl's Guide to Exercise and Other Incendiary Acts*, by Hanne Blank, 2012.

*Women En Large: Images of Fat Nudes*, by Laurie Toby Edison and Debbie Notkin, 1994.

*Yoga XXL: A Journey to Health For Larger Bodies*, by Ingrid Kollak, 2013.

*Eat, Drink, and Be Mindful*, by Susan Albers, 2009.

*Body Respect*, by Linda Bacon and Lucy Aphramor, 2014.

*The Obesity Myth*, by Paul Campos, 2004.

*The Food and Feelings Workbook*, by Karen Koenig, 2007.

*The Diet Survivor's Handbook*, by Judith Matz and Ellen Frankel, 2006.

*Eat What You Love, Love What You Eat*, by Michelle May, 2011.

*Fat Politics*, by J. Eric Oliver, 2006.

*What's Wrong with Fat?*, by Abigail Saguy, 2014.

*Embody*, by Connie Sobczak, 2014.

*Intuitive Eating*, by Evelyn Tribole and Elyse Resch, 2012.

## References

Berman, M. I., Morton, S. N., & Hegel, M. T. (2016). Health at every size and acceptance and commitment therapy for obese, depressed women: Treatment development and clinical application. *Clinical Social Work Journal, 44*(3), 265–278.

Borckardt, J. J., Nash, M. R., Murphy, M. D., Moore, M., Shaw, D., & O'Neil, P. (2008). Clinical practice as natural laboratory for psychotherapy research: A guide to case-based time-series analysis. *American Psychologist, 63*(2), 77–95.

Chesney, E., Goodwin, G. M., & Fazel, S. (2014). Risks of all-cause and suicide mortality in mental disorders: A meta-review. *World Psychiatry, 13*(2), 153–160.

Crow, S. J., Peterson, C. B., Swanson, S. A., Raymond, N. C., Specker, S., Eckert, E. D., & Mitchell, J. E. (2009). Increased mortality in bulimia nervosa and other eating disorders. *The American Journal of Psychiatry, 166*(12), 1342–1346.

de Ridder, D., Adriaanse, M., Evers, C., & Verhoeven, A. (2014). Who diets? Most people and especially when they worry about food. *Appetite, 80*, 103–8.

Lambert, M. J., & Finch, A. E. (1999). The Outcome Questionnaire. In M. E. Maruish (Ed.), *The use of psychological testing for treatment planning and outcomes assessment* (pp. 831–869). Mahwah, NJ: Lawrence Erlbaum Associates.

Lambert, M. J., & Shimokawa, K. (2011). Collecting client feedback. *Psychotherapy, 48*(1), 72–79.

Puhl, R. M., & Brownell, K. D. (2006). Confronting and coping with weight stigma: An investigation of overweight and obese adults. *Obesity, 14*(10), 1802–15.

Tryon, G. S., & Winograd, G. (2011). Goal consensus and collaboration. *Psychotherapy, 48*(1), 50–57.

# Index

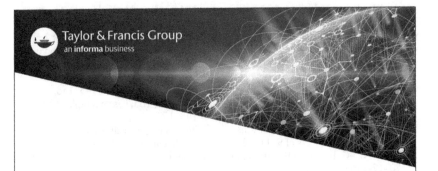